Battling Bias

Also by Ruth Sidel

On Her Own:
Growing Up in the Shadow of the American Dream

Women and Children Last:
The Plight of Poor Women in Affluent America

Urban Survival:
The World of Working-Class Women

Families of Fengsheng:
Urban Life in China

Women and Child Care in China:
A Firsthand Report

Battling Bias

The Struggle for
Identity and
Community on
College Campuses

Ruth Sidel

VIKING

VIKING
Published by the Penguin Group
Penguin Books USA Inc., 375 Hudson Street,
New York, New York, 10014, U.S.A.
Penguin Books Ltd, 27 Wrights Lane,
London W8 5TZ, England
Penguin Books Australia Ltd, Ringwood,
Victoria, Australia
Penguin Books Canada Ltd, 10 Alcorn Avenue,
Toronto, Ontario, Canada M4V 3B2
Penguin Books (N.Z.) Ltd, 182–190 Wairau Road,
Auckland 10, New Zealand

Penguin Books Ltd, Registered Offices:
Harmondsworth, Middlesex, England

First published in 1994 by Viking Penguin,
a division of Penguin Books USA Inc.

10   9   8   7   6   5   4   3   2   1

Copyright © Ruth Sidel, 1994
All rights reserved

LIBRARY OF CONGRESS CATALOGING IN PUBLICATION DATA
Sidel, Ruth.
Battling bias: the struggle for identity and community
on college campuses / Ruth Sidel.
p.   cm.
Includes bibliographical references and index.
ISBN 0–670–84112–9
1. Discrimination in higher education—United States.
2. College students—United States—Attitudes.
3. Pluralism (Social sciences)—United States.   I. Title.
LC212.42.S53   1994
378.1'981—dc20   94–2382

Printed in the United States of America
Set in Postscript Bodoni Book
Designed by Ann Gold

To Vic,

who is there every step of the way,

with my love.

Contents

Acknowledgments

First, my appreciation to the college students who gave so generously of their time, their experiences, and their views about recent events on their campuses. Their seriousness of purpose, their concern about issues affecting broad groups of people, and their efforts to have an impact on some of the fundamental issues of our time illuminate these pages.

My gratitude as well to all those who have contributed to this book, in so many ways. To Lynn Chancer, who has explored these issues with me throughout the writing of the book and has commented on the manuscript in all of its various stages, my deepest appreciation. To Marque Miringoff, who went far out of her way to support this project; to Terry Arendell, who helped me develop contacts at the University of Wisconsin/Madison; and to her and Laurie Kramer, both of whom read and made valuable comments on the manuscript—my special thanks.

And to all those who shared their thoughts, their work, and their research, to those who referred me to students, faculty members, and administrators, and to those who lent support and friendship—this book could not have been written without you. My thanks to Betsy Halpern Amaru, Alice Axelbank, Lance Bennett, Pierre van den Berghe, Johnnetta Butler, Leslie Calman, Robert Carter, Naomi Chase, Flora Davidson, Troy Duster, Nancy Dye, Lee Edwards, Harvey Fladd, Sally Freeman, Judith Friedlander, Natalie Friedman, Elayne Garrett, Robyn Gittleman, Sol Gittleman, Gail Green, Jerome Grossman, Margot Haas, Nancy Hartsock, Zaineb Hasan, Freddye Hill, Marilyn

Jackson, Anthony Johnson, Colton Johnson, Janet Jones, Linda Kalof, Natalie Kampen, Temma Kaplan, Pauline Katz, Eileen Leonard, Hubert Locke, Anne Loustau, Lawrence Mamiya, Thomas Matos, Brina Melemed, Darrell Millner, Ernest Morris, Paula Nesoff, Howard Pinderhughes, Edward Pittman, Janet Poppendieck, Marjorie Pryse, Paula Rayman, Susan Reverby, Timm Rinehart, Mary Roark, Terry Rogers, Paula Rothenberg, Janet Saunders, Beverly Solochek, Mary Dean Sorcinelli, Pamela Stone, Jaimie Trautment, Patricia Wallace, David Ward, and Bill Wassmuth.

And, finally, to my editor, Mindy Werner, who unfailingly gives support and encouragement even when she's swamped and always asks the tough questions, to Michael Hardart, who facilitated the publication process with efficiency and good humor, and to Anne T. Zaroff-Evans, who copy-edited the manuscript with great skill and sensitivity, my heartfelt gratitude.

Battling Bias

Introduction

I went to Wellesley in the 1950s. It was the only college I really wanted to attend. Having grown up in downtown Boston, I felt somehow that Wellesley and Smith (to which I also applied) were close enough to home for me to keep in touch but also far enough away for me to gain some independence. When I visited Smith for the obligatory interview and tour, it seemed just too small-town, *too* traditional. One Sunday afternoon during my senior year in high school, I visited Wellesley. The Wellesley senior who showed me around must have pointed out administration buildings, classrooms, the chapel, the path down to the lake (or perhaps she even walked me down to see the lake), but all I remember from that visit is Tower Court, a large, stone, Gothic-esque dorm in the center of campus.

Tower was really for upper-classmen (as we called them then), but Wellesley was planning an experimental freshman corridor there the following year. After walking through the elaborate stone portico, we entered the main public room: huge (to my eyes, at least), paneled in dark wood with high-vaulting ceilings, a portrait of Madame Chiang Kai-shek on one wall, Oriental rugs on the floor, and carved tables and chairs placed around the edges of the room. It was just after Sunday dinner, and students were sitting in small groups talking, drinking coffee, some smoking (the ultimate sign of worldliness in that era), and others sitting at card tables or on the floor playing bridge. It was to me, a sixteen-year-old senior from a small, conservative, all-girl school at the foot of Beacon Hill, the epitome of sophistication, a dream come true. Others might have gone to Wellesley to study French literature, economics, or mathematics, but I went to be transformed into one of those bright, animated "girls." I would be witty, wise, thin, and, above all, knowing.

As with many initial impressions, particularly ones so vivid that they can be seen, heard, smelled, and nearly tasted decades later, the reality of going to Wellesley in that era was both different from and similar to the images evoked that afternoon. Yes, we played a lot of bridge. And drank a lot of coffee, and even, I am ashamed to say, smoked many, many packs of Pall Malls. Some of our endless conversations were dotted with wit, filled with philosophical debates about religion and the meaning of life, and sometimes heated by political differences. But the Wellesley of the 1950s was also a Wellesley of homogeneity and uniformity. It was a Wellesley of the Korean War, of Eisenhower, of Joseph McCarthy. It was a Wellesley of mixers (oh, those dreadful mixers), of tennis racquets and white socks and sneakers, of male visitors to your room only on Sunday afternoons with the door always open, of the freshmen (sic) class obsession with finding and stealing the sophomore class banner, of seniors rolling hoops at graduation. The magnificent Wellesley campus was unruffled by dissonance, by harsh debates or protests, or, for that matter, by diversity. The model Wellesley student then was fresh-faced, hardworking, upper-middle-class, and usually well behaved. Of course, there were a few who did not quite fit the mold: some of us mocked the rah-rah, good-girl, sweater-set-with-pearls image; others were barely scraping by financially and managed only by working in the library or elsewhere on campus and watching every penny. Some did not fit the image in still other ways: a few were Jewish (in the early 1950s, Wellesley and other colleges stopped using an official quota for Jewish students); a very few were African-American or Asian-American, and there was a sprinkling of international students; but white, Anglo-Saxon, Protestant culture was dominant.

Most students identified themselves as Republicans, some were Democrats, but almost no one ventured beyond the two mainstream parties in her thinking. Though religious differences were endlessly discussed in those late-night marathon sessions, to be an atheist was literally to be beyond the pale. This was not only a Protestant school but one that required first-year students to attend chapel. Not an ecumenical, take-from-many-religions-in-order-to-make-everyone-feel-at-home chapel service, but a straight Protestant version of religion, complete with those magnificent, unforgettable hymns with their great alto harmony:

> *A might-y fo-r-tress i-s our God,*
> *A bul-wark ne-ver fa-a-ai-ling;*

Or the stately

> *Praise God, from whom all bless-ings flow;*
> *Praise him, all crea-tures here be-low;*
> *Praise him a-bove, ye heaven-ly host;*
> *Praise Fa-ther, Son, and Ho-ly Ghost.*

Academics and other observers of the college scene didn't talk about political correctness in those days, but in the fifties most students made sure they held the "correct" opinions and behaved in highly acceptable ways. Assimilation—at least as far as was possible—was the goal. One could believe in a religion other than Protestantism, but one was expected not to make too much of it. One might be Asian-American or Asian or even "Negro," but fitting in was *de rigueur.* You might be managing somehow to have sex with your boyfriend, but you kept it pretty much to yourself, and you certainly only slept with one guy, the one with whom you were "going steady" and whom you were planning to marry. If you behaved in any other manner, you were talked about as "that kind of girl."

And, of course, politically you had to be very "correct." At a time when congressional committees were investigating the political beliefs and behavior of State Department employees in order to determine who "lost" China, were examining the political affiliation and patriotism of writers, actors, professors, and many others, at a time when many lost their jobs because of alleged political beliefs, merely questioning the merits of capitalism was enough to earn you a questioning look. Anything to the left of Adlai Stevenson was suspect, and many were not so sure about him. After all, he was divorced and spoke in that intellectual way of his.

Most students never felt that political uniformity was being forced down their throats; they never questioned it at all. Few, inside or outside of the classroom, spoke of racism—of segregation, the poll tax, or lynchings, or separate and grossly unequal schools; few spoke about anti-Semitism, even though everyone had recently lived through the Second World War and the revelations about the Holocaust; and no one, to my knowledge, objected to mandatory chapel attendance, even though many believed in other religions and a few believed in no religion at all. No, it wasn't called political correctness, but our daily lives were infused with it.

Many who attended college in that era now look back at it as a simpler time. Campuses were peaceful; no one questioned the assigned texts. Homogeneity, conformity, and predictability characterized the decade. Students did not rail at studying "dead white males" (even though much of what we did was just that); they read what they were supposed to read, turned in their papers on time, and hoped for good grades. Many who are actively involved today in the debate around higher education had their image of the collegiate experience formed by this earlier era, when elite colleges served the fortunate few and any "outsiders" tried desperately to minimize their differences and, above all, to fit in. What was once seen, and is still viewed by some, as a time of calm and civility was, in reality, a time of exclusion and suppression of difference.

This image of academia as a sheltered, ivory-tower existence, far from the turbulence and hostility of the real world, where professors thought and taught and students studied and partied, was, of course, dramatically shaken by the campus rebellions and protests of the 1960s and 1970s. The early 1980s brought a quieter time, but one in which student self-absorption and materialism were decried by many. Then, during the late 1980s and early 1990s, bias incidents started to occur with alarming regularity on college campuses. Many observers felt, and still feel, a sense of shock when these incidents occur. Why are they happening? What are the beliefs, the values, the pressures that motivate students who perpetrate racist, sexist, homophobic incidents? What do such incidents tell us about the broader society? What is the impact on the victims? To begin to explore these issues, let us start by listening to some of the students who have themselves experienced bias.

Francesca Wilkinson, a senior at Tufts University in Medford, Massachusetts, a suburb outside of Boston, describes an incident that occurred her first day at college:

> I was skipping through the dining hall with a white boy I've known since I was four and a frat boy said, "Look at that nigger bitch with that white boy." I hated it there that whole first semester! I went home every weekend. I was angry at everything. There were only a hundred African Americans out of forty-eight hundred students and it angered me. It was the first time I had been in that kind of environment and I had a real feeling of iso-

lation. My roommate and I were the only people of color in the dorm; I felt like people were staring at me. A lot of freshmen had never been among black people before.

Two Asian-American students discuss anti-Asian incidents in and around the University of Washington in Seattle. They recall the professor of one of them who stated, "All Asians are overachievers," or the recent incident at a community college in Seattle when a sign was put up that read "Speak English or Die, Squinty Eye," or the two Asian students "walking down Greek Row" when someone called out, "Do you want to eat sushi?"

Marcella Rosario, a junior at Hunter College (a public institution that is part of the City University of New York) whose family originally came from Southern Europe and settled in Canada during her childhood and young adulthood, says, "Here at Hunter people think I'm Latina." Marcella describes a recent conversation with an academic adviser about a master's-degree program. Without asking any questions about her academic record (she is part of the prestigious Honors Program at Hunter), her grade-point average (her academic record is superior), her interests, or her career goals, the adviser told her, "This is for our more high-powered students." She stated in no uncertain terms that for Marcella the program would be "too hard, too, too hard." Looking back on the experience, Marcella allowed that, generally, "if I want to do something, I do it, but this adviser took my confidence right away."

Pierre, an African-American senior at Vassar College in Poughkeepsie, New York, recalls posting flyers in his dorm during his first year and being questioned by a security guard who implied that he was not a Vassar student but, rather, a "young man from Poughkeepsie." Pierre describes his feelings about this incident:

I'm thinking to myself, This individual has seen me at dorm events. It's a very alienating feeling when you're a freshman.

These people have accepted you, they've said, "We want you to come and contribute. . . . You can be part of this." Then, when you get there, that happens. It puts you on notice that you're in, but you're not *in*.

He recalls a time when he tried to enter a female dorm and, as others were let in unchecked, the security person asked to see his ID. When he presented it, the guard said, "This does not look like you," and asked for a second ID. He gave her his meal card with the same photograph and was finally admitted. The fact that African-American male students are always being "carded" is a source of concern for many at Vassar, students, faculty, and administrators alike. Pierre feels that these incidents send out a double message: " 'Yes, come to Vassar, but. . . .' If they bring students from different backgrounds to the campus, it is their responsibility to make them feel like every other student," Pierre states, quietly but emphatically.

All these students, very different people seeking an education in very different settings, have been told in a variety of ways that they do not quite belong. Whether by fellow students, by members of the faculty, by administrators, or by people in the local community, they have been informed, clearly and distinctly, that admission is often a far cry from acceptance, and that, because of the color of their skin rather than the "content of their character," they are suspect, they are indeed outsiders within. Given that status, what do these students make of their college years? How does their prior experience prepare them for sorting out the complex, often coded messages they both receive and transmit in this new environment in which they are seen—by some, at least—as the interlopers, the "others"? How do they protect themselves and yet participate in ways meaningful to them and to the larger community?

During the last decade, college campuses have been rife with what have come to be called "hate incidents." Between the fall of 1986 and the winter of 1990, the National Institute Against Prejudice and Violence, a private, nonprofit organization established in 1984 with a seed grant from the State of Maryland and later financed by individuals, corporations, and foundations, monitored incidents of "ethnoviolence" at approximately 250 colleges. According to the institute, "Campus ethnoviolence covers the spectrum of violent acts including potentially lethal assaults, classroom and dormitory harassment, personal insults, graffiti, property damage, and so on." The institute's research indicates that about 20 percent of minority students experience some form of bias attack during an academic year and that at least one-quarter of these students are victimized more than once. The acts include racist, anti-Semitic, homophobic, and sexist incidents and range from repeated, overt harassment that virtually any observer would consider offensive to onetime remarks that the speaker might consider humorous but the recipient perceives as slurs.

Many would have us believe that these recent developments in colleges and universities are aberrations, the work of extremists. I suggest, to the contrary, that higher education in the United States today mirrors, just as it did in earlier eras, the values, the divisions, and the debates within the larger society, and, in fact, that college campuses are often the arenas in which the schisms and conflicting values of the larger society are played out and become crystallized. Because many institutions of higher learning are enclosed, somewhat isolated communities in which very different kinds of people spend an unusual amount of time together, highly charged issues and incidents are quickly magnified and erupt into full-blown conflict. Many colleges, in fact, resemble "total institutions," as described by Erving Goffman, in which the participants eat, sleep, work, and play in the same environment, and feelings and actions can quickly escalate until they are very nearly out of control. Despite this highly volatile situation that has, particularly over the past few years, produced hostile encounters that are often shocking to the rest of the society, I suggest that these incidents are nonetheless a reflection of the values, attitudes, and conflicts of that wider society. A fundamental question, therefore, is: how do the attitudes and values of the broader society shape attitudes and actions on college campuses?

Our colleges and universities are lightning rods for conflict in part because there are so few other avenues for effective protest in the wider society. Academic institutions are often, moreover, in the nearly impossible position of trying to bridge some of those schisms and resolve some of the conflicts, not only within their own environment but within the larger society as well. Institutions of higher education have, in limited ways, attempted to compensate for some of the gross inequalities of income, education, and opportunity in American society. Many colleges and universities have made efforts to recruit students of color, who have traditionally suffered discrimination in the wider society and in the admissions process. Others have tried to recruit additional faculty of color. Still others have admitted students who are not fully prepared for college-level work and then provided remedial education to help these students catch up. Many such initiatives have led to friction among groups vying for that exceedingly valuable yet scarce resource: access to higher education, and the power, status, and opportunity it can confer.

Institutions of higher education, moreover, frequently bring together within the academic community people who have, prior to this experience, led quite separate and very different lives and therefore often have conflicting perspectives and worldviews. Administrators, teachers, and students then face the critical task of finding new ways to facilitate communication among disparate groups, of helping people from different backgrounds live together, and of creating a sense of community among those for whom there is frequently little sense of connectedness in the outside world.

In recent years, we have heard from journalists, political ideologues, elected officials, and college administrators and faculty members about conflict on college campuses, diversity, multiculturalism, political correctness, race relations, and gender issues, but amid the debates and the diatribes what have been missing are the voices of the students. This book will focus on their thoughts and feelings, their actions and reactions when faced with these complex issues on their campuses. How have students experienced the hostility and divisiveness around race, gender, sexuality, and entitlement that have stirred so much passion? What does it mean to be an African-American student on a predominantly white campus? What does it mean to be Chinese-American or Japanese-American when stereotypes about Asian Americans abound? What does it mean to be gay or lesbian in an era when homosexuals are vilified by segments of the larger society and beaten up on the streets of our cities? What does it mean to be Jewish at campuses where black student organizations invite as speakers African-American leaders who are widely known to have expressed anti-Semitic ideas? What does it mean to be a white, middle-class male student from a conservative background and feel that one's values and attitudes are under siege?

To feel like an outsider is, of course, extraordinarily difficult at any age or stage of life. To be openly reviled or more subtly judged unworthy because of ascribed membership in one or more groups is painful to virtually everyone, but for a young person who is actively exploring his/her own identity, who is engaged in the crucial tasks of differentiating self from others and of developing knowledge, skills, and the equally essential self-confidence, it is even more painful to feel outside the mainstream of society. Whereas many Americans think of identity in purely individual, psychological terms, in reality our identity, both in the eyes of others and in our own eyes, is an intricate

web of our particular individual characteristics and our place
in the social and economic hierarchies of our society. In fact, in
this era when nations are so thoroughly interconnected and in-
terdependent, our identity is also predicated on our position in
the *world's* social and economic hierarchies. The place that we
come to occupy is determined, in large part, by our race, class,
gender, and ethnicity, as well as by our educational level, our
physical appearance, and myriad other details of our history and
our lives. If we assume, therefore, that identity is inseparable
from issues of race, gender, class, and sexual orientation, then
the treatment of all groups in the larger society, and within the
academic community, has a direct impact on how students view
themselves.

If a student, for example, belongs to a group (or groups) about
which the broader society, and in all likelihood elements of the
college community as well, holds largely negative images, how
does that young person come to terms with these negative images and feelings, which must include her/him? How does the
young man or woman resolve the conflict between being a member, generally through no action of his/her own, of a group that
is openly reviled, and developing some measure of the pride in
self that is essential for emotional, economic, and social survival? With whom does that student identify? The larger, mainstream society? His/her own reference group? Which reference
group (for, in this complex world in which we live, we all belong
to many)? With whom will that individual choose to spend time?
What area of study and what occupational goal will s/he pursue?
Food preferences, style of dressing, choice of language, leisure
activities all express our statement of who we are and how we
wish to be perceived by others. In some instances, in our highly
charged society, in which individuals are constantly labeled and
judged by their ascribed status, the quest for identity may merge
with a quest for an ideology that will make some sense out of the

harsh and often conflicting messages so many students receive, and day-to-day life-style choices inevitably become symbolic political statements.

The traditional college years, the late teens through the mid-twenties, are years of extraordinary maturation and growth. These are the years when many young people leave home, often for the first time, meet very different kinds of people (also often for the first time), come upon previously unheard ideas, and have the opportunity, and indeed the task, of defining for themselves and others who they are—what they think, the values they hold, their place in a world beyond the one in which they grew up. They often move out of their family circle, their group of friends, and their community, and cross boundaries—intellectual boundaries, economic boundaries, racial boundaries—they have never crossed before, sometimes never even dreamed of crossing. This experience is often exhilarating, but it can also be unsettling, anxiety-provoking, frightening, and occasionally simply too much to bear. Crossing boundaries always entails a journey, even if those boundaries are in close physical proximity. One student merely took the ferry and the subway from one borough of New York City to another, but in so doing discovered another world and other sides of herself. A student from the University of Washington made a very different kind of journey; he became deeply involved in an internal political issue at the university and also discovered another world and another self. Yet another student made the journey from a suburb in Washington State to Columbia University in New York City and discovered a commitment to conservative political action within him that he had not known existed.

This book will explore these issues largely through the words and experiences of college students. I have discussed with students from a variety of backgrounds their attitudes about the current issues on their campuses, the ways they have attempted to survive and, in many instances, taken major leadership roles on their campuses, and the ways these issues have affected their sense of themselves. I found many young people not only learning and making plans for their future lives but feeling a sense of responsibility for their fellow students and for the future of their colleges, students of uncommon courage and wisdom who are trying to sort through the many complex dilemmas and contradictions they face on a daily basis. These students shared their thoughts, their lives, and their dreams with incredible generosity.

During the academic years 1991–92 and 1992–93, I talked at length with one hundred college students, members of the faculty, and administrators from seventeen colleges and universities. The majority of the schools are located on the East Coast, several are on the West Coast, and the remaining schools are located in the South and the Midwest. Nine of the institutions are public, eight private. The students included African Americans, Latinos, Asian Americans, non-Hispanic Caucasians, and one Native American; a broad spectrum of ethnic, religious, socioeconomic and political beliefs was represented.

For the most part, I was referred to the students by faculty members, administrators, or other students. Clearly, this sample of students contains more activists than do student bodies generally. I invariably asked my contacts for the names of students who would be interesting to talk to, who would have views on the subjects about which I was particularly concerned, and who might be willing to share their experiences and views with me. Everyone with whom I talked was informed at the start of our conversation that I was writing a book about bias incidents on college campuses.

Many of the interviews with the students were single sessions that lasted from one to two hours. More than one-third of the student interviews, however, took place over a period of time— several weeks, or in some instances several months—and provided an opportunity for students to reflect on an ongoing basis on the events at their campuses, on their personal reactions to these events, and on the impact of their college years on their views of themselves, on their ideology, and on their lives. For logistical reasons, the majority of these multiple-session interviews took place on the East Coast, but many of these students grew up in other parts of the country, one of them in Canada. Does the book have an East Coast bias because so many of the in-depth interviews were conducted there? I believe not. I did not find any marked difference between the attitudes and behavior of students I interviewed on the East Coast and those of students elsewhere in the country. The specific issues, of course, vary depending upon the geographical area. The conflict between African Americans and Jews was only mentioned on the East Coast; bias against Asian-American students was discussed on both coasts but seemed more intense on the West Coast; and homophobia seemed to be everywhere.

The specific events taking place on their own campuses and the broader issues facing higher education today constituted the central focus of the open-ended interviews: bias incidents, relations among students of different races, religions, and ethnicities, gender and class issues, homophobia, affirmative action, multiculturalism, and political correctness. I also asked about their personal lives: where they came from, their family background, their prior education, and their hopes for the future. I have attempted to weave together these two strands, their personal lives and their undergraduate experiences, in an effort to shed some light upon the volatile issues on college campuses today, upon the impact their college years have had on these students, on their attitudes and values, and, finally, upon the impact they have had on events on their campuses. Many of these students are actively battling bias—within themselves, within their college communities, and within the larger society.

This book is divided into three parts. The first raises the question "Who shall learn?" and asks what conditions are necessary to facilitate students' learning, achieving, and developing into active, participating, thoughtful members of society. It examines some of the central characteristics of our educational system, from primary school through postgraduate education, some of the key issues facing higher education today, and raises the question of who shall have access to the education so essential for active participation in the economic, political, and civic life of the United States in the twenty-first century. Part I also explores some of the central issues in American society that have significant impact on higher education: recent patterns of immigration and the extent to which the United States has truly become a multicultural society, and an examination of the issues of racism, sexism, anti-Semitism, and homophobia in the wider society. Finally, part I describes some of the "hate incidents" that have occurred on college campuses in recent years and raises questions about the impact of these events on individual students.

Part II examines the above issues largely through the words and experiences of college students. In these chapters, I have attempted to present the students as they presented themselves to me—as complex, sometimes conflicted players in a drama that is not, for the most part, of their making, but is nonetheless one for which many of them feel genuine concern and a sense of responsibility. To protect their confidentiality, the names of all of the students, as well as a few details of their personal lives, have been changed, but every attempt has been made to present them, their experiences, and their words accurately and without embellishment. Some view themselves as agents of change, as activists who hope to make a lasting impact on their schools, on their fellow students, and even on members of the faculty and administration. Others see themselves as private individuals trying to learn and make some sense of their educational experiences and their lives. But, no matter how they view their roles during their undergraduate years, many of them care deeply about their colleges, their friends and colleagues, and the urgent issues we discussed. Finally, part III attempts to sort out the problems and dilemmas that face American education at the end of the twentieth century and the beginning of the next, and to point the way to possible solutions. It is my hope that this book will shed light upon the recent phenomenon of hate incidents, particularly upon their impact on students and the ways students are coping with hostility and bias. I also hope that this book will clarify some of the critical issues facing higher education and encourage genuine debate about the role of education in a democratic society.

A note on language: Throughout the book I have used the terms "African American" and "black" as well as "Latino" and "Hispanic." Since the United States Bureau of the Census uses "black" and "Hispanic" in its data, for clarity whenever I deal with such data I also use "black" and "Hispanic." In addition, I am aware that controversy exists between the use of the terms "American Indian" and "Native American." The one student I interviewed for whom these designations are relevant, herself a member of the Oneida tribe, used both terms, with perhaps more emphasis on the word "Indian." In my material about her and her experiences, I attempt to reflect her usage.

Part One

1

Who Shall Learn?

We are living through a transformation that will rearrange the
politics and economics of the coming century. . . . Each nation's
primary political task will be to cope with the centrifugal forces
of the global economy which tear at the ties binding citizens
together—bestowing ever greater wealth on the most skilled and
insightful, while consigning the less skilled to a declining standard
of living.   Robert B. Reich,
                                    The Work of Nations

We have a school in East St. Louis [Illinois] named for Dr. [Martin
Luther] King. The school is full of sewer water and the doors are
locked with chains. Every student in that school is black. It's
like a terrible joke on history.
              Fourteen-year-old student quoted in Jonathan Kozol,
              Savage Inequalities:
              Children in America's Schools

Recent events on college campuses and recent debates
about the nature, quality, and goals of American education raise fundamental questions about the function of
education in a complex, postindustrial, democratic society. How
accessible must education be for a society to provide equality of
opportunity to those who dwell within its borders? Should we be
focusing on educating the best and the brightest, or at the very
least the better and the brighter, or are virtually all Americans
entitled to an education that will enable them to live productive
lives in the twenty-first century? What do we mean by "accessi-
bility"? Is a democratic society required to provide education

19

that is financially accessible? Geographically accessible? In a society with a highly diverse population, must education incorporate material from many cultures and belief systems, or should educational institutions in the United States teach primarily the cultural, philosophical, and historical roots of the Western tradition?

These exceedingly difficult and controversial questions have been debated widely over the past decade, both within academia and in the larger society. Before examining these issues, I must stress that over the past hundred years the United States has made an extraordinary commitment to mass education. In 1900, approximately 7 percent of all Americans graduated from high school; today approximately 80 percent receive high-school diplomas. The proportion of high-school graduates attending college has also risen dramatically, from 4 percent in 1900 to over 50 percent by the late 1980s. American commitment to mass education becomes even clearer through cross-cultural comparisons. In the countries of Western Europe, approximately 20 percent of the young people attend college; in Canada, fewer than 30 percent of eighteen-to-twenty-one-year-olds go on to higher education. But, even though the United States has made a far greater commitment to education than have countries with similar political structures and economic conditions, the quality of that education varies significantly depending on the class, race, ethnicity, gender, and geographical base of the students.

To examine the questions who shall learn and what conditions are necessary to facilitate and maximize students' learning experience, we must clarify at the outset who we are as a nation. All too often, our images of the United States lag behind the reality, reflect an earlier era. The pace of change—demographic, social, economic, and political—is so swift in late-twentieth-century America that we can often barely comprehend the magnitude of that change and the essential character of our world. Since education is central to the fundamental concept of democracy and the functioning of a democratic society, we must be clear about the composition of our diverse population and then raise questions about who is being educated, the effectiveness of that education, the inequalities within the education system, and the impact upon individual students of feeling like outsiders within the very institutions that can provide a passport to the new world, that of the twenty-first century.

The twentieth century has been called the American century, but for much of that time it has been unclear what we in the United States mean by "American." For generations, American meant Anglo-American or White Anglo-Saxon Protestant. These were the real Americans. The term "American" was redefined to some extent by the surge of immigration that ushered in the twentieth century and is once again being redefined by the surge of immigration that is ushering out the century. The 1990 census found nearly twenty million foreign-born residents, the most in the nation's history. During the 1980s, moreover, when over seven million legal immigrants came to this country, both Asian-born and Latino immigrants outnumbered the European-born. According to a researcher from the Urban Institute, "As recently as the 1950's, two-thirds of legal immigrants to the country were from Europe and Canada, with the bulk from Europe. That ceased being true in the 1960s and it is not even close now. European and Canadian immigration is less than 15 percent of total immigration." Not only did the nationality of the majority of immigrants change during the most recent wave, but the port of entry changed as well. As many immigrants entered California during the 1980s as entered New York State from 1901 to 1910.

According to recent projections, if current levels of immigration continue, the number of Latino residents will reach 38.2 million in 2010, surpassing African Americans as the largest minority group, and the number of Asians, which doubled during the 1980s to seven million, will double again over the next two decades and reach 38.8 million by 2050. The number of non-Hispanic blacks is expected to reach 38.2 million in 2010 and 57.3 million in 2050, 15 percent of the total population.

Further evidence corroborating the multicultural nature of the United States population in the 1990s is the increasing number of residents for whom English is a second language. According to Census Bureau data, nearly thirty-two million Americans, one person in seven among the nation's population over the age of five, grew up or is growing up speaking a language other than English. These numbers have increased by over 38 percent between 1980 and 1990. Spanish speakers far outnumber speakers of other foreign languages, but the number of speakers of Asian languages has increased sharply over the decade: of Korean, by 127 percent; Chinese, 98 percent; and Tagalog, the primary language of the Philippines, 87 percent.

The impact of this recent influx of immigrants on education in the United States has been significant. A study conducted by the College Board and the Western Interstate Commission for Higher Education found that the increasing racial and ethnic diversity of the U.S. is being reflected in dramatic increases in the number of Hispanic and nonwhite students in the classroom. The study predicts that by 1995 one-third of American public-school students will be members of minority groups. It further predicts that Asians and Pacific Islanders will increase their enrollment in elementary and secondary schools from 1985 to 1994 by 70 percent; that Hispanic enrollment will increase 54 percent; that black students will increase by only 13 percent but will remain the second-largest racial or ethnic group, behind whites; and that American Indians and Alaska natives enrolled in school are expected to increase by 29 percent but will nonetheless remain the smallest group.

Since members of minority groups will constitute an increasing proportion of the nation's students and work force, issues such as the provision of adequate education to these groups, their high-school dropout rates, and the percentages of minority students attending college become even more crucial for American society. Traditionally, blacks, Hispanics, and Native Americans have higher high-school dropout rates and lower college-enrollment rates than do whites. With new projections on the patterns of school attendance by region and by racial and ethnic group, "For the first time," according to a research associate from the Western Interstate Commission, "officials can pinpoint the patterns of the increasingly multi-cultural student body and then make plans to better educate underserved, but increasingly significant, racial and ethnic groups."

The situation in New York City provides a particularly vivid example of changes taking place in many cities across the country. Between 1989 and 1992, 120,000 immigrant children entered the New York City public-school system. The largest number, 23,000, came from the Dominican Republic, 10,000 came from Jamaica, 8,000 from Russia, and 7,000 each from Guyana and China. Significant numbers of students enrolled in New York schools also come from Haiti, Trinidad, Mexico, Ecuador, Colombia, and Korea. One elementary school, P.S. 19 in Queens, has 2,100 students from 45 different countries and is so crowded that its enrollment is the same size as that of many high schools that draw from far larger geographical areas. One economist suggests that the numbers might increase further before they level off. Many of the immigrant couples who are bringing children will be bearing more children, and many of the children they already have will soon be approaching childbearing age themselves.

"We the people" is clearly a rapidly changing entity—not only nationally and on the East Coast but perhaps most dramatically on the West Coast. As recently as 1970, nearly 79 percent of California's population was Anglo; by 1990, the Anglos had dropped to 56 percent; by the year 2000, they will account for only 48 percent of the population, while non-Anglos will make up 52 percent of the population. Between 1970 and 1990, the Latino population grew from 11 to 26 percent, the black population remained at 7 percent, and the Asian population went from 3 to 10 percent. According to a study conducted by the UCLA Chicano Studies Research Center, during the first decades of the twenty-first century Latinos will outnumber Anglos in California. Low Anglo in-migration combined with high Latino in-migration, and low Anglo fertility combined with high Latino fertility, have contributed significantly to these massive demographic shifts.

In his book entitled *Who Shall Live?*, Victor Fuchs raises the complex and controversial question of how the United States should spend its resources in health care and how the resolution of that multilayered, multifaceted issue of medical and public policy ultimately determines who lives and who dies. If we spend a substantial percentage of our finite resources on coronary-bypass surgery and organ transplants, middle-aged or older people are likely to benefit; if, on the other hand, we shift some of our resources from highly technological medicine that focuses on the end of the life cycle to prenatal care and the social and economic well-being of pregnant women and preschool children, the numbers of low-birth-weight babies and the infant mortality rate are likely to decline. Indeed, through our social policy we as a society decide who shall live and who shall die every day.

Our educational system may not decide quite so directly who shall live and who shall die, but, in a very real sense, the structure and funding of our primary and secondary schools, and the structure, funding, and admissions policies of our colleges and universities, determine which students will be given a chance to survive economically, which will have the opportunity to work their way into the middle class, which might be able to develop the skills that will, in turn, enable them to live relatively comfortable lives and pass on not only material but also social and cultural advantages to their children.

The educational system is, furthermore, of central importance in determining who will be able to participate fully and meaningfully in our democratic society. The ability to grasp complex ideas, to comprehend even in a rudimentary way the implications of constant scientific and technological change, to evaluate the trade-offs between economic expansion and environmental deterioration, and to acquire the knowledge necessary to evaluate differences in political and economic philosophy is in a modern, complex society dependent to a significant extent upon the level and quality of one's education. If democracy, the "rule of the people," is predicated on popular participation, that participation is predicated, as we move into the twenty-first century, on a system of education that truly enables the people to understand the issues of our time and to feel as though they can participate in meaningful ways in the democratic process.

Moreover, as Andrew Ross has stated, "Education (which covers much more than formal schooling), and not material prosperity, is our culture's way of 'earning' respect." It is the primary vehicle by which Americans raise their social class, by which they see themselves and others see them as individuals worthy of attention, entitled to a voice in determining public policy. In our highly technological late twentieth century, where the cliché "Knowledge is power" is truer than ever, the amount of education individuals have truly establishes their place in society.

Robert Reich has pointed out that, though Americans like to think of themselves in one economic boat, rising and falling together with the vicissitudes of the economy, the reality is that we are sailing in very different boats. In 1960, a chief executive of one of America's hundred largest corporations earned after taxes, on average, approximately twelve times a factory worker's wages; by the end of the 1980s, a chief executive earned on average, again after taxes, approximately seventy times what the average factory worker earned. By 1992 the average income of CEOs in the United States was $3.8 million while the average income for workers was $24,400; for teachers, $34,100; and for engineers, $58,200. The CEOs who were among the top twenty in salaries, bonuses, and stock options all earned over $10 million; the CEO of the Hospital Corporation of America earned an incredible $127 million. Moreover, "the income disparity has widened fastest between people who graduate from college and those who graduated only from high school or dropped out."

Data from the 1990 census indicate exactly how crucial higher education is in determining earning power. Whites who received doctorates had the highest median monthly income, $4,679. (It should be noted that there were too few black and Hispanic recipients of doctoral degrees in the census sample to determine their valid monthly income levels.) Recipients of master's degrees earned the second-largest income: whites earned $3,248; blacks, $2,786; and Hispanics, $2,840. It was at the master's level that black and Hispanic workers earned the closest to parity—that is, the closest to what white workers earn; in 1990, they earned just over 85 percent as much as white workers. At the bachelor's-degree level, whites earned $2,552, only 55 percent of the earnings of white workers with doctorates, and blacks and Hispanics earned only 76 percent of white bachelor's-degree recipients' income. For those with a high-school diploma, monthly earnings were $1,405 for whites, 55 percent of the earnings of white college graduates, and approximately $1,000 for the other two groups. The level of education at which blacks were furthest from parity, 71 percent of white income, was "some high school." All three groups at that level earned incomes that were just at or below the poverty line for a family of four.

If we examine these data for gender differences, we see that at all levels women earn considerably less than men. Among those with doctorates, women earn 64 percent of what men earn ($3,162 and $4,915 respectively). Among those with master's degrees, women are closest to parity, earning $2,614, or 69.7 percent of what men earn ($3,748). As with blacks and Hispanics, women with only "some high school" are furthest from parity; they earn less than half, 49.7 percent, of what men earn, a gap of $579 monthly. Although the educational system along with social and economic policy may not be deciding directly who shall live, these forces are surely determining to a significant extent who will survive economically and perhaps even achieve a moderately comfortable life-style.

In the sometimes bitter, often agonizing debate about who shall learn, many claim that the only just criterion for admission to institutions of higher education should be merit. The concept of merit has a deceptively simple and enticing ring, tied as it is to Americans' desire to see ourselves as a society that believes in and practices equality of opportunity, but merit is an extraordinarily difficult concept to define. Does the young person who has the good fortune to be born to affluent parents and therefore attends first-rate primary and secondary schools, learns readily, achieves academic recognition, and gains admission to a first-rate college accomplish this feat on the basis of merit? And what of the converse—the perhaps equally bright child who is born to poor or working-class parents and therefore attends mediocre or, more likely, abysmally poor schools, does not perhaps learn with quite the same rapidity, and achieves above-average but hardly noteworthy SAT scores? How must the same school judge that student's application? Let us postulate, for the moment, that this second young person not only comes from a low-income family but is a member of a minority group as well. Perhaps his/her more modest achievements are indeed due to hard work and a love of learning. In other words, perhaps that young person's more modest accomplishments have been achieved more completely through merit.

There is no question that these are exceedingly delicate and controversial determinations and that there are no easy solutions. If we accept that we are, in large part, the product of our social, psychological, economic, and political environment, what, then, does the concept of merit signify? With the gross inequities that exist within American society, can the concept of merit have any intrinsic meaning?

In his recent study of public education, *Savage Inequalities: Children in America's Schools*, Jonathan Kozol describes the virtually side-by-side existence across the United States of inferior, underfinanced, often physically dangerous schools in poor communities, and lavish, state-of-the-art schools in affluent neighborhoods. Of central importance in the shocking inequalities within our public-school system are not only the vast differences on the basis of class but the "remarkable degree of racial segregation that persisted almost everywhere," particularly outside the Deep South. Many of the urban schools Kozol visited were 95-to-99-percent nonwhite, and, what is perhaps even more disturbing, few people in positions of power were interested in addressing the issue of segregation. As Kozol states, "The dual society, at least in public education, seems in general to be unquestioned."

The U.S. public-education system is not only virtually separate but grossly unequal. Kozol describes conditions in many of the Chicago schools: a shortage of teachers (on an average morning, 190 classrooms, with fifty-seven hundred children, have no teacher); a shortage of supplies (chemistry labs without beakers, running water, or Bunsen burners; playgrounds and gyms without rudimentary equipment; toilets without toilet paper); and a system that has long ago given up on its students. ("If a kid comes in not reading," according to one Chicago high-school English teacher, "he goes out not reading.")

Kozol points out that poor children in some of the worst inner-city schools often start their education with faith and optimism and that many thrive during the first few years. But by the third grade, their teachers see signs of failure; by the fourth grade, the children themselves see failure looming; and by fifth or sixth grade, many are skipping school, and, as Kozol states, the route from truanting to dropping out is "direct and swift."

In contrast, the principal of the New Trier High School in Winnetka, Illinois, just outside Chicago, states confidently, "Our goal is for students to be successful." The school, situated on twenty-seven suburban acres, offers Latin and six other foreign languages; the senior English class is reading Nietzsche, Darwin, Plato, Freud, and Goethe. In addition to seven gyms and an Olympic swimming pool, New Trier operates a television station. Every freshman is assigned a faculty adviser who counsels roughly two dozen students. In contrast, at DuSable, a high school in Chicago, each guidance counselor advises 420 students.

These conditions are duplicated in and around cities all over the country. In New York City, two schools barely fifteen minutes apart by car reveal the same patterns. Public School 261, in the North Bronx, is located in what was once a roller-skating rink. No sign identifies the building as a school; the building has no windows. Four kindergartens and a sixth-grade class of Spanish-speaking children share one room. One full-time and one part-time counselor are available to work with the thirteen hundred children, 90 percent of whom are black and Hispanic. Textbooks are scarce, and students must often share those that are available.

In contrast, just a few miles to the west, in the same school district, is P.S. 24, situated in the Riverdale section of the Bronx, a residential area with parks, libraries, large cooperative apartment buildings and many beautiful, expensive homes. The school serves 825 children, from kindergarten through the sixth grade. Kozol describes essentially three groupings within the school: one for special classes for the mentally retarded in

which most of the students are poor and black or Hispanic; one
for mainstream students, the vast majority of whom are white
and Asian; and a third track for "gifted" students. As Kozol observes, the fourth-grade gifted class is "humming with excitement." The class, according to the teacher, emphasizes "critical
thinking, reasoning and logic." The students were at that time
writing a new Bill of Rights, examining the very concept of a
right, a concept their personal experience clearly helps them to
understand.

Report after report has shown that the poorest districts in
New York City receive significantly lower allocations than the
wealthier districts, and that per-pupil expenditures within the
city of New York ($5,500 in 1987) are dramatically lower than
comparable expenditures in the affluent suburbs surrounding
the city (more than $11,000 in communities on Long Island).
The same differentials exist, of course, in virtually all metropolitan areas. The per-pupil expenditure in the late 1980s in Chicago secondary schools was, for example, $5,500, compared
with $8,500 to $9,000 in the highest-spending suburbs, to the
north. But the ultimate meaning of these inequalities is their impact on the lives, feelings, and self-image of the children themselves. The children in Kozol's book speak movingly of the
enormous discrepancies between schools for the affluent and
schools for the poor, between schools for white children and
schools for children of color. A Latino boy from a high school in
the South Bronx says, "People on the outside may think that we
don't know what it is like for other students, but we *visit* other
schools and we have eyes and we have brains. You cannot hide
the differences. You see it and compare. . . ." Or an eleventh-
grader from Camden, New Jersey: "So long as there are no white
children in our school, we're going to be cheated. That's America. That's how it is."

The children in these schools may not acquire the skills so
necessary for living in a postindustrial society, but they are cer-

tainly learning the explicit meaning of living in a profoundly racist and class-biased society. Moreover, children in affluent neighborhoods are also absorbing the message of living in a grossly unequal society in which individual success is the highest good. Students in the affluent New York City suburb of Rye for the most part oppose busing, suggest a "separate-but-equal" solution to the problem of inequality in education, and blame the victim in their analysis of differences in educational opportunity. When Kozol asks about the possibility of raising taxes in order to equalize educational opportunities one student succinctly summarizes the ideology of American individualism: "I don't see how that benefits me."

Despite substantial advances over the past two decades, gender inequality continues to permeate the entire field of education. From elementary school through graduate school, substantial evidence exists that girls and women are treated differently from boys and men, are frequently harassed, and often suffer overt discrimination. As a study commissioned by the American Association of University Women, published in 1992 by the Wellesley College Center for Research on Women, states:

> The absence of attention to girls in the current education debate suggests that girls and boys have identical educational experiences in school. Nothing could be further from the truth. Whether one looks at achievement scores, curriculum design, self-esteem levels, or staffing patterns, it is clear that sex and gender make a difference in the nation's public elementary and secondary schools. There is clear evidence that the educational system is not meeting girls' needs.

Significant gaps continue in the overall performance of girls, despite the narrowing of the gender gap in verbal and mathematical performance. Girls do not do as well as boys in physical sciences, and even girls who take the same science and math courses as boys and perform equally well on tests are "much less apt to pursue scientific or technological careers than are their male classmates." An analysis of the semifinalists for the 1993 National Merit Scholarships corroborates these observations. Even though well over half of the high-school seniors taking the qualifying exam were girls, and girls get higher grades on average then boys in both high school and college, three out of five semifinalists were boys. Moreover, boys outnumbered girls in every state. As the AAUW report states, "This is a 'gender gap' our nation can no longer afford to ignore."

Many factors, of course, contribute to the continuing gender gap in education. One of these is surely the formal school curriculum. The emphasis has been placed overwhelmingly on political and military events and leaders, on public events and the heroes (or villains) associated with them. Since women have traditionally been excluded from positions of power in the public sphere, they are rarely actors of consequence in our history books. Only when history also focuses on the "cyclical nature of daily life" do we see women represented as more than mere tokens. These issues may be exceptionally clear when applied to the study of history, but they also apply to the study of literature, social studies, and even math and science.

Not only does the formal structure of the curriculum all too often exclude and denigrate women, but classroom interaction is itself a crucial component of an individual's learning experience. As the AAUW points out, "Whether one looks at preschool classrooms or university lecture halls, at female teachers or male teachers, research spanning the past twenty years consistently reveals that males receive more teacher attention than do females."

In addition to teacher-student interaction, the way students treat one another is a key element in the development of their self-images and in the education process. Barrie Thorne, professor of sociology at the University of Southern California, has studied interaction between boys and girls in elementary schools. In her recent book, *Gender Play: Girls and Boys in School*, she states:

> On school playgrounds boys control as much as ten times more space than girls. . . . Boys invade and disrupt all-female games and scenes of play much more often than vice versa.
> . . . power is central to the social relations of gender. . . . Boys . . . treat girls as contaminating [and] participate in larger structures of male dominance.

Studies indicate, moreover, that sexual harassment among junior-high-school and high-school students is rising. A 1993 study commissioned by the American Association of University Women Education Foundation and carried out by Louis Harris & Associates surveyed over sixteen hundred students in grades eight through eleven in seventy-nine schools across the country. The study found that two-thirds of the students say they have experienced unwelcome sexual behavior at school, that 65 percent of girls and 42 percent of boys reported that they were touched, grabbed, or pinched in a sexual way, that 57 percent of girls and 36 percent of boys were intentionally brushed up against in a sexual way, and that 38 percent of girls and 28 percent of boys had their clothing pulled at in a sexual way. It is important to note that nearly one-quarter of the boys were called homosexual, the form of harassment they reported as most upsetting. Approximately 80 percent of the unwelcome sexual behavior was found to be by students toward other students; the remainder came from teachers, custodians, coaches, and other adults.

There is general agreement that sexual harassment is fundamentally about power and that the less powerful—females, or boys perceived to be weaker—are likely to be the harassed. As sociologist Lynn Chancer has noted in her pathbreaking book, *Sadomasochism in Everyday Life: The Dynamics of Power and Powerlessness*:

> ... gender relationships have been steeped in routinized patterns of power and powerlessness that permeate many aspects of day-to-day life. Broad and clear-cut examples are easy to cite: sexual harrassment is almost always the expression of men's disproportionate ability to control the economic and social conditions of women's lives, often in a sadistic manner; domestic violence from battering to rape as well as violence outside the home continue to be aimed predominantly at women by men.

This sadomasochistic behavior can be observed routinely in secondary schools across the country. As the AAUW report states, "The clear message to both girls and boys is that girls are not worthy of respect and that appropriate behavior for boys includes exerting power over girls—or over other, weaker boys."

As widespread as sexual harassment is in the broader society, it should come as no surprise that it is endemic in the nation's high schools as well. Examples are ubiquitous: female students were subjected to vulgar writing about them in the boys' bathroom at a high school in Duluth, Minnesota; a California girl taunted by a group of boys whose suggestive remarks escalated until she transferred out of her computer class; another California high-school student complained of boys' lifting up her cheerleading skirt yet wondered if she had "asked for it" by wearing revealing clothes. A female high-school student who felt she was harassed by the band director complained to her principal, but he tried to discourage her from filing a lawsuit by telling her that it would be her word against the band director's and indicated that the man in question had always had excellent evaluations. The young woman filed a lawsuit anyway. She is, however, the exception. Most high-school students, and many college students as well, find it exceedingly difficult to complain about such behavior. As one young woman said, "It's negative to speak up for yourself. A strong guy is a strong guy. A strong girl is a bitch." Virtually all experts agree that most cases of harassment occur when boys are in groups and, moreover, that school personnel rarely take action. One California boy acknowledged, "It's their word against yours, and boys lie."

A variety of factors have made it ever more complex—some would say convoluted—to achieve some measure of equity in our system of higher education in recent years. Of central importance are recent demographic shifts in the pool from which colleges must pick their first-year classes. A key problem has been the decrease in the number of high-school graduates. According to the Center for Education Statistics, the number of high-school graduates fell from 3.15 million students in 1977 to 2.58 million in 1990. As a result, many colleges are competing with one another and using a variety of recruiting tools to woo the so-called best and brightest. Several colleges have advanced the date for mailing acceptances to give themselves more time to compete with other institutions; many schools are using financial-aid packages to lure top students, often without regard to need. With the cost of a single year at Ivy League institutions approximately $25,000 for the academic year 1993–94, the amount of financial aid offered has become more central to students' decisions about which school to attend. At many schools the overwhelming majority of students receive some aid—including students whose families are clearly middle- or even upper-middle-class.

The competition for high-achieving students has become so intense that the rather impersonal, carefully choreographed, traditional minuet between college and student—formal application, interview, tour of the college, and, on a designated day, receipt of a "fat" or a "thin" envelope—has, in some instances, given way to sales pitches, open disparagement of other schools, and even what many would consider inappropriate interaction with the students and/or their families. In one instance, a Missouri high-school senior with a 4.0 average was aggressively wooed by the associate dean of admissions at the University of Southern California. The student had not even applied to USC but was contacted by the admissions office because he had performed well on the Scholastic Aptitude Test. In his letter to the student the dean included his home telephone number. The student called, and "a friendship blossomed." When the student decided to visit USC in Los Angeles, the dean took him on a tour of Universal Studios and on a day trip to Mexico. Clearly, a bright student from a small town in Missouri would help geographically diversify the first-year class at USC. Perhaps an even more unusual example of the aggressive courting of prospective students is the experience of a Long Island high-school senior who also had a perfect 4.0 grade-point average. After she was accepted by the University of Pennsylvania, Haverford College, the University of Michigan, and Cornell University, Penn was so eager for her to enroll that some Penn alumni—complete strangers to her family—visited her father in the hospital where he was recovering from surgery! As the dean of admissions and financial aid at USC, which recently opened offices in New York City, Detroit, and San Francisco, stated, ". . . we have to run twice as fast as we did yesterday to keep even."

Colleges have been aggressively wooing select African-American and Hispanic students as well. As more colleges pursue racial diversity, both in response to accusations of exclusion and in order to recruit students who better reflect the demographics of the country, and with the pool of black students who have achieved academic excellence still relatively small, some colleges are resorting to techniques they once used only with star athletes, "special financial aid, free campus visits and aggressive promotional tactics." In 1992, only 1 percent of all black high-school students, or 1,493 people, scored 600 or above, out of a maximum of 800, on the verbal part of the Scholastic Aptitude Test, and only 2 percent, or 3,404, scored 600 or above on the math portion. Among white students, 8 percent, or 55,224, scored over 600 on the verbal portion, and 19 percent, 132,846, scored that high on the math portion.

Many colleges and universities, such as the University of Virginia, Duke University, and Rutgers University, have resorted to merit scholarships to woo the best students rather than only relying on scholarships based on financial need to attract black students. One of the central repercussions of this policy is that institutions that only offer scholarships based on need are finding that many black students are choosing to go elsewhere.

A survey by the National Association of College Admission Counselors in 1990 found that 13 percent more colleges and universities had openings in their first-year classes as of May 1 than had openings at that time the previous year. Of the eight hundred colleges surveyed, approximately 670 reported that they still had openings by May 1 of that year. Some institutions have responded by downsizing—that is, by reducing the number of incoming students—but this course of action creates both financial and personnel problems. Many colleges and universities are faced with the unenviable choice of laying off untenured faculty, and thus diminishing the numbers of women and people of color on the faculty, or firing tenured faculty, and thus provoking anger and anxiety among the rest of the faculty. Another response has been to dig deeper than usual into waiting lists or to lower admissions standards. According to one report, high-school counselors have observed that many colleges and universities have admitted students they probably would not have considered a few years ago.

While many colleges and universities are searching and competing harder than ever for students from their traditional pool—high achievers who can pay at least part of their own way—many other young people are suffering financially and searching with equal diligence for a way to continue their education. The recession of the early 1990s played a significant role in college enrollment. According to the Higher Education Research Institute at UCLA, the number of first-year students who chose colleges because of low tuition or financial aid or in order to live near home reached a record high in 1991. Over one-fourth of the students surveyed said they chose colleges based on low tuition and because of the amount of financial aid that was available. In 1991, one-fifth of the students surveyed selected colleges in order to live near home, while over 7 percent said they were attending college because they could not find jobs. The recession and the cost of tuition, room, and board have caused many students to choose public institutions over private ones; still others are choosing community colleges over four-year schools. During the 1970s and 1980s, older, nontraditional students fueled the growth of community colleges, but during the early 1990s significant numbers of eighteen-to-twenty-four-year-olds who ultimately want to receive a baccalaureate degrees are spending the first two years at lower-cost institutions and living at home.

As students are searching for affordable ways of financing college, access to higher education in both public and private colleges has been significantly limited by the impact of economic recession and stagnation. In recent years public schools have turned away thousands of students. In many cases formal enrollment policies have not been changed but *de facto* limits have been set, often without public acknowledgment, a legislative vote, or board-of-regents decree. Some institutions have raised admissions requirements; others have set earlier application dates or not provided enough course sections to meet students' needs. In 1989, Oregon reduced enrollments in its four-year colleges by two thousand, and further reductions were planned. In 1991, the State University of New York at Albany reduced the number of spaces for incoming first-year students by 5 percent, even though applications were up by 8 percent. In 1992, the California State University laid off hundreds of lecturers and cut approximately ten thousand classes at the twenty campuses in the system. San Francisco State President Robert Corrigan stated, "This will translate into thousands of students being denied classes this fall. This is the single worst catastrophe in the history of California higher education."

Public-college tuition, moreover, has risen steadily during the past decade, most dramatically during the severe recession of the early 1980s and again in 1991–92. In 1981–82, tuition at public institutions rose 16 percent; in 1982–83, 20 percent; and in 1983–84, an additional 12 percent. After several years of further tuition increases, the rise reached 12 percent in 1991–92 and climbed an additional 11 percent in 1992–93. Public education is clearly being rationed in a variety of ways—through cutbacks in course offerings, through faculty layoffs, and through increases in tuition. Tuition has also been raised at many community colleges, leading, according to the president of the American Association of Community and Junior Colleges, to "the potential of shutting the door to higher education for some disadvantaged students."

While public institutions are suffering cutbacks and many private institutions are rethinking their financial-aid policies, reducing the number of faculty, and, in some cases, eliminating departments, what is happening to those students who are traditionally the most favored in the admissions process of private institutions? The practice of admitting so-called legacy students, the sons and daughters (or grandsons and granddaughters) of alumni, is a long-standing, venerated policy of virtually all private colleges and universities in this country. According to Henry Rosovsky, former dean of the Faculty of Arts and Sciences at Harvard University, the definition of "legacy" varies from school to school. At Harvard, legacies are the sons and daughters of the graduates of Harvard and Radcliffe colleges; at Stanford they are defined as the children of all alumni, including the professional and graduate schools. Rosovsky points out yet another category of privilege—the children of faculty members—and estimates that approximately 16 to 20 percent of Harvard's first-year class belong to one of these two categories. Rosovsky claims that these students are admitted on an " 'all other things being equal' " basis—that is, that they are "given preference provided that their other qualifications are as strong as those with whom they have to compete."

According to the Office of Civil Rights of the U.S. Department of Education, 15.6 percent of all applicants of the class of 1992 at Harvard were accepted, and 35.2 percent of children of alumni were accepted. Rosovsky raises the question whether these preferences can be justified and provides a forthright answer:

> Private universities depend on alumni financial donations and other forms of support to ensure continued or rising levels of economic and intellectual prosperity. There is some relationship between a school's wealth and its quality, and the bulk of that wealth consists of gifts made by graduates. For these reasons, it is vital for a private university to strengthen its ties with individuals and families. This is done—across generations—by encouraging the presence of legacies in the student body.

An indication of exactly how important a college or university's "ties with individuals and families" can be is the amount of money these institutions raise yearly. In 1990, for example, Cornell University raised over $160 million, Yale raised $130 million, Columbia over $120 million, and Princeton approximately $75 million. During 1990–91, Wellesley College raised a record-breaking $32.3 million, the only liberal arts college other than Smith to raise over $30 million in one year. Moreover, in its five-year Campaign for $150 Million, which ended January 31, 1992, Wellesley raised $172 million, breaking all fund-raising records for national liberal arts colleges.

Fund-raising is, of course, a crucial and constant effort for all institutions of higher education, and is dependent on the good-will and sense of allegiance of alumni(ae) and friends of the in-stitution. The maintenance of the legacy system is a central method of encouraging multigenerational institutional loyalty. Moreover, while fund-raisers must constantly seek out and woo prospective donors, administrators must also be constantly aware of walking the delicate line between innovation and the promotion of social change, on the one hand, and moving too far ahead of their traditional constituency, on the other.

Having noted the importance of legacies to the financial well-being of colleges and universities and the preference they are consequently given, let us look at that other group of students who are said to be given preferential treatment in the admission process, students of color, most specifically African-American and Hispanic students. Affirmative action as an admissions strategy as well as a hiring strategy has become the *bête noire* of many critics of higher education in recent years, but what has, in reality, happened to minority admissions over the past de-cade? Before examining college enrollment, we must look at high-school completion rates. Among African-Americans, 75.1 percent of eighteen-to-twenty-four-year-olds completed high school in 1991, an increase of over 15 percentage points since 1970 but a decrease of nearly 2 percentage points from the pre-vious year. In comparison, whites had a high-school completion rate of 81.7 percent in 1991, essentially the same rate as twenty years earlier, and Hispanics had a shockingly low completion rate of 52.1 percent. This marked the fourth decline registered by Hispanics in the last five years, a rate below the 55.2 percent in 1973 and markedly lower than the rate of 62.9 percent in 1985.

According to a 1992 report by the American Council on Education, the percentage of black and Hispanic high-school graduates enrolled in college declined sharply during the 1980s. The report, based on Census Bureau data, indicates that the percentage of black high-school graduates between eighteen and twenty-four years of age who were enrolled in college dropped from 33.5 percent in 1976 to 28.1 percent in 1988. Among Hispanic high-school graduates of the same ages, the rate fell from 35.8 percent to 30.9 percent over the same period. The percentage of comparable white graduates enrolled in college rose from 33.0 to 38.1 percent, and for all races and incomes college enrollment increased from 33.1 percent in 1976 to 37.3 percent in 1988. As the researchers stated, "Since the mid-1970s, the college participation of African Americans and Hispanics has been a picture not of progress but of major regression."

In the late 1980s, however, the percentage of African-American high-school graduates attending college rose. By 1991, among eighteen-to-twenty-four-year-olds, 31.5 percent were attending college, up from a decade low of 26.1 percent in 1985. Though most of the increase was among black women, the attendance rates of black men increased 6 percent between 1985 and 1991, reversing a decline over the previous eight years. Hispanic participation rates increased slightly as well, from 26.9 percent in 1985 to 34.4 percent in 1991. During the same period of time, the rate of white high-school graduates attending college rose from 34.4 percent to 41.7 percent.

Many factors limit the number of Hispanic students who go on to higher education and remain to graduate: inferior secondary education, financial barriers, continuing discrimination, feelings of loneliness and isolation, and the reluctance of some families to see their children go far from home. Juan Morales, for example, graduated from high school in California but wanted to attend Oberlin College in Ohio. With substantial financial aid and faith in his academic potential, Oberlin admitted him, but

Juan found he was incredibly homesick during his first year. Now a senior chemistry major, he described how he felt at first: "I was so desperate for my community. . . . I came here, and there were no Mexican people, and I felt alone. But I thought, If I'm to improve my life, this is my chance." Increasingly, many Catholic institutions and the so-called public Ivies like the University of Michigan send their representatives and alumni recruiters into the Southwest and the West, hoping to persuade Hispanic students to consider their schools; nonetheless, Latino college attendance and completion rates remain relatively low.

Although college still eludes the vast majority of black and Hispanic students in the United States, the number of foreign students attending U.S. colleges has soared in recent years. During the academic year 1960–61, a total of 53,107 foreign students attended U.S. institutions; thirty years later, in 1990–91, the number had risen to 407,530. In the early 1960s, just over one-third of all foreign students (37.6 percent) came from Asia. By 1990, Asian students constituted over half (56.4 percent) of all foreign students. Despite new restrictions on foreign study, China led all countries, with 39,600 students in the U.S., an 18.6-percent increase over the previous year. The other countries that sent the most students to the United States were Japan, with 36,610, an increase of 22.7 percent over the previous year; Taiwan, 33,530, an 8.3-percent increase; India, 28,860, a 10-percent increase; and Korea, 23,360, a 7.6-percent increase. Miami-Dade Community College again enrolled the largest number of foreign students, followed by the University of Southern California, the University of Texas at Austin, Boston University, and the University of Wisconsin at Madison. The institutions with the largest percentages of foreign students in 1990–91 were the Massachusetts Institute of Technology and the New Jersey Institute of Technology, both with 21.8 percent; Columbia University, with 16.2 percent; the University of Pennsylvania, with 15.5 percent; and Stanford, with 14.9 percent.

The statistics for black, Hispanic, and foreign students at Ivy League schools indicate the critical problems within the U.S. educational system. At these schools, black students constituted no more than 5.8 percent of the total student population during the 1991–92 academic year. Cornell had the lowest percentage, with 3.9 percent; Brown and Yale had the highest percentage, 5.8. During the same year, the largest percentage of Hispanic students at Ivy League schools was at Cornell, where they constituted 4.6 percent; the smallest was at the University of Pennsylvania, where they constituted 2.8 percent. In contrast, the percentage of foreign students ranged from a low of 7.3 at Dartmouth to a high of 14.2 at Princeton.

One issue that crystallizes some of the fundamental problems in the American education system is that of the awarding of doctorates. Because several recent studies have predicted a shortage of professors in the 1990s, many groups have closely monitored the supply of American doctoral-degree recipients, those who form the pool from which academics are drawn. Overall, U.S. citizens received 9 percent fewer doctorates in 1989 than in 1979. Among whites, the decrease was 5.6 percent; among blacks, an alarming 23.2 percent. Though Hispanics, Asians, and Native Americans increased their share, their overall numbers remain small.

In the same year, among the recipients of doctorates whose citizenship was known, 73.9 percent were U.S. citizens. This percentage has been steadily declining since 1960, when U.S. citizens earned 87.8 percent of all doctorates awarded in this country. In 1989, women increased their share of doctorates, from 28.6 percent a decade earlier to 36.5 percent.

Data released in 1992 indicate that there has been a 13-percent rise in the number of African Americans receiving doctoral degrees between 1989 and 1991. But, despite the increase, the actual number of black Ph.D.'s is still lower than in 1980. Of particular interest is the fact that most black Ph.D.'s still receive their degrees from black colleges. According to Frank Matthews, publisher of *Black Issues in Education:*

> African-Americans do better at historically black colleges and universities, Asian-Americans at Berkeley, Hispanics at the University of Texas at Austin and in Puerto Rico and Native Americans increasingly at Southeastern Oklahoma State University. Instead of us moving closer and closer to integration, we seem to be moving closer to racial polarization.

As the statistics demonstrate, whereas the percentage of American citizens, particularly African Americans, receiving doctorates has decreased over the past decade, the percentage of foreign students receiving Ph.D.'s has risen significantly. Many educators have suggested that these trends are the result, at least in part, of a greater willingness on the part of universities to support foreign students, both financially and in other, tangible and intangible, ways, rather than American students from minority backgrounds. According to Frank L. Morris, Sr., president of the Council of Historically Black Graduate Schools and dean of graduate studies at Morgan State University, a historically black university in Baltimore, "At the heart of it is a fundamental aspect of American culture that really does value some immigrants over some American minority groups. University departments just don't believe many minorities can be successful."

An examination of financial-aid patterns for American, African-American, and foreign students indicates, moreover, that foreign students receive considerably more financial support from universities than do either of the two other groups. In 1990, for example, universities provided 68.8 percent of the financial support of foreign students while the individual students provided 13.8 percent of their own support. Among black doctoral candidates, university aid accounted for only 24.8 percent of their financial support while the students themselves had to provide 62.6 percent on their own. Some analysts claim that foreign students receive far more university support because they are more likely to be studying in fields such as science and engineering, in which research grants are plentiful. Black students tend more often to study the humanities and education, in which less research money is available. Even in the field of education, however, support is skewed in favor of foreign students. According to a 1990 report published by the National Research Council, 28 percent of the foreign students who earned doctorates in education received university support while only 12 percent of black students received similar support. Dr. Morris suggests that many of the senior faculty members who often make these decisions have "an irrational fear" of black men and that the image of "aggressive black males in the laboratories" contrasts sharply with that of the "model Asian immigrant scholar." In a speech to graduate-school officials Dr. Morris stated, "There clearly seems to be a move afoot to freeze out American minorities, especially black American males, from future faculty positions."

These views are shared by many educators. Dr. Israel Tribble, Jr., president of the McKnight Doctoral Fellowship program, which provides fellowships for black students in the sciences and engineering, has stated that, if institutions of higher learning spent the same energy recruiting and helping black scholars that they do recruiting and helping black athletes, the universities would be filled with black faces.

It is evident that, although the United States has made a clear commitment to mass education, many groups are being overlooked, neglected, and even excluded from the opportunity to receive the passport so essential for travel into the twenty-first century. Despite multifaceted efforts to include and welcome diverse groups to the halls of higher education, transforming once-elite social institutions into more democratic ones that are responsive to the needs of diverse groups has been a formidable task. Whether we are talking about prestigious law firms, which for decades, or in some cases for generations, were dominated by upper-class white males, or elite medical schools, which prior to the Second World War were largely the preserve of Protestant white males, or "restricted" neighborhoods and private secondary schools, or golf courses, tennis clubs, and prestigious men's clubs, opening these facilities to more than the token outsider, be he (and it has usually been a "he") Jewish or black or Asian-American, has taken years of struggle, knocking on closed doors, and usually major change in demographics and economics. Jewish students were held to quotas in virtually all elite colleges and universities until the late 1940s and early 1950s, when there were just too many qualified Jews who could afford the tuition to keep them out en masse any longer. According to the noted sociologist E. Digby Baltzell, author of *The Protestant Establishment: Aristocracy and Caste in America*, even among the faculty, "throughout the thirties and well into the forties, our major universities were still staffed almost entirely by old-stock Protestants." There have been (and still are in many places) quotas on Asian Americans in American higher education that are only starting to break down as the number of qualified Asian Americans soars, and, as we have seen, the number of African-American students admitted to elite colleges and universities in recent years has remained static or, in some cases, diminished. But even schools that have admitted significant numbers of nontraditional students often retain the feel of elite institutions.

Even the architecture seems to symbolize privilege—soaring Gothic-style stone buildings, rolling stretches of lawn dotted with old, magnificent trees, lakes on which students practice rowing for intercollegiate competition. One has only to think of Princeton, or Wellesley, or Harvard, with its timeless brick buildings, topped with blue, white, and golden domes to feel the presence of the Lodges, the Roosevelts, and the Lowells. In

Geoffrey Wolff's novel *The Final Club*, the central character, Nathaniel Clay, a part-Jewish public-school graduate from Seattle, goes east to Princeton in the mid-1950s. In a letter to his maternal grandparents he describes Ivy Club, one of the most prestigious of the well-known Princeton eating clubs, which chose its new members during sophomore year by the now infamous process of "bicker": ". . . an understated, handsome, deep-red old-brick building at 43 Prospect Avenue, predictably stained-glass windowed, furnished with leather, hunting printed, paneled with carved—oh, you know."

When Nathaniel doesn't really understand the importance of being among the chosen, of being selected by one of the eating clubs, preferably Cottage or Ivy, a friend tells him exactly how it is:

> "Because if you don't get in, you're out. Because if you're out . . ." Booth made a nasty slashing motion at his throat. "You don't want to be out, buckaroo, unless you choose out. . . ."
>
> "No! No! You don't understand," Booth said. "Let me tell you how it is!"
>
> And he told how it was. Taught the Iron Law of Clubmanship that holds: many are outside looking in, a few are inside looking . . . in. This Darwinian model of the feral world requires fewer us's than thems, or why be an us?

How is it possible to transform such closed, hierarchical institutions into ones that truly welcome people from many backgrounds? During the past two decades women and significant numbers of Jewish students have been admitted to formerly all-male, overwhelmingly Protestant Ivy League colleges. Moreover, private colleges and universities have reached out for many, many years to those "deserving" students who could not afford to meet all of their educational expenses. Students on partial scholarship, and students working on campus to help pay for tuition or room and board, have been relatively common at least since the 1950s. At Wellesley in the 1950s, these were students who seemed much like everyone else—middle-class, white, eager, hardworking. The only difference was that their families could not quite meet all the expenses connected with college. But reaching out to low-income populations and to members of minority groups in an attempt to include new people, students who could never have imagined attending a private, four-year college, is a relatively recent phenomenon.

Both public and private colleges have reached out over the past two decades to selected students from traditionally underrepresented groups. These efforts and the programs established on campuses to attempt to incorporate diverse students into what was once a remarkably homogeneous population has proved to be extraordinarily difficult and controversial. The admission of women, of people of color, and of students from low-income backgrounds, the establishment of student organizations devoted to their concerns, the attempts to modify the curriculum so that it incorporates the history, philosophy, culture, and concerns of previously underrepresented groups, have met with strong resistance on many campuses. Moreover, over the past decade outbreaks of overtly racist, sexist, anti-Semitic, and homophobic incidents have plagued campuses across the country. As we think about who shall learn in our incredibly diverse society, these "hate incidents," as they have come to be called, must be viewed as yet another barrier, and a formidable one at that, to the education of students in the United States. Since these incidents started to take place with startling regularity, academic administrators have attempted to quell the disturbances, protect the victims, and create a greater sense of community through a variety of measures, including the limitation of inflammatory speech, diversity requirements, and multicultural programs. But if we are to understand recent events on college campuses, these events must be viewed as part of the social, economic, and political picture of the country as a whole. Before analyzing the impact of bias incidents on individual students, the ways these young people have dealt with experiences of denigration and exclusion, and the leadership roles many have taken, let us first examine the broader societal context in which these events are occurring.

2

The Societal Context

Historically, the middle classes have felt deeply betrayed when
their wants have outpaced expectations or their aspirations have
been thwarted by austerity. Betrayal easily turns into soured
cynicism or worse, nationalist mania and race-baiting.

> Jonathan Rieder,
> *Canarsie: The Jews and
> Italians of Brooklyn
> Against Liberalism*

The barriers to education do not lie only in the increasingly inequitable class structure, or in the vastly unequal system of primary and secondary education, or in
the formidable problems of financing higher education. The attitudes of policymakers, educators, and students about who is
worthy of being educated, and about economic entitlement, and
the deep-seated attitudes about race, class, and gender, also
constitute real barriers to educating all the varied groups and individuals within American society.

Many debates about the goals and methods of education in
the United States and about recent conflicts on college campuses are framed as though academic institutions are walled-off
city-states, each with its own individual culture and social dynamics. Though these institutions do indeed have their own his-
tories, social structures and customs, they are also integral parts
of the larger society, and consequently reflect, at least to some
degree, the values, prejudices, and conflicts and the social, economic, and political realities of the United States today. There-

fore, in order to begin to comprehend the struggle over access to higher education and the dynamics operating within specific institutions, we must examine the larger society's attitudes toward equity, toward diversity, and toward the multiplicity of groups that together make up the United States. What have college students learned, as they were coming of age, about racial and ethnic conflict and cohesion in late-twentieth-century America? What are the central messages about equality of opportunity and about race, anti-Semitism, homophobia, and gender that they have absorbed from family members, from political leaders, from popular culture, from daily life?

In addition to examining attitudes toward this complex, pluralistic society, we must examine the economic reality students face as they prepare to forge their future. The headlines of the early 1990s tell the story: "Economic Trend for the 90's: Fear"; "Middle-Class and Jobless, They Share Sorrows"; "Graduates Facing Worst Prospects in Last 2 Decades"; "Graduates March Down Aisle into Job Nightmare"; and "Pay of College Graduates Is Outpaced by Inflation." What have the economic conditions of the late 1980s and early 1990s, particularly the severe unemployment and underemployment of the early nineties, meant to college students, to their vision of the American Dream, and to their prospects for the future? In June 1992, when many of the students interviewed for this book were graduating from college, the official U.S. unemployment rate had reached 7.8 percent. Ten million Americans were out of work and an additional seven million were part of the "hidden" unemployed—six million working part-time out of necessity and over one million "discouraged workers" who had stopped even looking for work. With a national rate of 7.8 percent, the rate for African Americans was nearly 15 percent (14.9), for Hispanics just over 12 percent (12.1), and for teenagers aged sixteen to nineteen, 23.6 percent.

Job prospects were dim for graduates in 1990 and 1991, but 1992 offered opportunities more dismal than they had been for twenty years. According to studies conducted at Northwestern and at Michigan State University, many large companies reduced their hiring, and nearly one-third of the entry-level jobs for new graduates evaporated during the first three years of the decade. In the New York region the job market was the worst it had been for fifty years, and it was not much better in the rest of the Northeast, in Michigan, and in California. In 1988, for example, American Telephone and Telegraph Company recruited seniors on three hundred campuses and hired two thousand graduates; in 1992, the company recruited on 155 campuses and hired a thousand graduates. What made the job search particularly difficult for college graduates in 1992 was that they were competing with over nine hundred thousand unemployed managers and professionals, whose unemployment rate had increased 60 percent in two years. Liberal-arts graduates had the most difficult time finding jobs; those with engineering and scientific specialties fared the best.

Many Ivy League graduates found themselves tending bar and driving taxicabs, law-school graduates were marking time while sending out as many as a hundred résumés, and recent Ph.D.'s were feeling lucky if they found year-to-year teaching posts. As one student from the University of Chicago indicated, students' concerns about the economy are adding to an already weighty list of worries they face: "If we're not the best, we don't get the jobs. If we sleep with the wrong person, we end up with AIDS. If we don't come up with a financially sound policy for the future of this country, we'll suffer the consequences."

But even college graduates with jobs were less well off in the early 1990s than they were during the 1980s. A study by the Economic Policy Institute, a Washington-based research organization, found that wages of college-educated people had failed to keep pace with inflation between 1989 and 1991. The study suggests that, as many high-paying jobs have vanished, college graduates have been forced to lower their sights and accept em-

ployment with lower pay. Today more Americans may be working in white-collar jobs than in blue-collar jobs, but income as
well as health and pension benefits have declined significantly
over the past several years. Moreover, the job climate for college
graduates in 1993 was characterized by economists as one of the
harshest in the past quarter-century. Graduates in the social sciences and the humanities have had trouble getting jobs for several years; in 1993, graduates in science and engineering, even
those from prestigious institutions such as the Massachusetts Institute of Technology, Stanford, and the California Institute of
Technology are having problems lining up positions. By the
week before graduation, only six of Caltech's graduates had received job offers from the once-lucrative southern-California
aerospace industry; over half of the graduates planned to go on
to graduate school, and twenty—eighteen more than in the previous year—planned to go to medical school. The importance of
higher education to the economic future of young people becomes clear when we note that the only groups whose average
pay continued to rise at a faster pace than inflation were black
women with bachelor-of-arts degrees and all men and women
with at least two years of postgraduate study.

Recent graduates cannot help being affected by the specter of
General Motors, IBM, Boeing, Sears, Roebuck, and many other
large companies eliminating thousands of jobs, teachers being
laid off in New England, and middle-class white-collar workers
joining support groups to share their sorrow over losing their
jobs, their homes, and their dreams. There were so many support groups for unemployed professionals in Connecticut during
the early 1990s that statewide gatherings of such groups were
held once a month. Even those who had jobs found their standard of living and their real income dropping. The pay of most individuals and the pooled earnings of most families bought less
in 1990 than in 1973. The only group exempt from this decline
was the top 20 percent of the population, whose incomes contin-

ued to rise throughout the 1970s and 1980s, and who finished the latter decade with real incomes well above their earnings in 1973.

In other words, while the vast majority of Americans have been losing ground, the richest among us have been getting even richer. According to researchers at the Federal Reserve Board and the Internal Revenue Service, the richest 1 percent of American households owned an even bigger share of total private wealth in 1989 than they had in 1983. In that year, the top 1 percent owned 31 percent of total private wealth; by 1989 they owned 37 percent, more than the total private wealth of the remaining 90 percent of Americans. The richest 10 percent of the population owned and controlled an incredible 68 percent of total private wealth in 1989, "a jump in inequality," according to Paul Krugman, an economist at the Massachusetts Institute of Technology, "to Great Gatsby levels." Claudia Goldin, a Harvard University economic historian, stated, "Inequality is at its highest since the great leveling of wages and wealth during the New Deal and World War II."

Given such dramatic inequality, how much social mobility really exists within the U.S. class structure? Moving up the economic ladder is, of course, one of the central tenets of the American Dream. Doing better than one's parents is viewed by many as almost an American birthright; the reality is that the best predictor of economic status is the status of one's parents. Recent studies indicate that rags-to-riches remains the exception rather than the rule and that, though it became easier in the 1980s for some in the middle class to become rich, it also became harder for the poor to climb out of poverty. There is no doubt that higher education, particularly scientific and technical education, is the key not only to upward mobility but even to merely securing employment and keeping up with inflation.

If the economic outlook during the early 1990s seemed problematic for many young people and perilous for some, the quicksand of race threatened the well-being of virtually all Americans. According to social scientists Michael Omi and Howard Winant, "To study race in the United States is to enter a world of paradox, irony and danger. In this world, arbitrarily chosen human attributes shape politics and policy, love and hate, life and death."

How does one possibly capture the flavor of race relations in a society as diverse as the United States? Interaction and attitudes differ so widely from one area to another, from cities to rural areas to suburban enclaves, from sections of the country with incredibly diverse populations to homogeneous small towns in the Midwest. But the media, particularly television, bring home to each of us, sometimes all too vividly, the often horrifying, at the very least disturbing, events on the racial landscape.

The last few years have often seemed defined by paradox—by the celebration of African-American stars, athletes such as Magic Johnson and Michael Jordan, entertainers like Bill Cosby, Oprah Winfrey, and Whitney Houston, movie stars like Eddie Murphy, Whoopi Goldberg, and Denzel Washington, and, at the same time, by the tragic, violent encounters that invariably involve race and have come to symbolize the tensions under which we all live, day to day: the unprovoked killing of Yusef Hawkins in Bensonhurst, New York; the vicious attack upon "the Central Park jogger"; the bitter conflict between blacks and a Jewish sect in Crown Heights, Brooklyn, following the automobile accident that killed a young African-American boy, and the subsequent fatal stabbing of a young Hasidic scholar from Australia; and, pre-eminently, the beating of Rodney King, the 1992 acquittal of the police officers, and the rioting in Los Angeles that followed including the brutal beating of Reginald Denny. These mythic, larger-than-life events inevitably become part of our consciousness, part of the way we view our world, and they affect, whether we know it or not, whether we want them to or not, the way we think about and relate to one another. They contain in concentrated form the suspicion, the fear, the anger, and the hatred that groups in the U.S. so often feel toward one another. These incidents tap into our most primitive fears: the unwelcome, even despised stranger murdered in an insular, homogeneous urban village; young black men going out of control—"wilding," as it came to be called—and brutally sexually attacking a white woman; two groups of outsiders venting their fury at one another; those we depend on to protect us viciously abusing that trust; and the poorest, most desperate among us giving expression to their rage and impotence. How we fear these explosions and try to protect ourselves from them!

But these deeply disturbing, psyche-battering eruptions provide only part of the backdrop for the development of popular attitudes about the allocation of educational resources, and for the incidents that have taken place on college campuses over the past few years. Another element is the continuing presence of organized white supremacists in our society and the violence they perpetrate. Whether it is David Duke capturing 55 percent of the white vote in his 1991 campaign for governor of Louisiana, or neo-Nazi skinheads and Klansmen marching through Birmingham, Alabama, in 1992, they are a real force in American society. According to the Southern Poverty Law Center, a record number of white-supremacist groups were active throughout the United States in 1991. The number of hate groups jumped from 273 in 1990 to 346 in 1991, and, for the fourth consecutive year, the Klanwatch Project of the Center recorded a surge in hate violence.

The Anti-Defamation League has also closely monitored the rise of neo-Nazi skinheads in the United States and found a 50-percent increase in the number of racist skinheads during the late 1980s. By the early 1990s, racist skinheads were active in thirty-one states and were actively recruiting and promoting racially motivated incidents in high schools. In 1988–89, at Groves High School in Birmingham, Michigan, a suburb of Detroit, three nonstudent skinheads joined with three students, roamed the halls, and confronted two other students; eventually a brawl broke out. The skinhead students were expelled and transferred to another high school, but the problems at Groves were far from over. During the spring of that academic year, racist flyers were found taped to a tree, a fence, a telephone pole, and doors outside the school. Two weeks later, several black students found the word "nigger" scrawled across their lockers; other lockers were defaced with swastikas. In mid-May, swastikas and the words "White Power" and "Skins" were spray-painted on the outside of the school. Police believe skinheads were responsible for these acts.

At the Douglas County High School in Castle Rock, Colorado, in 1989, a black student was harassed by skinheads shouting racial epithets at her and following her to a nearby store, where they threatened and pushed her. Later that spring, skinheads harassed the artist who created an antiracist poster with threats such as "Any day now, any time now, we're going to get you." The following fall, during homecoming weekend, a noose was hung on a black student's locker with a sign, "Wanted: Three Blacks, Reward." At Sprayberry High School in suburban Atlanta, over two dozen skinheads shouted "Heil Hitler!" during the pledge of allegiance and had Nazi insignias scrawled across their lockers and books.

In recent years, white supremacists, right-wing extremists, and other groups have used the forum of public-access cable channels to spew forth racial and religious hatred. According to one 1991 report, fifty-seven such programs were running in twenty-four of the hundred largest cable markets. Ku Klux Klan leaders produce shows in Kansas City; the White Aryan Resistance puts on a "popular program" in California; and Herbert Poinsett, "swastika-sleeved neo-Nazi," describes the Holocaust as a fiction and calls for the deportation of blacks to Africa on a cable station in New York City. On a Westchester County cable

station Ta-Har, who calls himself a high priest of Black Israel-
ites, threatens, "We're going to be beating the hell out of you
white people. . . . We're going to take your little children and
dash them against the stones. . . . We're also going to rape and
ravish your white women."

And, of course, the activities of hate groups in this country
mirror political developments in other parts of the world: the re-
surgence of neo-Nazi groups in Germany; the "ethnic cleansing"
and widespread use of rape as an instrument of terror in what
used to be Yugoslavia; attacks on immigrants in Italy; anti-
immigration political parties gaining support in Austria and
Switzerland; a rising tide of hate crimes in Toronto and increasing xenophobia in Canada, accompanied by moves to restrict
immigration; growing numbers of voters supporting Jean-Marie
Le Pen's racist National Front in France; and ethnic violence in
Kenya and in parts of what used to be the Soviet Union.

Hate groups in the United States and individuals who use
their techniques do not, of course, focus only on race. Calls to
restrict immigration that sometimes have the ring of xenophobia
have been heard from such disparate quarters as presidential
candidate Patrick Buchanan, Senator Robert Byrd, Democrat of
West Virginia, and former presidential candidate and Senator
from Minnesota Eugene McCarthy, Representative Charles
Rangel from New York, and the Sierra Club. There is considerable debate about the extent of anti-Semitism in the United
States today, with some experts claiming it has diminished significantly in recent years; the Annual Audit of the Anti-
Defamation League indicates, however, that anti-Semitic
incidents in the United States rose during 1991 to a record total
of 1,879. This 11-percent increase over 1990 represents the
highest level of anti-Jewish attacks in the thirteen years the
league has been compiling the nationwide survey. Moreover, for
the first time there were more attacks on people than on property. During 1992, the number of such incidents declined by 8

percent, but for the second straight year attacks on individuals were more frequent than attacks on property. In addition, the Asian American Legal Defense and Education Fund has reported a recent rise in anti-Asian violence, particularly in New York City.

Incidents of violence against homosexuals also rose in 1991. A survey of five cities by the National Gay and Lesbian Task Force Policy Institute found that the number of reported incidents, including harassment, threats, physical assaults, vandalism, arson, police abuse, and murder, rose 31 percent, from 1,389 reported incidents in 1990 to 1,822 the following year.

The brutal murder of an American sailor highlights the level of hostility felt by some toward homosexuals in this country. On September 30, 1992, Allen R. Schindler, a twenty-two-year-old naval radioman stationed on the USS *Belleau Wood*, a large amphibious assault ship, "ended months of inner turmoil and told his commanding officer that he was homosexual." A month later, he went to a park near the naval base in Japan where the ship had pulled into port and "was battered to death against the fixtures of a public toilet." The following day, two other sailors from the ship were arrested. The lenient punishment of the first sailor to be brought up on charges indicates the U.S. Navy's response to the murder of one of their own who also happened to be homosexual. After admitting his involvement in the murder and agreeing to testify for the prosecution, he was given a four-month sentence and a bad-conduct discharge. In May 1993, the other sailor—originally charged with premeditated murder, which carried with it a possible death sentence—was permitted to plead guilty to the lesser charge of murder with intent to commit great bodily harm and was sentenced to life imprisonment.

Just one month before sentencing of the sailor for Navy Radioman Schindler's murder, three marines were acquitted of charges that they had assaulted three men at a Wilmington, North Carolina, bar that caters to homosexuals. The three marines allegedly dragged one man out of the bar and beat him while shouting, "Clinton must pay," apparently referring to President Clinton's efforts to lift the ban on gay men and lesbian women serving in the military.

Also during the spring of 1993, the Bremerton High School student council, in Washington State, approved a measure that would prohibit openly gay students from serving in school government. The amendment to the school's constitution would bar from office any student practicing "immoral activities," such as indecent exposure, homosexuality, and sexual harassment. According to the school's principal, the amendment was proposed by a group of religious, conservative students. One supporter, the president of the Young Republicans Club, addressed the student council wearing a T-shirt that read, "On a mission from God"; he stated, "This sends a message to the school that homosexuality is wrong." Randy Shilts, in an interview at the time of the publication of his book, *Conduct Unbecoming: Lesbians and Gays in the U.S. Military*, analyzes the status of homosexuals in the United States in the early 1990s: ". . . straight people are in tremendous denial about the existence of prejudice against gay people. Even those supportive of gay rights don't get it. They don't realize what a despised minority we are in America."

Tension and incidents of violence between minority groups have also escalated in recent years. The most vivid and disturbing example took place during the riots in Los Angeles following the Rodney King verdict, when Korean businesses became the targets of black looting and violence. Ironically, this intergroup rage was predicted by the rapper Ice Cube in an album released on Halloween 1991. As Jon Pareles has stated:

> The album included "Black Korea," which revealed the deep resentment between Korean shopkeepers (whom Ice Cube, in one ignorant flourish, described as "chop-suey-eatin' ") and blacks, who felt they were being treated more like potential

criminals than customers. . . . The album was vengeful and divisive, airing deep-seated prejudices and treating ethnic groups as
if they were warring gangs that could never share turf. But it was
also prophetic. . . .

But violent incidents give us only one perspective of the complexity of racial conflict in American society; to probe the nature
of intergroup interaction one must examine day-to-day life more
closely. One of the myths that have developed over the past two
decades is that African Americans are being given preferential
treatment in the United States. In part because of the way Republicans have used race as a wedge issue to mobilize the anger
of the white working and middle classes, the idea that blacks are
benefiting while whites are suffering is widespread. As Thomas
and Mary Edsall have pointed out in their influential book, *Chain
Reaction: The Impact of Race, Rights, and Taxes on American
Politics*, "Under the aegis of conservative principle, the Reagan
administration produced an agenda that placed the interests of a
substantial segment of black America against the interests of
a substantial segment of white America." Using "ostensibly neutral language," Ronald Reagan developed a "powerful tool with
which to advocate stands that polarized voters on race-freighted
issues—issues ranging from welfare to busing to affirmative action." The repeated slurs against mothers receiving Aid to Families with Dependent Children, the Willie Horton advertisement
during the 1988 presidential campaign that so cleverly played on
people's fears about black men and crime, George Bush's disdain-
ful articulation of the word "quotas," playing on white workers'
fears of losing their jobs to members of minority groups, all have
reinforced the image of blacks as lazy, worthless, even savage people who are nonetheless getting ahead, not on the basis of merit
and hard work, but, rather, because of handouts from "liberal" pol-
iticians.

This analysis has been foisted on the American people during a period of intermittent recession and economic stagnation when the working class and middle class have lost ground, and, as we have seen, a period during which the rich and very rich have increased their income and share of the nation's wealth to what some consider obscene levels. This strategy of encouraging the middle classes to blame the poor and people of color for their losses—not only their economic losses, but the deterioration of their schools, their neighborhoods, and the quality of their lives—is both a political ploy to drive a wedge between traditionally Democratic voters and the Democratic party, and also a tactic to divert blame for the growing inequality within American society and the deterioration of the quality of life for the majority of Americans from those in power to the least powerful among us.

In his book, *Race and Class in Texas Politics*, Chandler Davidson gives a vivid example of this diversion of blame from elected officials to poor people of color. Davidson describes a conversation between two working-class men standing waist deep in the swimming pool of a Houston, Texas, apartment building:

Bob stared at his beer can for a moment, and then savagely, to no one in particular, he said, "That son-of-a-bitch Reagan put me out of a job. That's who did it."

Al stiffened. "Wa-a-a-it a minute," he said. "You're talking about my man, now. You're talking about my man."

"I don't care if he's your man. That son-of-a-bitch is the reason I'm standing in this goddamn pool tonight, drunk on my ass. . . ."

"Just a minute," he said. "You don't talk about the president like that."

"To hell with the president!" . . .

"Listen, Bob," Al said, suddenly calm. "You've got it wrong. You've got it all wrong. You want me to tell you who's taken your job away? You really want to know?"

Bob glared at him.

"It's the goddamn niggers, who'll work for lower wages. And it's these goddamn wetbacks. That's who's taken your job. You can't blame that on Reagan."

Bob was silent for what seemed like a long time, staring straight at Al. "Now you're talking sense," he said, finally. "Now you're talking something that I can relate to. You've put your finger on something now."

In his powerful book, *Canarsie: The Jews and Italians of Brooklyn Against Liberalism*, sociologist Jonathan Rieder quotes an analyst of lower-middle-class rage and fear: "They feel the pressure, like everything is fading away. It's all in danger: the house you always wanted is in danger, the kids are in danger, the neighborhood is in danger. It's all slipping away."

The residents of Canarsie whom Rieder interviewed, many of them former liberals who supported the civil-rights movement and the War on Poverty during the 1960s, spoke again and again, often with brutal and undisguised venom, of how they were losing ground and the blacks were benefiting from the social policies of the 1970s. A city worker "explodes":

These welfare people get as much as I do and I work my ass off and come home dead tired. They get up late and they can shack up all day long and watch the tube. With their welfare and food stamps, they come out better than me. . . . So why should I work? I go shopping with my wife and I see them with their forty dollars of food stamps in the supermarket, living and eating better than me. . . . Let them tighten their belts like we have to.

Another man exclaimed, "Who's feeling sorry for me? The colored have gotten enough. Let them do for themselves like we do!"

But the reality for many African Americans is far different from the images of angry middle-Americans. Study after study indicates that structural racism continues to permeate American society. A judicial commission that spent three years and $1 million studying evidence concluded in June 1991 that the New York State court system is "infested with racism." The report stated, "This commission is constrained to draw the basic conclusion that there are two justice systems at work in the courts of New York State, one . . . [for] whites and a very different one for minorities and the poor." A research group established by the American Bar Association studied some three hundred car dealerships in the Chicago area and found that salespeople who bargain with customers over the price of a new car make significantly lower final offers to white men than to women or blacks. Other studies indicate that African Americans regularly suffer harassment when they are shopping. According to Dr. Joe R. Feagin, professor of sociology at the University of Florida, who has studied discrimination in public places, "Blacks are seen as shoplifters, as unclean, as disreputable poor. No matter how affluent and influential, a black person cannot escape the stigma of being black even while relaxing or shopping."

A study by researchers at the Medical College of Wisconsin of the records of over eighty-six thousand Medicare patients who underwent heart-bypass surgery in 1986 concluded that such operations are performed on older black patients only about one-fourth as often as on similar white patients. Medical reasons do not explain the difference. Blacks, particularly black males, are underrepresented in medical schools across the country. The percentage of all minority students enrolled in medical school has remained at around 10 percent over the past two decades, but in 1990, 23 percent fewer black men were enrolled than in 1971.

In May 1993, six African-American Secret Service agents assigned to protect the safety of the President of the United States were kept waiting an hour for breakfast as all other patrons were being served in an Annapolis, Maryland, branch of Denny's restaurant. They have filed a federal discrimination suit. In Boston, at 2:00 A.M. on a December night in 1992, a black man hailed a taxi and asked to be taken to his home in Roxbury, a predominantly black neighborhood. The driver, a white woman, refused, saying it was too dangerous, and told him to get out of her cab. He refused. After she radioed for help, another driver arrived, ordered the man to get out of the cab, and, when he would not, "grabbed him, jerked him out and called him a 'nigger.' " The passenger turned out to be Bruce Bolling, a member of the Boston City Council and a "scion of the most prominent black family in Massachusetts."

Lawyers who are members of minority groups are grossly underrepresented in law firms nationally. In 1991, thirty-five major law firms, recognizing the gravity and persistence of the problem, pledged to hire more black, Hispanic, Asian-American, and Native American lawyers and to treat them equally in assignments and promotion once they arrive. The president of the New York City Bar Association acknowledged, "There are problems at every level—at recruitment, at retention and promotion, and the only way to make sure that changes occur is to address them all at the same time." And even in the military, which has recently been celebrated as one of the more integrated institutions within American society, evidence was found in 1991 of pervasive racial discrimination. After touring six American military bases in Germany, Arthur A. Fletcher, chairman of the United States Civil Rights Commission, reported to senior Pentagon officials that discrimination was occurring in the hiring and promotion of both enlisted personnel and civilian defense employees. He also reported that racial discrimination was endemic in the schools of employees' children.

Although *de jure* segregation has been outlawed since the Civil Rights Act of 1964, *de facto* segregation continues to exist in many aspects of American society. In 1954, four decades ago, the Supreme Court decision *Brown* v. *Board of Education* stated that "separate but equal" was fundamentally unequal.

The crucial issue, as Andrew Hacker has stated, was "that segregation based on race sent a message to black children that whites did not want them in their schools. And that exclusion, the Justices concluded, 'generates a feeling of inferiority as to their status in the community that may affect their hearts and minds in a way unlikely ever to be undone.' " According to studies done by the National School Board Association, as recently as the late 1980s two-thirds of all black children still attended segregated schools. In Illinois, New York, and Mississippi over 80 percent of black children attended segregated schools; in Michigan, California, New Jersey, Maryland, and Wisconsin over 70 percent attended such schools.

Much of the segregation of the schools is due to the continuing segregation of residential patterns all over the country—not only in major cities, which have increasingly become nonwhite, but in suburbs as well. Even affluent blacks are choosing to live together rather than move into predominantly white suburbs. By 1990, 32 percent of all black Americans in metropolitan areas lived in suburban communities, a record 6-percent increase over 1980. In explanation for their choice of suburbs in which a significant percentage of the residents were black, one senior administrator stated, "I don't want to come home and always have my guard up." An urban planner recalls being one of the few blacks attending the University of Connecticut in 1970:

> I was called a nigger the first week there and held by the police until this white girl told them I hadn't attacked her. You want to call me a separatist, so be it. I think of myself as a pragmatist. Why should I beg some cracker to integrate me into his society when he doesn't want to? Why keep beating my head up against a wall, especially when I've been there.

Following the savage beating of Rodney King, the acquittal of the four policemen, and then the conviction of two of the four, many middle-class African Americans around the country expressed their anger, sadness, and frustration at the status of blacks in the United States. One Chicago writer and consultant said, "When I heard the verdict, I couldn't stop crying. It was crying of the deepest sadness. One piece of it was release. The other was, 'Will our children ever know the absence of racism?'" A Los Angeles architect reflected, "We have had to look in the mirror of our society. What I see is very ugly." And a professor of sociology from the University of California at Los Angeles analyzed the impact of the Rodney King ordeal: "We carry around a rage in us. We carry the weight of the race and the weight of racism. The Rodney King case has radicalized black folks that used to be mild-mannered. It has brought people face to face with the country's racial caste system."

Although so many Americans echo the feelings of the middle-class Americans of Canarsie—that blacks and other minority groups have profited over the past two decades while they themselves have suffered—the reality is dramatically different. Significantly more African Americans did move into the middle and upper-middle classes during the 1980s; nonetheless, millions of black and Hispanic families remained locked in deprivation.

Data from the 1990 Census document the continuing disparity in income between whites and blacks in the United States. Nationally, the 1990 median household income was $36,915 for whites and $21,423 for blacks. In other words, blacks earned 58 cents for every dollar whites earned. In 1970, blacks earned 61 cents for every dollar whites earned. Thus, throughout the 1980s, the gap in earnings has increased.

Even if many whites may feel they are losing ground because blacks and Hispanics are gaining ground, virtually all studies indicate that this is rarely the case. Although two-thirds of all poor people in the U.S. are white, the proportion of African-American and Hispanic families living in poverty is disturbingly high. Moreover, the accompanying social ills of decrepit housing, dangerous deteriorating neighborhoods, inferior schools, and inadequate health services make it exceedingly difficult for African Americans and Latinos to enroll in institutions of higher education, to achieve academically, to complete their course of study and obtain a degree. These problems constitute nearly insurmountable barriers to the educational achievement that is so necessary in postindustrial America.

When we consider the issue of bias in higher education, we must, of course, analyze the role of women within the educational system and in the larger society as well. An examination of the status of women in the United States during the late 1980s and early 1990s yields a complex mélange of continuing advances along with continuing discrimination and violence. As women have moved in significant numbers into law, medicine, business, politics, and a wide variety of other fields, they have also been victims of high-profile, often brutal crimes of violence—the attack on the Central Park jogger, the rape of Desiree Washington by Mike Tyson, and the assault of over thirty-five women by navy and Marine Corps pilots at the Tailhook convention in Las Vegas. A study by the Senate Judiciary Committee stated that in 1990 rape was at "epidemic proportions" in the U.S. In that year, 100,433 rapes were reported, but the study suggests that almost two million rapes go unreported annually. As New York City Assistant District Attorney Linda Fairstein stated, "Sadly, our society tolerates attitudes that lead to violence against women."

Indeed, the Anita Hill–Clarence Thomas case brought home to millions of Americans the disregard, disbelief, and disdain of the all-male Senate Judiciary Committee toward a highly educated, respected professional woman who brought out into the open the pervasiveness of sexual harassment. Though her story was discounted and disbelieved at the time, in much the same way that black women's stories about sexual aggression and rape have been discounted and disbelieved for generations,

Anita Hill taught Americans the importance of women in positions of power. Who could doubt that, if one or two female senators had been sitting on that committee, Arlen Specter would not have set out to denigrate and humiliate Professor Hill in quite the same vicious way, that Alan Simpson would not have referred to "this sexual harassment crap" with obvious disdain, that the committee would have been forced to treat Anita Hill with greater respect? The 1992 political process demonstrated the impact of this dramatic episode on the electoral politics. Most analysts agree that the Anita Hill–Clarence Thomas television spectacle was the proverbial wake-up call in American attitudes toward women in power. Whether one believed Anita Hill or not, American voters, particularly women, finally saw with their own eyes how unrepresentative one of our central governing bodies was, and took action. What followed was the so-called 1992 Year of the Woman: the primary victory in Illinois of Carol Moseley Braun defeating the incumbent Senator Alan Dixon, who had voted for the Thomas nomination, and her subsequent election as the first African-American woman to the United States Senate; the victories of two female candidates to the Senate from California, Representative Barbara Boxer and former San Francisco Mayor Dianne Feinstein; and the victory of Patty Murray, the "Mom in tennis shoes," to the Senate from Washington State. In addition, forty-seven women were elected to the House of Representatives, a record number.

Over the past few years, the widespread nature of sexual harassment has become clearer. In a 1989 study by *The National Law Journal*, 60 percent of the nine hundred female lawyers surveyed said they had experienced some form of sexual harassment in the workplace. Several major law firms have recently enacted codes of conduct to delineate appropriate behavior and to ward off official complaints.

A survey of interns and residents in internal medicine at the University of California at San Francisco published by *The New*

England Journal of Medicine in February 1993 found that three-fourths of the women and one-fifth of the men believed they had been sexually harassed during their medical training. Another survey of two thousand graduate students and two thousand faculty members in four scientific disciplines at ninety-eight major U.S. research universities found that 32 percent of female graduate students and 40 percent of female faculty members have direct evidence of sexual harassment by faculty members at their universities. Funded by the National Science Foundation, the study's findings were presented at a preconference session of the 1993 annual meeting of the American Association for the Advancement of Science. These data are consistent with previous studies. A 1986 survey by the Association of American Colleges, for example, reported that 49 percent of untenured women and 32 percent of tenured women at Harvard had reported some form of sexual harassment.

In May 1991, Dr. Frances Conley, a professor of neurosurgery at the Stanford University School of Medicine, resigned her academic position, charging sexism on the part of individual colleagues and a quarter-century of subtle and not-so-subtle sexism at the medical school. Like Anita Hill, Dr. Conley is highly educated and well respected in her field, and therefore was heard—at Stanford and across the country. Dr. Conley complained of being called "honey" when she was heading the surgical team in the operating room, of being sexually propositioned, of being accused of having premenstrual stress syndrome when she disagreed with a colleague, and of having male doctors run their hands up her leg at meetings. As Dr. Conley stated, "The most frustrating part of this whole thing is that most of the harassment is an attitude where male faculty members are in a time warp. . . . They believe in male superiority and female subservience." She subsequently returned to her position, after changes were made in the administration of her department.

In 1990, the Pentagon reported that a major study of sexual harassment in the military showed that more than one-third of the women surveyed experienced some form of serious harassment, include touching, pressure for sexual favors, and rape. The Pentagon study was based on responses from more than twenty thousand men and women on active duty, took two years to complete, and was, according to researchers, the largest effort to measure sexual harassment in the workplace, public or private. Fifty-two percent of the women surveyed reported harassment in the form of teasing and jokes, 44 percent reported looks and gestures, 38 percent reported touching and cornering, 15 percent pressure for sexual favors, and 5 percent actual or attempted rape or sexual assault. One of the most important findings was that 71 percent of the women said they had suffered three or more forms of harassment.

A highly publicized incident of harassment occurred in September 1991, at the thirty-fifth annual convention of the Tailhook Association, a private group of retired and active-duty naval pilots. At least thirty-six women, several of them officers, were assaulted while the secretary of the navy stood nearby on a patio chatting with colleagues. According to *The New York Times*, "On each of the three nights . . . groups of officers in civilian dress suddenly turned violent, organizing with military precision into drunken gangs that shoved terrified women down the gantlet, grabbing at their breasts and buttocks and stripping off their clothes." One woman, a thirty-year-old helicopter pilot who was also an admiral's aide, recalled approaching a group of officers:

". . . one officer shouted, 'Admiral's aide! Admiral's aide,' while another grabbed me by the buttocks with such force that it lifted me off the ground and ahead a step.' . . ."

Others grabbed her, too, and one man put his hands down her bra. "I then turned my head to the left and sank my teeth into the fleshy part of the man's left forearm, biting hard," she said.

The lieutenant kicked and punched her assailants but was overpowered. After being pawed for about 20 feet of the hallway, she managed to escape through an open door into a hotel room.

When the lieutenant filed a complaint with her boss, Rear Admiral John W. Snyder, Jr., he is reported to have told her, "That's what you get for going to a hotel party with a bunch of drunk aviators."

After a prolonged period of cover-up, a "stone wall of silence among a brotherhood of aviators who said they could not recall what they had seen," Navy Secretary H. Lawrence Garrett 3rd was forced to resign, two navy inquiries were established, an admiral was reassigned, the promotions of thousands of navy and marine officers were delayed, and a new training program was initiated. The Tailhook scandal illustrates the intricate interconnections between the attitudes and norms of the wider society and those of young people just coming of age. The tolerance of sadistic, sexist behavior in the society at large clearly sets the tone for acceptance of such behavior by some males and females at all levels of the educational system.

Any examination of attitudes in the United States around the issue of equality, and particularly around class, race, and gender, must include a discussion of popular culture, for, whether it distills and reflects societal attitudes, helps to form them, or fulfills both functions, often simultaneously, popular culture is a potent force within American society. If we observe American popular culture overall, particularly television, films, and music, the overriding impression is of violence that is constantly and relentlessly depicted, described, and detailed. From the obscene and frankly misogynist, racist, and homophobic performances of Andrew Dice Clay in the late 1980s; to the ubiquitous reports of murder and other generalized mayhem on local-television news programs; to the aggression embedded within American athletics, particularly football and hockey; to the lurid discussions of sadomasochistic exploitation and abuse on talk shows; to the cop shows and endless made-for-TV movies that feature demented lovers and crazed killers stalking their prey; to movies that, in the spirit of equal opportunity, feature unbalanced, obsessed women who kill alongside similarly obsessed, brutal men—violence, often coupled with kinky sex, is virtually inescapable.

Perhaps *Falling Down*, the 1993 film starring Michael Douglas, is the prototype of the violent film of the angry 1990s. Douglas plays an ordinary man who "breaks down one hot Los Angeles morning in a freeway traffic jam and blazes a trail of violence across the city. It is a movie filled with fury, human scum and hatred in the metaphorical urban sewer that the city of angels has become." As one observer has described it,

> Steeped in hatred, "Falling Down" flings intolerable ethnic and homophobic insults, with one character proudly showing another a can that once held the Zyklon B gas the Nazis used to exterminate Jews in death camps. With eerie timing, the movie was being filmed on a downtown Los Angeles street the day . . . [the] riots [following the first Rodney King verdict] began.

As one detective on Barry Levinson's television program entitled *Homicide* states, "It's homicide, the one thing this country is still good at."

If, as Andrew Ross, author of *No Respect: Intellectuals and Popular Culture*, has written, popular culture incorporates "popular perceptions, aspirations, and resentments," perhaps no aspect of American culture more clearly articulates these perceptions, aspirations, and resentments than does popular music.

According to a *Newsweek* article entitled "Rap and Race,"

While plain talk about race and our real racial divisions has been absent from the [1992] campaign, it has become the rhetorical center of pop music. After nearly three decades of reflecting the promises of integration, pop music—from country to hard-core rap—has become our most pointed metaphor for volatile racial polarization.

Whether we are listening to Ice-T and his song "Cop Killer," or the California rap crew N.W.A. (Niggers with Attitude) and their "——— Tha Police," or Public Enemy's emphasis on "pure confrontation," "race has replaced the generation gap as the determining force" in pop music. The violence that characterizes so much of American society, particularly the violence that is experienced by people living in inner-city ghettos, also characterizes much of rap: N.W.A. peppers their raps with "tales of gang brutality and misogyny" and "pitch themselves—to a largely white audience—as 'Real Niggaz.' " Their album, *NIGGAZ4LIFE*, became the top one in the country within two weeks of its release during the summer of 1991. Are these young musicians acting out the larger white society's images and stereotypes of black youth, particularly black young men, capitalizing on white fear and fascination with violence and with African-American culture, in order to make it big in America? Are they saying, If this is the way they see us, this is the way we'll be—we'll give them what they want? Or are these groups expressing their own and their communities' genuine rage and, at the same time, striking an incredibly powerful chord of rage in other young Americans, regardless of race?

There are some who claim that rap isn't just entertainment—that it is reportage. Chuck D, Public Enemy's main writer and rapper, has characterized rap as black America's CNN, the documentary news service of the inner cities. Others, such as Cornel West, director of Princeton's Afro-American Studies Program, claim:

Rap is an attempt to socialize black children by young black artists. When . . . KRS-One . . . and Public Enemy speak of themselves as a cable channel for the black community, they are saying that we will socialize, acculturize ourselves, given the breakdown in the black family, community and nurturing system. . . .

In fact, *Apocalypse 91 . . . the Enemy Strikes Black*, the 1991 album of Public Enemy, focuses largely on "black pride and black nationalism" and insists that "the black community must unite to claim what it has earned." And Queen Latifah, a major rap star of the late 1980s and early '90s, "stands for goodness, hard work and saying no to racism and sexism."

A recent phenomenon in rap, as well as in films and even television, is the increasingly common use of the once taboo word "nigger." As a *New York Times* headline spelled it out, it is truly "speaking the unspeakable." The front-page article began, "One of America's oldest and most searing epithets— 'nigger'—is flooding into the nation's popular culture, giving rise to a bitter debate among blacks about its historically ugly power and its increasingly open use in an integrated society." Rap artists have used the term widely in their lyrics; in a major-studio film, *Trespass,* about an inner-city treasure hunt, gang members portrayed by black rappers call one another " 'nigger' almost as often as they call one another by their names." On Home Box Office, every Friday night, black "cutting-edge comedians" on *Russell Simmons' Def Comedy Jam* frequently use the term in their acts.

The word has been used extensively within the black community, but what is new is its open use in the larger society. It is that wider use that has spawned controversy within and outside of the black community. There are those like Kris Parker, the rap artist known as KRS-One, who predict that "nigger" will be demystified and deracialized by its broader use and will become just another word. Paul Mooney, a comic and writer, agrees. On a comedy tape entitled *Race*, he does routines called "Nigger Vampire," "1-900-Blame-a-Nigger," and "Nigger History." He explains, "I say nigger all the time. I say nigger 100 times every morning. It makes my teeth white. Nigger-nigger-nigger-nigger-nigger-nigger-nigger-nigger-nigger. I say it. You think, 'What a small white world.' "

Others feel that Americans, black and white alike, should never forget what the term has meant historically and, in fact, what it still means today. As one civil-rights leader stated, "That term made us less than human, and that is why we must reject [its] usage. . . . We cannot let that term be trivialized. We cannot let that term be taken out of its historical context." Still other observers point out the danger of using language in order to demystify it while it is still being used within the large society to wound and to legitimize violence and discrimination. One person queried, "Does it signal a new progressive step forward toward a new level of understanding or a regressive step back into self-hate?" He continued, "I fear it is the latter."

Concern about legitimizing a term that has been used for so many centuries to demonize and dehumanize an entire group of people, and to treat them with almost unimaginable cruelty, becomes particularly relevant in light of the January 1993 incident in which a fraternity, Phi Kappa Psi, at Rider College in New Jersey, organized "nigger night," during which prospective new members were required to perform chores at the fraternity house while dressed as and behaving in ways illustrating denigrating stereotypes of blacks. For over the past decade, as the United States has become ever more diverse, as the economy has weakened and slid repeatedly into recession, as violent episodes of racism, sexism, anti-Semitism, and homophobia have increased in the larger society and in the rest of the world, so have colleges and universities been beset by widespread episodes of intolerance.

Before turning to in-depth interviews with individual students who have experienced intolerance or have been active on campuses that have been beset by bias incidents, let us examine some recent events on campuses across the country that have shocked observers and given rise to renewed efforts to educate and sensitize students, administrators, and faculty alike to live and work together with greater understanding and mutual respect.

3

Conflict Within
the Ivory Tower

Either/or dichotomous thinking categorizes people, things, and
ideas in terms of their difference from one another. . . . This emphasis
on quantification and categorization occurs in conjunction with
the belief that either/or categories must be ranked. The search
for certainty of this sort requires that one side of a dichotomy be
privileged while its other is denigrated. Privilege becomes defined
in relationship to its other.   Patricia Hill Collins,
                                     Black Feminist Thought:
                                     Knowledge, Consciousness, and the
                                     Politics of Empowerment

Admission to college or university is, as has been noted,
a first but crucial step in an individual's preparation for
meaningful participation in the social, economic, and political life of postindustrial America. But admission is merely the
first hurdle a student must clear in higher education. Financing
college education, achieving academically, and maneuvering
around the multitude of social, psychological, and political obsta-
cles that impede the path to a bachelor's degree are often much
higher hurdles than admission. Among the barriers that many students have had to face in recent years are virtually continuous
clashes stemming from prejudice, ethnocentrism, and fear—fear of
the unknown, of the stranger among us. At root these clashes are
about entitlement and power, and about students' concerns with
the precariousness of their position in the social structure.

Although colleges and universities have since the end of the
Second World War been to a considerable extent transformed
from elite bastions of privilege to increasingly open, heterogeneous communities, a wave of overt intolerance has recently swept
over the academic community. There is little doubt that students
today are more tolerant than their grandparents and their parents, yet clashes—some involving vocal or written assaults,
some involving violence—continue to plague academic institutions and to shock observers. One of the reasons these so-called
hate incidents are so shocking is the increasing unacceptability
of overtly racist, sexist, anti-Semitic, and homophobic language
and behavior in much of the wider society; another is the contrast between the violence of these incidents and the open expression of hatred and bigotry on the one hand, and the
expectation of at least minimal civility in academic settings on
the other.

Two relatively recent incidents that deal with the incendiary
combination of race and gender point up the depth and pervasiveness of intergroup hostility on campuses all over the country.
In the small rural town of Olivet, Michigan, at Olivet College, a
school founded in 1844 by the abolitionist minister the Reverend John Shipherd as a "bastion of racial tolerance," a "racial
brawl" involving approximately forty white students and twenty
black students broke out one night in early April 1992. According to one report:

> Racial epithets were shouted at the black students as the two
> sides rumbled on the gray linoleum. Two students, one black,
> one white, were injured and briefly hospitalized.
>
> Afterward, blacks and whites who had crammed together for
> midterms and shared lunch money and dormitory rooms could
> not look each other in the face and were no longer on speaking
> terms.

This incident was the culmination of increasing hostility among black and white students at Olivet. In the months prior to the incident, white male students had become more openly resentful of black men dating white women. Then, on April 1, a white female student claimed she had been attacked by four black students and left unconscious in a field near the campus. She was not hospitalized, and, despite a police investigation, no arrests were made. College officials were said to be skeptical about her accusations. Nonetheless, word spread, and later that night two trash cans were set on fire outside the dormitory rooms of black student leaders.

The specific incident that precipitated the brawl occurred the next night and again involved a white female student and black male students. Three male students, two black and one white, knocked on a female student's door to ask about a paper she was typing for one of the black students. The men later described the conversation as "civil." The woman, a sorority member, called her brother fraternity for help, saying she was being harassed by some male students. Within a few minutes, about fifteen members of the white fraternity Phi Alpha Pi arrived and confronted the two black men. More whites joined in, and black female students called more black males to even the numbers. Who threw the first punch is unclear; black students claim it was a white fraternity member. "What is clear," according to one report of the incident, "is that instead of seeing a roommate or a fellow sophomore, the students saw race." Davonne Pierce, a dormitory resident assistant who is black, stated that his white friends shouted racial epithets at him as he was trying to break up the fight. He said to them, "How can you call me that when we were friends, when I let you borrow my notes?" But, he later recalled, "At that point, it was white against black. It was disgusting."

After the incident, most of the fifty-five black students, who said they feared for their safety, left the college and went home.

They had made up 9 percent of the student body. Davonne Pierce stayed on campus but stated, "Obviously they don't want us here." Dave Cook, a white junior who was one of the fraternity members involved in the fight, later said, "There were a lot of bonds that were broken that didn't need to be broken." He talked about his friendship with a black female student: "We would high-five each other and study for tests. But I don't know what she thinks about me. I don't know whether she's hating me or what. I didn't say one word to her, and she didn't say one word to me. Now she's gone."

Racist behavior on college campuses is, of course, not limited to students. An incident involving a campus in New York State reveals the deep-seated stereotyping and bigotry of some college administrators, police officers, and citizens in communities all over the country. In the early morning of September 4, 1992, a seventy-seven-year-old woman was attacked in the small town of Oneonta, New York. She told the state police that she thought her attacker was a black man who used a "stiletto-style" knife and that his hands and arms were cut when she fended him off. In response to a request from the police, the State University of New York at Oneonta gave the police a list of all of the black and Hispanic males registered at the college. Armed with the list, state and city police, along with campus security, tracked down the students "in their dormitories, at their jobs and in the shower." Each student was asked his whereabouts at the time the attack occurred, and each had to show his hands and his arms.

Michael Christian, the second of five children from a family headed by a single mother, grew up in the Bronx. His mother encouraged him to go to Oneonta to get him away from the problems of the city. Shortly after the attack, two state-police officers and representatives of campus security went to his dormitory room and woke him at 10:00 A.M. After asking him where he was at the time of the attack and demanding to see his hands, they said they wanted to question him downtown, and then they left. His roommate, Hopeton Gordon, a Jamaican student who had gone to high school in the Bronx with Mr. Christian, was questioned in front of other students from their dormitory. When the police asked to see his hands and he demanded their reasons, they responded, "Why? Do you have something to hide?" He said that he had felt humiliated in front of his suite mates and in front of female students.

This is not the first time black students, faculty, and administrators have been humiliated and have seen their civil rights trampled in Oneonta. Edward I. (Bo) Whaley, who went to the small town in upstate New York in 1968 as a student, remained, and is currently an instructor and counselor in the school's Educational Opportunity Program for disadvantaged students, recalls being followed by salespeople in Oneonta shops because they feared he would shoplift. He remembers the two minority ball players—one of whom he was trying to recruit—who were picked up as suspects in a rape case and had to pay for DNA testing even though someone else was convicted for the crime.

An admissions coordinator, Sheryl Champen, who is also black, was herself stopped by the state police the night of the attack. They demanded to see her identification before she could board a bus to New York City. It is unclear why the police questioned her and three other black women traveling with children, who also had to show identification before boarding the bus, since the attacked woman had reported that the person who assaulted her was a man. Their only common characteristic was race. When she heard about the treatment of the students of color, Ms. Champen said, "I was devastated, ashamed of being an admissions coordinator. Am I setting them up?" She feels that the behavior of the police was not an example of overeagerness to solve a crime. After recounting thirteen years of incidents that had begun when she was a first-year student at

SUNY/Oneonta, she stated, "I know what it was. It was a chance to humiliate niggers."

The release of the names of the 125 black and Hispanic students not only violated their privacy (and their right to be presumed innocent until proved guilty) but also violated the Family Educational Rights and Privacy Act of 1974 (also known as the Buckley Amendment). Following the incident, the vice-president who authorized the release of the names was suspended for one month without pay and demoted. The president of SUNY/Oneonta called using the list in the investigation "an affront to individual dignity and human rights."

Though each of these events is unique and a product of the particular social environment, demographics, personalities, and stresses at the particular institution, during the late 1980s and early 1990s campuses were rife with similar episodes. A Brown student describes one incident at her university:

> It was April 25, 1989, the end of spring term. . . . Students . . . were preparing for Spring Weekend, an annual fling before final exams. That day, found scrawled in large letters across an elevator door in Andrews dormitory were the words, NIGGERS GO HOME. Over the next 24 hours, similar racial epithets were found on the doors of several women of color living in that hall; on the bathroom doors WOMEN was crossed out and replaced with NIGGERS, MEN was crossed out, replaced with WHITE. And in that same women's bathroom, a computer-printed flyer was found a day later which read: "Once upon a time Brown was a place where a white man could go to class without having to look at little black faces or little yellow faces or little brown faces except when he went to take his meals. Things have been going downhill since the kitchen help moved into the classroom. Keep white supremcy [sic] alive! Join the Brown Chapter of the KKK."

Seven years earlier, *The Dartmouth Review* had set the standard for racist denigration by publishing an article ridiculing black students. The article was entitled "Dis Sho' Ain't No Jive, Bro," and read in part: "Dese boys be saying that we be comin hee to Dartmut an' not takin' the classics. . . . We be culturally 'lightened, too. We be takin hard courses in many subjects, like Afro-Am studies . . . and who bee mouthin' bout us not bein' good read?"

During the late 1980s, the University of Michigan experienced several racist incidents. One of the most infamous took place in 1988, when a poster mocking the slogan of the United Negro College Fund was hung in a classroom. It read "Support the K.K.K. College Fund. A mind is a terrible thing to waste— especially on a nigger."

Violent behavior has also been part of the cultural climate over the past decade. In February 1991, two black students from the University of Maine were allegedly assaulted by nine white men. The two students, both twenty-one, were driving in downtown Orono when approximately a dozen white men attacked their car and shouted, "Nigger, get out of here." When they got out of the car to see what was going on, the two men were kicked and beaten. Three students from the university were among those who attacked the students.

Incidents have not been limited to one kind of school, but have occurred at private as well as public, urban and rural, large and small, at Ivy League as well as less prestigious, little-known institutions. A survey conducted in 1992 by three Princeton students, for example, concluded that "racism is a serious problem at Princeton." The report that documents their findings includes an appendix with 108 anecdotes by Princeton students of racial or religious harassment or discrimination. The following are excerpts from those anecdotes:

> —I've been told to go back where I came from. I've been called a "chink." I've been told that they should have kept my parents in concentration camps during WWII.

—A fellow first-year student . . . said, "God only knows how many qualified whites were left out because of quotas like you."

—I ran into some guy who called me a "Latino piece of shit."

—I've been the butt of a couple of Jewish jokes, but I wouldn't say that's harassment.

—I've been referred to as a WASP in a derogatory tone.

—I've seen posters in the Woodrow Wilson School defaced with racial slurs, and the harassment of black faculty.

At a May 1992 rally in front of Firestone Library at which five hundred students protested the first Rodney King verdict, numerous minority students spoke about the racial harassment they had experienced at Princeton. Some cited being excluded from classroom discussions, others having their complaints ignored by faculty members and administrators. At another time, a Princeton student described being stopped by a university security guard looking for a homeless man who had been loitering on campus. According to the student, "I was stopped because I was black. I know who they were looking for, and I can tell you I look nothing like the guy."

In response to these problems and others, President Harold Shapiro appointed Vice-Provost Ruth J. Simmons to study race relations at Princeton. After three months of investigation, Simmons found that "persistent stereotyping and bias" toward minority students is "both a severe impediment to their academic success as well as a deterrent to healthy, unforced, unstructured association with members of other races on campus." Vice-Provost Simmons noted: "Members of all groups appear to feel that there are too few 'safe' spaces within the university in which discussions on race can take place among different ethnic and racial groups without accusations, hostility, and recriminations."

According to the Anti-Defamation League, anti-Semitic incidents on college campuses have risen sharply in recent years, from fifty-four in 1988 to over double that number, 114, in 1992. In February 1990, at American University in Washington, D.C., anti-Semitic graffiti were spray-painted on the main gate and on a residence hall. On the gate were painted a Star of David, an equal sign, and a swastika. On the dormitory was sprayed an expletive followed by "Israel Zionist." In 1991, at California State University at Northridge, a ceremonial hut used to celebrate the Jewish holiday of Sukkoth was vandalized with anti-Semitic writing. In addition to swastikas, "Hi' [sic] Hitler" and "Fuckin [sic] Jews" defaced the informative signs and flyers that decorated the hut. Two months earlier, Dr. Leonard Jeffries, Jr., then chair of the African-American Studies department at the City College of New York, delivered a speech at a black cultural festival in which he spoke of "a conspiracy, planned and plotted and programmed out of Hollywood" by "people called Greenberg and Weisberg and Trigliani." He went on to say that "Russian Jewry had a particular control over the movies and their financial partners, the Mafia, put together a financial system of destruction of black people."

Gay bashing has also been widely visible on college campuses. A Syracuse University fraternity, Alpha Chi Rho, was suspended by its national organization in 1991 for selling T-shirts with antihomosexual slogans, including one advocating violence against gays. On the front the shirts said "Homophobic and Proud of It!" and on the back, "Club Faggots Not Seals!" The picture illustrating the words was of a muscled crow, the fraternity's symbol, holding a club and standing over a faceless figure lying on the ground. Next to them is a seal hoisting a mug of beer.

During the same year, *Peninsula,* a conservative campus magazine at Harvard, published an issue entirely devoted to the subject of homosexuality. The magazine called homosexuality a "bad alternative" to heterosexuality and stated in its introduction that "homosexuality is bad for society." Within one hour of the magazine's distribution, the door of a gay student's room was defaced with antihomosexual words.

But, of course, discrimination does not need to be physical or perpetrated by students to wound, and to exclude some from mainstream college life. The football coach at the University of Colorado has called homosexuality "an abomination" and has supported a statewide group working to limit gay rights. In 1992, the governor of Alabama signed legislation prohibiting gay student groups from receiving public money or using buildings at state universities.

Sexual harassment and assault have also been reported on campuses across the country. The exploitation and objectification of women, so deeply embedded in traditional college life for so many generations, is often difficult to perceive, to diagnose, or to eliminate. Incidents at college campuses range from individual acts to institutionalized traditions. At the State University of New York at Binghamton a student who lived in a coed dorm was accused by the administration of lewd and indecent behavior because he displayed nude centerfold photographs from *Penthouse* magazine on the door to his room. The display was characterized by a member of the administration as "degrading and abusive to women." The student refused to remove the pictures, claiming, "My act of expression is clearly covered by the First Amendment."

At George Mason University in Virginia, as part of their fund-raising efforts in 1991, a fraternity ran an "ugly-woman" contest in which the men were helped by sorority members to dress as women before they paraded in front of an audience of students in the university's cafeteria. One white male came out in blackface, wearing a black wig with curlers, and pillows tied to his chest and buttocks. The university suspended the fraternity for two years, during which it could not hold social or athletic activities. No academic penalties were imposed. The suspension was overturned by a federal judge on the grounds that the fraternity's actions were protected by the First Amendment.

The re-examination of once-hallowed traditions in the light of recent violence against women is exemplified by events at Carleton College. Carleton's football team each year selected the most attractive first-year female and tried to date her. During the mid-to-late 1980s, four Carleton students brought accusations of rape against male students, and in 1991 they sued the college for mishandling the entire issue of rape on campus. It is therefore not surprising that during this time the Carleton community was particularly sensitive to sexist behavior. In 1990, the student chosen as most attractive complained about the practice: "I was really surprised to find such a sexist, fraternalistic tradition on campus." According to the college chaplain, who brought the issue to light by criticizing it at a chapel service, "The football team is making a claim on her. It's an intimidating and demeaning thing to happen." The practice was stopped.

Perhaps the most disturbing account of sexual harassment has been described by Carol Burke, currently an associate dean at Johns Hopkins University, about events at the U.S. Naval Academy, where she taught for seven years. Marching chants—or "cadence calls," as they are called in the navy—provide a window into the macho male culture fostered at the academy, a culture that simultaneously celebrates the power of men and violence toward women. As Burke states:

Cadence calls not only instill mutual solidarity but resurrect the Casey Jones of American ballad tradition as a brave pilot who survives the crash of his plane only to subdue women with greater ferocity:

> *Climbed all out with his dick in his hand.*
> *Said, "Looky here, ladies, I'm a hell of a man."*

Went to his room and lined up a hundred . . .
Swore up and down he'd fuck everyone.

Fucked ninety-eight till his balls turned blue.
Then he backed off, jacked off, and fucked the other two.

Members of the academy's Male Glee Club while away the hours on bus trips back from concerts by singing a particularly sadistic version of the song "The Candy Man":

THE S&M MAN

Who can take a chain saw,
Cut the bitch in two,
Fuck the bottom half
and give the upper half to you. . . .

The S&M Man, the S&M Man
The S&M Man cause he mixes it with love
and makes the hurt feel good!

Who can take a bicycle,
Then take off the seat,
Set his girlfriend on it
Ride her down a bumpy street. . . .

Who can take an ice pick
Ram it through her ear
Ride her like a Harley,
As you fuck her from the rear. . . .

Lest we think that such lyrics are sung only at the U.S. Naval Academy, the following incident took place at the Phi Kappa Psi fraternity at UCLA in 1992:

A group of fraternity brothers waited outside the door. They serenaded the rape victim inside, cheering a brother on as if it were a football game. To the tune of "The Candy Man," they sang, "Who can take his organ / Dip it in vaseline / Ram it up inside you till it tickles your spleen / The S and M man, the S and M man / The S and M man can / cause he mixes it with love and / makes the hurtin feel good."

UCLA's administration looked the other way this spring as Phi Kappa Psi fraternity brothers distributed a songbook with lyrics glorifying necrophilia, rape and violent torture of women. Although a 1991 suspension for violation of alcohol and other policies forced the fraternity to implement pledge education programs and forums on sexism and homophobia, the recent songbook controversy reveals the inadequacies of such programs.

In March 1992, *Together*, a feminist magazine at UCLA, "exposed" the songbook that was left anonymously in their office. When asked about the songs, an assistant vice chancellor of the university first responded, "What's the problem? They are just erotic lyrics." Later, when questioned by the media, he stated, "I was horrified, revolted, shocked and embarrassed. This book is sexist, homophobic and promoted violence." The president of Phi Kappa Psi claimed that the "lyrics are a joke [and] so exaggerated that it is . . . ridiculous to say these songs promote violence against women."

Nevertheless, it is clear that fraternities have been in the forefront of bias-related incidents. Among the most serious incidents occurred at a University of Rhode Island fraternity. An eighteen-year-old female first-year student claimed she was raped during a fraternity party while at least five other men watched. During the investigation a former student committed suicide just hours before he was to be questioned by the police. In this case, as in many others, not only had the fraternity members been drinking heavily but often the victims as well.

Indeed, much of the overt sexist behavior, harassment, and physical violence toward women on campuses occurs in environments infused with alcohol or other kinds of drug use. In March 1991, as the governing board of the University of Virginia was enjoying a black-tie dinner in the Rotunda, the "crown piece" of architecture designed by Thomas Jefferson when he founded the university in 1819, two blocks away federal marshals and local police officers conducted drug raids on three fraternities. Long known for its academic excellence, more recently for its athletic excellence, the university is also known as a party school where "noisy, sloshy weekend beer parties along fraternity row were tolerated by officials who knew that, come Monday, academic order would return." After a six-month investigation during which undercover agents were able to buy drugs from fraternity members on seventeen occasions and "witnessed numerous instances of 'open and notorious' drug use in the houses during 'Midnight Madness' parties," the raids resulted in the arrest of at least 12 students, the seizure of the three fraternity houses, and the confiscation of a dozen sandwich bags of marijuana, LSD tablets, hallucinogenic mushrooms, and drug paraphernalia.

Of greater importance than the immediate results of the raid, the action highlighted the anomalous relationship between fraternities and the academic institutions with which they are affiliated. Because fraternities are privately owned and run, they are for the most part beyond the jurisdiction of academic institutions. This arrangement, which enables the fraternities to be essentially autonomous, also protects colleges and universities from direct responsibility for what takes place along various Greek rows all over the country. The special status leads many students to believe that they are somehow above or beyond the law and, moreover, that they are above or beyond the norms of the wider society. As Larry J. Sabato, a professor of government at the University of Virginia, has stated:

> There is a pervasive and longstanding belief among students that fraternities are sanctuaries and that the entire university is a sanctuary, where we live by our own rules and are permitted to

do things that are not right so long as they are part of the student life style, or are tolerated by the student community. That's wrong.

The chief of police of Charlottesville, who led the raid, also pointed out the students' sense of immunity:

Up there in academia they're not always living in the real world. The students had gotten to where they thought they could do anything they wanted in their fraternity houses, and the school administration was saying that it had no control over the fraternities because they were technically not on the university's grounds. That's just not the way the real world works.

But, of course, that is often exactly the way the real world has worked for fraternities and their members over the years.

As colleges and universities have attempted to crack down on fraternities and sororities, there is evidence that the hazing of prospective members has moved underground. Many "Greek" organizations are conducting initiation rituals in secret in order to avoid sanctions from administrators. In addition to the increasing use of racial and ethnic taunting and mocking, serious physical injuries continue to occur. During an initiation meeting in March 1992 at Southern University in Baton Rouge, Louisiana, a pledge was hit on the head by a fraternity member wielding a frying pan. The pledge was blinded. One University of Alabama student "told his mother that he had been forced to drink excessive amounts of beer, that he had been slammed against the wall by fraternity members and punched. . . ." He refused to leave the fraternity, because of peer pressure. His mother's reaction was: ". . . the fear you have is 'My child is going to get killed.' "

A 1991 survey of over a thousand undergraduates at the University of Virginia undertaken just months after the drug raid, a fatal drunk-driving accident involving one student, and the alcohol-related drowning of another, found that nearly half of the students are heavy drinkers. The survey classified heavy drinkers as those consuming five or more alcoholic drinks in a row at one sitting on at least one occasion within a two-week period. Forty percent of the heavy drinkers acknowledged that alcohol use had caused them to drive unsafely, and more than half said that at some point they had had sex with someone they would not have had sex with if they had been sober.

Studies by the university's Institute for Substance Abuse Studies, which was formed as part of the university's response to the 1986 scandal involving three football players indicted on charges of distributing cocaine, indicate that alcohol and drug use at the University of Virginia is similar to that of college students nationally. According to a 1990 study, 74 percent of students nationally drank alcohol; 14 percent of the national sample used marijuana; 1.2 percent used cocaine; and 1.1 percent used LSD.

A 1989–90 survey of fifty-six four-year schools and twenty-two community colleges found that students at small colleges drink more alcohol than do students at larger schools, and that students with lower grades drink significantly more than students with high grades. The study found that approximately 42 percent of the students said they had gone on a drinking binge at least once in the past two weeks, and that among daily drinkers 49 percent said they would like to have drugs available at social events.

There is little doubt that alcohol and drug use is correlated with the rising number of crimes and increasing amount of violence on college campuses. A 1989 survey of over a thousand colleges and universities by the Center for the Study and Prevention of Campus Violence at Towson State University in suburban Baltimore reveals that there is a subculture on many campuses nationwide of victims and victimizers. Both crime vic-

tims and perpetrators drink and use drugs significantly more often than other students. Dorothy G. Siegel, a vice-president and
associate professor of psychology at Towson State, estimates that
"over 90 percent of campus crime is alcohol-related." A Harvard study of over sixteen hundred college freshmen released in
1992 found that since 1977 there has been a dramatic increase
in students' drinking to get drunk. The study indicated that one
student in three, including many women, drink primarily to get
drunk. One article describes weekend drinking at Arizona State
University in Tempe:

> Two bull-necked boys (wearing T-shirts with the slogans, "Take
> Me Drunk, I'm Home," and "From Zero to Horny in 2.5 Beers")
> hoist the disoriented and giggling girl by the ankles over a
> nearby keg. She seizes its plastic hose and, hanging upside
> down, begins to gulp.

The only substance-abuse counselor for forty-three thousand
students, Dr. Ellen C. Yoshimura, explains:

> This is a huge commuter school, where it's easy to be lonely and
> alienated. They join fraternities and sororities to make friends,
> or hang out in bars for 1-cent drink nights and wet T-shirt con-
> tests. . . . Some experiment with hallucinogens, including Ec-
> stasy and LSD, or IV cocaine, or heroin. Yet the typical student
> I treat looks astonishingly clean-cut—a hearty, sunny, polished,
> perfect child.

Over the past several years, an increasing number of rapes
have been reported at campuses across the country. From Brown
University to the University of Southern California, from Southern Methodist University in Dallas to the University of Rhode
Island, from St. John's University in Queens, New York, to
Carleton College in Minnesota, rape has become a major issue
for today's undergraduates. Most studies indicate that alcohol is

involved, on the part of the victim as well as the perpetrator. A national study of women at thirty-two institutions of higher education in the U.S. found that 15 percent of college women said they had experienced attempted intercourse by the threat of force and 12 percent said they had experienced attempted intercourse by the use of alcohol or drugs. Recent data plus in-depth studies of individual cases have made it clear that acquaintance rape is far more common than stranger rape in the United States. According to David Beatty, the public-policy director of the National Victim Center, a Washington-based advocacy group, "There is no question that acquaintance rape is more common than stranger rape. No one has the exact numbers, but the consensus is that probably in 80 to 85 percent of all rape cases, the victim knows the defendant."

Many questions have been raised about acquaintance rape since the surge of reported cases has been noted across the country. Notorious cases such as the one involving William Kennedy Smith, in which rape was not proved, and the one involving Mike Tyson, in which the verdict was guilty, have also raised many questions: What is rape? Must physical force be used? When does "no" mean "no" and when is it part of a mating ritual? What about plying a woman with drugs or alcohol and then, when she is too inebriated or out of control to protest effectively, having sex with her? Is that rape?

An incident that came to be known as the "St. John's case" is a vivid and heart-wrenching example of the difficulties of establishing the parameters of acquaintance rape and of prosecuting the alleged perpetrators:

As she recalled it, the evening of March 1, 1990, a Thursday, began ordinarily enough: the St. John's University student took target practice with another member of the school's rifle club and bantered with him and the coach about everything from the coach's shabby clothing to the other student's love life.

But when the evening ended about seven hours later, as the 22-year-old woman later testified, she had been "forced" to drink nearly three cups of a mixture of orange soda and vodka and had been disrobed, ogled, fondled, berated and sodomized by at least seven St. John's students, including her acquaintance from the rifle club. The debauchery began in a house near the Jamaica, Queens, campus; then she was transported, semiconscious and disheveled, to a second house where a party was underway and the assault continued.

Later, she said, she heard the men debating what to do with her. One asked, "What if she talks?" Another replied: "So what? Remember Tawana Brawley? Nobody believed her. Nobody will believe this one."

And, of course, he was partially right. After months of publicity and an extensive trial, after two students pleaded guilty to lesser charges while essentially corroborating the young woman's story, three of the defendants were found not guilty and the final defendant interrupted his trial to plead guilty to sharply reduced charges but, in so doing, admitted that he had done everything he had been accused of.

As newspaper accounts stressed, the case "rocked" the ten-thousand-student university, the country's largest Roman Catholic institution of higher education, and the surrounding community. Adding to the explosive nature of the accusations—that someone the female student knew took her back to a house where several of the accused lived and plied her with alcohol, and then, when she was on the couch with her eyes closed, appearing helpless, he and other male students fondled the woman and made her perform oral sex on them—all six defendants were white and the young woman was black. None of the six defendants were convicted of the original felony charges against them.

Perhaps the most disturbing analysis of rape on college campuses is anthropologist Peggy Reeves Sanday's shocking study

of fraternity gang rape. Also known as "gang banging," the phenomenon of "pulling train" refers to a "group of men lining up
like train cars to take turns having sex with the same woman."
Bernice Sandler, one of the authors of a report issued in 1985 by
the American Association of American Colleges, has reported
finding more than seventy-five documented cases of gang rape in
recent years. These incidents, which occurred at all kinds of
institutions—"public, private, religiously affiliated, Ivy League,
large and small"—share a common pattern:

> A vulnerable young woman, one who is seeking acceptance or
> who is high on drugs or alcohol, is taken to a room. She may
> or may not agree to have sex with one man. She then passes out,
> or is too weak or scared to protest, and a train of men have sex
> with her. Sometimes the young woman's drinks are spiked with-
> out her knowledge, and when she is approached by several men
> in a locked room, she reacts with confusion and panic. Whether
> too weak to protest, frightened, or unconscious, as has been the
> case in quite a number of instances, anywhere from two to
> eleven or more men have sex with her.

The specific case that is the centerpiece of Sanday's study in-
volves a young woman, Laurel, who was known to have serious
drinking and drug problems. The evening in question, she was
drunk on beer and had taken "four hits of LSD" before going to
a fraternity-house party. According to her account, she fell
asleep after the party in a room on the first floor. When she
awoke, she was undressed. One of the fraternity members
dressed her and carried her upstairs, where she claimed she was
raped by five or six "guys." She said, in Sanday's words, that she
was "barely conscious and lacked the strength to push them off
her." This account was corroborated by another woman, a friend
of the fraternity members, who felt that, because Laurel was in-
capable of consenting to sex, she had been raped. The fraternity

brothers never publicly admitted to any wrongdoing; they claimed throughout the investigation that Laurel had "lured" them into a "gang bang," which they preferred to call an "express."

In this study, Sanday claims that "coercive sexual behavior" is prevalent on college campuses and that rape is "the means by which men programmed for violence and control use sexual aggression to display masculinity and to induct younger men into masculine roles." Sanday continues her analysis:

> [The] male participants brag about their masculinity and . . . [the] female participants are degraded to the status of what the boys call "red meat" or "fish." The whole scenario joins men in a no-holds-barred orgy of togetherness. The woman whose body facilitates all of this is sloughed off at the end like a used condom. She may be called a "nympho" or the men may believe that they seduced her—a practice known as "working a yes out"—through promises of becoming a little sister, by getting her drunk, by promising her love, or by some other means. Those men who object to this kind of behavior run the risk of being labeled "wimps" or, even worse in their eyes, "gays" or "faggots."

As we have seen, a variety of groups have been perceived and treated as "the Other"—in Patricia Hill Collins' words, "viewed as an object to be manipulated and controlled"—on college campuses over the past few years. Though many of the bias incidents have involved racial enmity and misunderstanding, anti-Semitism, homophobia, and blatant sexism have also been catalysts for hostile acts. Many academic institutions, concerned about overtly demeaning, sometimes violent behavior as well as the far more subtle denigration of women and other minority groups, have attempted to address these problems through a variety of measures: speech codes; orientation programs for entering students that stress respect for diversity and the importance of civility; curriculum changes that focus on multiculturalism;

hiring policies whose goals are to increase the number of women and members of minority groups on the faculty and staff of the institution; and the recruitment of more students of color. These measures, often employed to counter the ignorance, ethnocentrism, and anger within the college community, have themselves become the subject of controversy and debate. Both academic and popular discourse have focused far more on political correctness, on affirmative action, and on changes in the curriculum than on the hate incidents and violence that continue to occur. Speech codes at the Universities of Wisconsin and Michigan became front-page news; discussions of what and who was p.c. seemed ubiquitous; and the pros and cons of a multicultural curriculum have been debated in university governing bodies and editorial meetings across the country. But what of the impact of overt bigotry and intergroup conflict on individual students? Does this conflict constitute a significant barrier to learning? What about the material taught and the attitudes of faculty members? What is it like to be a college student during a time of heightened tension, both within the larger society and within the more circumscribed academic environment?

Part II will attempt to address these issues via interviews with individual students. Through their experiences and their words perhaps we can gain a clearer understanding of the pressures college students face today, and the very real contributions they are making to the solution of some of these problems on their own campuses.

Part Two

As the state of higher education in the United States has been widely debated, the impact of racial, ethnic, religious, class, gender-based, and homophobic conflict on individual students has been virtually ignored. Choosing in these tense and turbulent times to attend a college—often one that is far from home at which students know they will be members of a small, distinct minority takes personal courage and genuine commitment. It must be noted, moreover, that many students are members of more than one traditionally underrepresented and all-too-often demeaned group: an African-American or Latino student may well also come from a family with limited economic resources, and therefore may not have shared the same social and cultural experiences or the same patterns of consumption as the majority of students. If we add gender to the variables, it becomes clear that attending Columbia, Tufts, or the University of Wisconsin as, for example, an African-American woman from a low-income family can be a very difficult and often alienating experience. By the same token, students may be members of a racial or religious minority and be gay or lesbian as well, thereby compounding their outsider status. Furthermore, the enormous variation in academic preparation for postsecondary education increases the feelings of separateness and the pressure that many students feel, and may diminish their self-confidence and self-esteem as well. In addition to these issues of difference, the widespread prevalence of both overt and covert intergroup hostility, prejudice, discrimination, and even violence on college campuses conveys to many individual students, and indeed in some cases to entire groups, that they are considered inferior and expendable.

Part II examines the impact of recent turbulence on college campuses from the perspective of individual students. Most of these young people have not faced the violence and extreme expressions of hatred described in chapter 3, but many have had to cope with the ramifications of these events, and virtually all have had to deal with some manifestation of prejudice, stereotyping, and intergroup conflict during their college years. All too often, moreover, tensions outside the academic community provoke and magnify tensions within it, and students must simultaneously grapple with hostility and discrimination from the larger society and from within the college community.

Recent events on campuses have an impact not only on members of minority groups; these events clearly have an important impact on those who are part of the mainstream as well. Students who never before concerned themselves with issues of privilege, inequality, and stratification within American society have started to question the fundamental meaning of the concepts of fairness, merit, and personal responsibility, as well as the role of higher education in a democratic society. Many have become politically active for the first time, spurred on by events and experiences—some of them wrenching—during their undergraduate years. In addition, all of these young people are struggling to discover who they are amid this ongoing turmoil. Some of the students interviewed are relatively privileged, others far less so, but all of them have been personally affected by recent conflicts and are struggling to understand both the nature of American society and their place within it.

Chapter 4 details some of the bias incidents the five students who were profiled in the introduction to this book have faced and the individual, and quite different, ways in which they have coped with hostility and discrimination. The students in chapter 5, in contrast with those in chapter 4, are far clearer about their need to speak out. Some are more comfortable with being assertive; others are less so but feel nonetheless that they must respond to a particular set of events and circumstances on their campuses. Yet another group of students, in chapter 6, take on major leadership roles within their schools. Certain students come to college hoping to make a difference; others gradually assume key roles within the student body. Whatever route they take, these young people often become important links between the faculty and the administration on the one hand and the students on the other, and many play an important part in bringing together various, often conflicting, groups on campus. Chapter 7 explores the experiences of students who are, in the words of a young Native American from Wisconsin, "walking in two worlds," recognizing their emotional ties and their obligations to their families and their identification with their subgroups but also simultaneously wanting and needing to interact and function successfully within the broader society. Whether Asian-American, African-American, Native American, gay, or lesbian, many are straddling cultural boundaries, attempting to understand who they are and where they belong at various levels of society. Finally, chapter 8 deals with students who have been significantly changed by coming into contact with people from very different backgrounds. These are students who consciously chose to move out of their homogeneous enclaves into undergraduate settings that are far more diverse, and in so doing have challenged themselves and been challenged by the social environment to think, react, and respond in ways that are quite different from those they have known in the past. It is their journey from the past to the present and the future that chapter 8 specifically, as indeed much of part II, attempts to document.

It should be noted that several of these students could have been profiled in more than one chapter. Many of the categories are overlapping, and, of course, the students are complex, multidimensional human beings who play varied roles and illustrate multiple issues on college campuses. Whereas students have often been portrayed simplistically and one-dimensionally, marching in lock-step with others who share their status, the students interviewed for this book were extraordinarily thoughtful, concerned about the major issues of our time, and surprisingly varied in their beliefs and actions. Part II attempts to let them speak for themselves.

4

Coping with Bias

To confront or not to confront? I wasn't raised to confront.

Marcella Rosario

Francesca Wilkinson, a senior at Tufts University, is an African-American woman from Washington, D.C. She is majoring in sociology and American studies, minoring in women's studies, and doing a Peace and Justice Studies certificate, an interdisciplinary program that focuses on the broad issues of conflict and social justice. As we sit in the student-center cafeteria to talk, I ask her how she happened to go to Tufts. She responds immediately and vehemently, "I got conned!" Francesca describes how she learned about Tufts:

> Tufts comes to my school and does their spiel. They throw the diversity thing around and I said, "That's it! That's the school for me!" The admissions person told me to apply early and send the stuff directly to her. I had medium grades, pretty good SAT scores, and was an activist in high school. And I visited here and had a good time. But I really got conned. They pushed diversity and I really believed it.

An only child of divorced parents, Francesca grew up in Washington with her mother. She describes herself as "worldly, but not as worldly as I thought. I was far too trendy for my own good." Francesca's mother is a nurse and "was not around that much. She was up at the crack of dawn and often not home until late. I was always a latchkey kid; she always trusted me."

107

Francesca dealt with her anger at the racism she felt at Tufts (being called a "nigger bitch" her first day there symbolized for her the widespread racism she felt) and her feelings of isolation in two ways: with a friend at Tufts whom she had known from high school she wrote a series of articles on "white people and racism" for one of the student newspapers, and then she retreated to a more familiar environment by going home to Washington every weekend she could. She now feels she "vented [her] anger" and then didn't stay around to deal with the repercussions.

Francesca states that she had a drug problem when she arrived at Tufts. She had thought leaving home would help, but going back and forth that first semester helped to keep her habit alive, and, in fact, she dealt drugs for a while to "frat people" and "made a lot of money. No one in Washington would pay those prices. It just made the gap between us even wider, because they looked so stupid to my worldly self."

After the first semester, Francesca found she couldn't get high anymore. She had smoked pot since she was twelve, and more recently had been using a form of cocaine known as Ecstasy. After three years of "consistent daily use I was at my saturation point physically, I had no more mucus in my nose, and I was emotionally wiped out." The second semester of her first year, Francesca stayed on campus but decided she wanted to go back to working in a club, as she had done during high school. She found a job four nights a week at the front door of a club in Boston, determining who should and who should not be admitted, and increasingly isolated herself from the Tufts community. That spring, she didn't finish any of her classes ("Everything was a mess, a big, big mess!"); the following fall, she didn't go back to Tufts at all. She lived in Boston, continued to work at the club, and was involved in what she now characterizes as a "battering relationship."

Despite her anger and alienation from Tufts, Francesca had

remained in touch with one of her professors from the Peace and Justice Program and decided to return to college the following January at least in part to get away from the abusive relationship. At that point, she began, in her words, to be "really active." She started raising money for a scholarship fund for black students, became a member of the board of the Peace and Justice Studies certificate and was active in a campaign to "kick the Greeks off campus" because of their homophobic behavior. During her junior year she was even more active, and the experience was particularly rewarding. She started working with another student:

> We teach together [this year they are teaching a course about rap music in the Tufts Experimental College], we give speeches together, we do everything together! It is great to be able to rely on a straight white man. It's the best, the best-est part about Tufts. It reaffirms my faith in humanity!

Francesca feels that one of her primary responsibilities is to "push people, particularly students, to recognize their privilege."

> There are lots of liberals here but they don't speak for me. They don't do enough processing about their own privilege. They have no idea what it means to go here. They think they're here because they worked hard—not because they went to good schools or can afford to pay for this education.

Francesca also feels the burden of challenging stereotypes in class. She was the only person of color in her "Contemporary Feminist Theory" class and felt she had to teach the professor and the students. "That is the burden of going to a white school." The administration has a responsibility, she believes, to "put the professors through diversity training," but, she says,

"They know we'll do it. It falls on every one of us to become politicized. It's a tremendous burden. If we don't do it, it doesn't get done. But I have enough stress just getting through myself."

Francesca continues, "It's good I came here, 'cause Tufts has to deal with my voice. The only reason I'm happy here is that I've made them deal with my voice. I can say what I need to say." When I ask if Tufts should perhaps get some credit for creating the kind of atmosphere that enables her to say what she needs to say, she responds, "I don't want to give Tufts credit for this. I give credit to Peace and Justice Studies, to the African-American Center, to the Women's Center, and to the Tufts Lesbian, Gay, Bisexual Committee. It was through these groups that I've gotten the encouragement, support, and role models that I've needed to make it here."

Though she couldn't see herself now doing anything but being politically active, Francesca says that she has been "really lonely at times. My social life has suffered. My reputation is such that people don't want to come near me. I'm known as a 'militant black activist, a separatist, a radical bitch.' It's amazing to me. It doesn't make any sense to me. Plenty of times I've walked down here [to the cafeteria] and not had a place to sit." But she sees her activism as "a matter of survival—my survival, my community's survival."

In discussing her swift and nearly total immersion in campus-based political activity, Francesca feels she "transferred my addiction from coke to activism." As part of her effort to get off drugs, she sought help from a counselor and "did A.A. [Alcoholics Anonymous] for a while," but she found the program "depressing, ridiculous, and male-oriented." She feels that the role of the sponsors in A.A. is crucial and that "the program only works if you work the program"—that is, if you really do the Twelve Steps—but may well not work if you don't embrace it wholeheartedly. In any case, Francesca feels she overcame her drug habit literally through her intense commitment to her political work at Tufts.

Echoing other activist students, Francesca talks about 120-hour weeks, and doesn't remember the last time she had a moment to herself:

> My day starts at eight A.M. and doesn't end until one or two in the morning. I've missed out on what college is all about—on the partying, the good times. It's more fun this year than the past three years, but being an activist has caused me a lot of pain, loneliness, and isolation. But at the same time, I've formed the most beautiful, lasting relationships. I don't know what else I would be doing.

Francesca feels that black students should really weigh the pros and cons of going to predominantly white schools, that they should "know the burden." "Why didn't they tell me?" she asks. High-school guidance counselors and friends who are already in college need to inform young people what they are getting into. Not only do black students have problems with white students and white institutions, but splits occur among the black students themselves. Francesca describes an African-American friend who came from a middle-class suburb of Atlanta and didn't identify with some of the other black students on campus. She was given a really hard time by the black community for not "acting black." Many of the students, she observes, are bilingual—they speak regular English and an urban black English that reflects the black experience across class lines. But her friend was not "bilingual" and had a very hard time.

There can also be real repercussions if you "call the black community out." When she and other students were demanding greater rights for gay and lesbian students, African Americans were conspicuous by their absence. Francesca feels that the black community is very hostile to gays; at a demonstration at which students were calling for a center for Tufts' gay-and-lesbian community, she made a speech asking them where they were on this issue. As other groups need to recognize their privilege, so do straight blacks, she feels.

Even though her years at Tufts have been difficult and demanding, Francesca says emphatically that she would do it "again—and again and again."

> I might change a couple of things along the way, but this has been the single most rewarding experience of my life. It has forced me to think in different ways. When I started, I felt no one could have it worse than me. But I have come to see *my* position of privilege—that I am middle-class and educated—and my responsibility to use that really, really powerful privilege of education.

As Francesca has so vividly pointed out, many on college campuses are bound by stereotypes and negative feelings about various groups and all too frequently articulate their prejudice in sometimes devastatingly hurtful ways. Many students and faculty members are similarly limited by narrow, rigid views about Asians and Asian Americans. How often, in speaking of people whose heritage is Asian, do we differentiate between Asians of Japanese background, Chinese background, Korean, or Vietnamese? And how often do we differentiate between Asians who have arrived in this country over the past ten years and fourth-generation Asian Americans who have been part of the fabric of this society during the greater part of the twentieth century? Moreover, as the *Final Report* of The Diversity Project of the University of California/Berkeley points out, though "Chinese Americans see important differences between Chinese from Taiwan and Hong Kong, Southeast Asia and the Mainland,

San Francisco and Walnut Creek, first or second generation, and so on," they and other Asian Americans are "likely to hold stereotypical views of the homogeneous character of 'others,' collapsing gentiles and Jews, working-class Irish Catholics and upper-middle-class Episcopalians as 'white.' "

Often preconceptions about Asian Americans may be "positive"—that they have a strong commitment to family, work hard, and are intellectually gifted, particularly in mathematics, science, and engineering—but the negative side of the stereotype exists as well: that Asian Americans are "academically narrow, grade grubbers, parochial, clannish, [and] forever consigned to be foreigners by a culture dominated by those of European descent, never fully Americans." These stereotypes, both positive and negative, often constitute a substantial burden for students of Asian ancestry. Several of them spoke about the problems of coping with these notions and about the pressures and difficulty of finding one's identity in an incredibly complex world.

Two students at the University of Washington discuss some of the difficulties of being both Asian Americans and activists on the huge Seattle campus. Camille Tecson, chair of the University of Washington chapter of the Asian and Pacific Island Student Union (APSU), discusses how the image of the model minority "really hurts":

> We are expected to be the compromising, sell-out minority. We are all lumped together and stereotyped as rich. People say, Well, you have already made it, especially Pacific Islanders and Filipinos. The scholarships, they feel, should only be for blacks, Native Americans, and Chicano Americans.

Susan Kim, a Korean American who is also active in APSU, feels the stereotype of hardworking, extremely bright Asian students creates still higher expectations; it is particularly upsetting to her, because she currently feels particularly "stupid" in an international-relations course that is part of her major. "These raised expectations only make me feel worse."

When Camille first came to the university, she experienced "little incidents." For instance, in the introductory speech class she took her first year:

> People came in with the wrong facts. I knew they were wrong— you know, things about the American Dream and how well people of color are doing. I wondered, Where are these people finding these facts and getting these attitudes? Things like "Affirmative action should be against the law." And how numerous and vocal these people were! I had to do my research and offer the other side.

She recounts far more serious examples of omnipresent racism, such as the incident in a residence hall at the university in which flour was poured over a Native American student as he was coming out of the shower. His assailants said, "Now you know what it's like to be white." Or the African-American student who had "nigger" written on his door during the fall of 1991. These events must be understood within the broader context of a significant ultraright presence in the Pacific Northwest. Within a few weeks of my conversation with these two students, a black man had been jumped and stabbed by local white skinheads. A protest rally followed during which skinheads marched through the community. They are constantly in the media— perhaps as often as three times a week in the Seattle area; skinhead literature is everywhere. Their mission, one student felt, is to create conflict. These students find it difficult to read ultraright literature. As one student said, "I can't read too much of it; I'm already so angry."

Camille describes how unprepared she was for the subtle instances of racism she feels in almost every class, and the not-so-subtle instances they all see outside of class. On one level, she blames her unpreparedness on her parents. Originally from the Philippines, they worked at one of the shipyards on the West Coast and found themselves and other Asian workers being "denied promotion, demoted, and finally weeded out. A court case was brought when I was twelve. Did my parents tell me and my brothers? No. I asked them, 'Mom, Dad, why didn't you tell me?' They answered that they didn't want to depress us." This was a common theme among many of the students of color whom I interviewed—that, because their parents had not wanted to upset them, they had not told them the extent of racism in the United States.

Both Camille and Susan analyze the variation in behavior and attitudes among students of Asian ancestry. Many Koreans, for example, hang out together because they speak the same language; they are reluctant to venture out into the English-speaking community because they are so insecure about their English. Many are uncomfortable speaking English that is not perfect, so, to stay in their "comfort zone," they must spend most of their time with one another. But, according to Camille, there are also some who reject the Asian part of themselves, who feel no connection with their ethnicity. "They are acculturated or sell-outs or whatever you want to call them." In Susan's opinion many feel like "bananas or coconuts—yellow or brown on the outside and white on the inside. More students need to understand that it is all right not to feel just American, that diversity can be brought into the spectrum."

Camille and Susan describe racism and the negative impact of stereotyping Asian Americans on and around the campus of a large public university on the West Coast; Marcella, a student at Hunter College, feels her academic opportunities were limited when an adviser discriminated against her, assuming she was a member of a minority group. Before describing the sometimes

subtle, sometimes open hostility and discrimination she has experienced, she discusses why she came to New York from
Canada:

> Why am I here? I fell in love with an American [woman] and
> gave up everything to come here to be with her. I decided to go
> to New York, and now that I'm at Hunter, I wouldn't want to
> go anywhere else. Everybody from the whole world is here. No
> other school is more multicultural than Hunter, and the differ-
> ences are exciting rather than frightening.

But, according to Marcella, people from various cultures interact primarily in class. Socially, she feels, the environment is
much more segregated; people tend to stay within their own
groups. In discussing political activism at Hunter, Marcella
points out that it develops within the larger context of New York
City activism—particularly around issues of race, gender, and
homosexuality. At Hunter, the students develop the political
agenda, and the primary issues, in Marcella's words, are "race
and gender—not homosexuality." The faculty "do better on gender, don't do so well on race, and are most horrendous on homophobia."

Marcella began attending Hunter in February 1989 and was
quickly tapped for the Honors Program. Though there are aspects of the program that she finds stimulating and rewarding,
she also feels that some of the students and faculty in the program behave in an arrogant, privileged manner. She tells of a
professor who, in discussing a specific academic journal, informed the students that they could subscribe to the journal on
their computers through their modems. Marcella was astonished
that a professor at a college with a largely immigrant, working-
class student population, many of whom do not even have access
to typewriters, would assume that everyone would own a computer and know what a modem is. To point out the inappropri-

ateness of his assumption, she asked, although she knew the answer, "What is a modem?" The professor answered her question in an "any-fool-should-know manner," and the students followed his lead and reacted with mocking amusement. One student even turned to her and asked, "Do you know what a microwave is?" She feels that she often points out what is "ridiculous," and when she does she gets labeled as antagonistic, a troublemaker.

Though she hates confrontation, she often feels she must speak out. At a recent meeting of a committee of which she is a member attended mostly by faculty, with only a couple of students, one of the professors said, "Please don't misunderstand me, but why do we always have to be the field nigger?" At the end of the meeting, as Marcella was debating whether or not to speak to the professor about her choice of language, an African-American faculty member approached the professor and spoke with her about her remark. Marcella, who in her role as student had been uncomfortable criticizing the professor, decided to say nothing, particularly since the incident seemed to have been dealt with. At the next meeting of the group, however, she felt as though she had chosen to walk away from a difficult situation and felt compelled to express her own view. She mentioned the earlier incident and pointed out that, anytime you have to apologize first for something you're going to say, you should think twice about saying it. During the ensuing discussion, the professor who had used the term "field nigger" began to cry, and the meeting became extremely upsetting for all those present.

Marcella shares her feelings about speaking out in this way:

> I hate confrontation! Yet I felt badly that I had not said anything during the original meeting and felt I had a second chance. This incident happened right after the Clarence Thomas–Anita Hill hearings, and Anita Hill's testimony—even though it wasn't voluntary—gave me the courage to speak up.

Most of the time, I want to speak out but fear keeps me back. It's scary but, most of the time, I don't want to run away from speaking out. But, you know, there is also a power imbalance in this situation. They are professors and I am a student.

Marcella continues talking about the problem of confrontation, particularly in response to homophobic remarks:

I was at a conference on gay and lesbian issues not too long ago and the woman signing in in front of me said, in response to a question from the guard, "No, I'm straight, thank God!" I didn't say anything. A colleague of mine constantly uses the word "faggot" as a generic swear word. I want to say, "How do you know that? How do you know that about his sexuality?" She is using the most despicable word she can think of. But I haven't said anything. Do you have to speak up all the time?

What does she do when these incidents occur? After stating with great feeling that these incidents were insulting, she stated with equal feeling, "I don't fight. I get tired of educating people. I get tired of educating professors. Many feel there is no point in protesting because nothing will change. Many students feel powerless to change things."

She continues in a rush of words:

I wasn't raised to confront. With each incident I have to think, To confront or not to confront. It's like talking back. I wasn't raised to talk back. It's not part of my culture. On an elevator filled with students, a faculty member tells "faggot jokes" to another faculty person. What makes him think he can tell that kind of joke? He didn't even look around to see who else was there. He just assumes that everybody hates "them." There is so much hostility toward this subject—so much arrogance. Everybody knows you're perverts anyway. But how do you work on resolving these issues if you don't say anything? Why are we protecting these fascists? I couldn't give a shit if people think it's free speech!

Though Marcella prizes the diversity at Hunter, she also sees the problems and suggests some solutions:

> Hunter is a wonderful place to be, but there is still pervasive and subtle racism, sexism, and homophobia, and it concerns me more when it's out of the mouths of faculty. They are truly our role models. There should be mandatory workshops where professors could work on their racism like you work on a marriage, continuously. They are done with their Ph.D.'s, done with their books, done with their tenure, and feel they don't have to work on their professional roles anymore. Staff would feel insulted if they were told they had to go to such workshops, so they must be mandatory.

Particularly sensitive about issues involving homophobia and class differences, Marcella is clearly conflicted about speaking out about the injustices and insensitivity she sees around her. On the one hand, she is reluctant to be assertive, particularly with professors and others whom she has been taught to respect and show deference to, but on the other hand, she feels guilty, as though she is not really behaving honorably if she remains silent, almost as though remaining silent means sanctioning the very attitudes she detests. Occasionally, the distress and anger she feels at the racism, classism, and homophobia she sees around her surge to the surface—sometimes almost before she knows it—and she speaks out, but not without suffering considerable anguish.

Interviewing Pierre LaCroix in the Retreat, the central eating place in Vassar's Main Building, is a bit like interviewing the very popular mayor of a small city. People stop by our table constantly. With apologetic glances and murmurs at me, students, faculty, and administrators alike need to speak to Pierre—to ask him a fast question, make a date to talk later, reconfirm the time and place for a meeting. He deals with each one in turn, calmly, reassuringly, modestly. His is a quiet presence, unassuming, but nonetheless a real presence. Several people touch him as they speak; he looks up, responds, and picks up right where we left off. He doesn't apologize for the interruptions; this is his work. Being available is a great deal of his job as president of the Vassar Student Association.

Born in Haiti, Pierre came to this country at the age of seven. His parents, both professionals trained in Haiti, came to the U.S. in the early 1970s, leaving their children with grandparents. When Pierre came to Philadelphia, he didn't speak any English, but he learned quickly by watching public television. After attending a mostly black Catholic elementary school, he moved to a predominantly white Jesuit high school where there was a mixture of students—students with Italian, Irish, and Polish backgrounds as well as a good number of Asian Americans and Latinos. In high school, he excelled athletically—played varsity soccer, managed the baseball team, ran track; during his senior year, he was the highest-ranking elected student officer in the school.

Pierre points out that he was the first person in his immediate family to go to college in this country and says that his parents did not take an active role in the selection process. He applied to colleges as varied as Northwestern, Syracuse, SUNY/Binghamton, Oberlin, and Vassar and was accepted by all of them. When he went to Chicago to visit Northwestern, the size of the city, of the university, and of the classes he visited "scared" him ("I got lost in the library"). In contrast, his visit to Vassar on a weekend devoted to minority students was very successful. He met many students, administrators, and members of the faculty, was paired with a "really involved sophomore who showed me a good time," and on the way home filled out his housing form. His parents had assumed he would go to a big university, major in science, and go to medical school; Pierre chose Vassar and is majoring in political science.

Active in student organizations since the beginning of his first year at Vassar, Pierre was vice-president of the Black Student Union during his sophomore year. He kept a low profile during the 1990 protest around an event at which Senator Daniel Patrick Moynihan spoke and felt he was therefore free to talk with all of the groups involved. During the reception following his speech, the senator reportedly told a Dutchess County official who had originally come from Jamaica and who had questioned him persistently, "If you don't like it in this country, why don't you pack your bags and go back where you came from?" Senator Moynihan later denied making the remark, but returned the $1,000 honorarium. This incident led to a takeover of Vassar's Main Building. Seventy-five students occupied the central administrative offices for thirty-five hours to protest what they said was a racist remark and to call for additional facilities and programs for minority students.

Though he has been incredibly successful at Vassar, Pierre has also had unpleasant experiences, such as being repeatedly questioned by security and "carded." Because of his color, it has been repeatedly assumed that he does not really belong at Vassar. This assumption is surely not because of his demeanor—which is invariably low-key and exceedingly polite—or his appearance, which is uncommonly neat and rather preppy. At a convocation in the fall of his senior year, Pierre spoke about the need to break down stereotypes. During the summer between his junior and senior years, as he was riding the New York City subway, he noticed a young woman staring at his Vassar ring. He watched her glance several times at the ring and then at his face; finally, she asked him, "Is that a Vassar ring?" He replied that it was, and she asked,

"Well, where did you get it?" It was clear to Pierre that because of his race the woman was suggesting that he had somehow acquired the ring illegitimately. When he explained that he was a Vassar student (Vassar has been coeducational since 1969), the woman acknowledged she was a recent Vassar alumna, and seemed embarrassed by the exchange. Pierre said, "I saw a change in her. She was thinking, 'I can't believe I said that to him.' "

But prejudice and stereotyping go both ways, Pierre points out. During the same summer, he was working in New York City. It was the summer of the turmoil in Crown Heights, and not long after the killing of Yusef Hawkins in Bensonhurst; Pierre decided to test how a black man would be treated by riding his bicycle through Bensonhurst, occasionally stopping to ask directions or the time. To his surprise, he was not treated with hostility. The experiment reinforced his conviction, which has stemmed in part from his personal experience of being perceived as a potentially dangerous and alien black man—that people must be treated as individuals rather than stereotyped as members of groups, and that blacks as well as whites can be guilty of such bigotry.

One of Pierre's central concerns is that, though twenty-seven African-American males were admitted to the class of 1995, only one decided to matriculate. This number is considerably lower than in previous years. Eleven African-American males enrolled in the class of '92, seventeen in the class of '93, and twenty in the class of '94. It is important to note that, while only one African-American male entered the class of '95, thirty-eight African-American *women* enrolled.

Pierre is critical of Vassar's recruitment efforts and feels that the college needs to expand its efforts, particularly to the nearby towns of Beacon and Poughkeepsie, which have sizable black populations. Pierre sometimes finds himself caught between his loyalty to Vassar and his feelings of loyalty to prospective students of color. When he gave tours to visiting students and their families, he found that parents were particularly appreciative if he tried to be candid with them and told them both the positive and the not-so-positive aspects of going to Vassar. He feels, however, that the administration would like him to emphasize only the positive. In fact, sometimes he feels the college is using him for its public relations. Around the time he was on the cover of the *Vassar Quarterly*, with an extensive, extremely positive article about him in the same issue, he said to me, "This year I'm a Vassar poster child."

The role of Pierre and others like him is exceedingly problematic. They work closely with members of the faculty and administration. They sit on many key college committees, have real prestige with many of the students and can therefore help to stir them up or cool them down. They are, in a college like Vassar, a key element in the smooth running of the school. A student leader told me that she could, with only a phone call, get an appointment with high-level administrators. It is clear that both faculty and administrators at Vassar believe in being accessible, in fostering real communication with students, especially with student leaders. Because of the intimacy of the institution, the air of informality, and the eagerness to incorporate students into the process of running the institution, it is very easy for students to feel co-opted. It must be particularly difficult for students like Pierre, products of educated, upper-middle-class families, to resist identifying totally with the institution that courts them, wants them, needs them, and to keep in mind the students who have not had their advantages. How easy it would be to spend four years at a beautiful, prestigious campus and then move on to virtually certain success while ignoring the plight of African-American and Latino students of the ghettos of Detroit and Los Angeles. How much more difficult it is to walk the thin line between working with the various constituencies smoothly enough to be effective, and simultaneously prodding the school to constantly do more—more imaginative recruiting of students of color, more outreach into low-income communities, more hiring of faculty of color.

The issue of recruiting larger numbers of minority students to Vassar was of concern to many of the students with whom I spoke. Though several of the students felt Vassar was not reaching out sufficiently, Thomas Matos, the director of admissions, pointed out that many factors contributed to the drop in black enrollment: demographics (fewer eighteen-year-olds and fewer high-school graduates); fewer black males going to four-year colleges, particularly private colleges; and the keen competition for talented African Americans among all of the first-rate colleges. The four schools that Vassar lost many prospective students to were Amherst, Brown, the University of Pennsylvania, and Wesleyan. Clearly, many of the student leaders, especially students of color, felt they needed to put pressure on the administration to increase their efforts to recruit all minority students, particularly blacks, and, after the disappointment of only one black male enrolling, especially black males. As another student leader, an African-American male originally from the South Bronx, stated, "As a black male, I don't feel good about this. At Vassar, it's important to have support and to be able to bond with other black males. . . . The commitment to diversity is on paper and it really isn't being carried out. That's the situation and I think the alarm signals should be going off now." And go off they did. By April 1992, Vassar had admitted 200 Asian students, 192 blacks (48 men and 144 women), 130 Latinos (44 men and 86 women), and 5 Native American students.

Many with whom I spoke felt that, though Vassar has made real efforts to recruit students of color, the college has not made the same attempt to provide a friendly atmosphere on campus for students from varied backgrounds. According to Lawrence Mamiya, professor of religion and African studies, Vassar still has not created a comfortable environment. He feels this is partly due to the nature of the larger society—that the students come from segregated neighborhoods, and consequently, "Blacks seem strange to whites, and whites seem strange to blacks. They have to get used to each other." Professor Mamiya spoke of racist grafitti on posters on the campus, security guards "carding" black male students, and the scarcity of people of color at every level of the Vassar hierarchy—among the maintenance workers, among the secretarial staff, and among the faculty. He and other faculty felt, furthermore, that Vassar's failure to create an environment truly friendly to people of color was reflected in other areas as well. Professor Mamiya spoke, for example, of an insufficient Latino presence, particularly students of Puerto Rican background, and a Hispanic Studies Program dominated by American and European white faculty. He spoke as well of weaknesses in the Asian Studies Program. During the academic year when I visited, 1991–92, there was no tenured Asian faculty member. A professor of women's studies described Vassar as "still, to some extent, a white women's elite college." She felt that the tone of the faculty is "WASP" and that there is an unspoken understanding that those who dress, look, and act "WASP" are better. She quoted a colleague who said that Vassar likes WASPS in all colors.

Another professor stated with real anger, "Vassar has become committed to multiculturalism and diversity but not to multicultural life."

It is the old liberal dilemma—they want different people to be here but they don't want particularism. They want these people because that's what you do these days, but they don't want to be financially troubled by it; they don't want to be emotionally troubled by it. The tone of this place is: we are committed to multiculturalism, but don't disturb my life. Once the kids are here, the minority is not part of the majority. I don't see any music, fairs, or festivals reflecting diversity. We have angry communities [groups of students] who feel the college is hostile to what they perceive as their interests. What's going to happen? Nothing.

This particular professor articulates a pessimism that was unusual among the people I interviewed at Vassar. Most of the students, faculty members, and administrators, while recognizing the many problems that remain to be solved, nonetheless seemed to feel that, with goodwill (which indeed did seem to exist on all sides) and perseverance, Vassar could, at the very least, move closer to a multicultural environment that would be more comfortable for the varied groups on campus. There is no doubt, however, that even on so-called liberal campuses people of color, gays and lesbians, and often women are made to feel as though they are outsiders and do not quite belong.

Each of these students has felt anger and outrage at the insults and slurs he or she have experienced. Each of them has felt diminished by discrimination. Though they have reacted to these incidents in very different ways, the most critical issue facing all of the students I interviewed is whether or not they allow expressions of bias to determine their perceptions of themselves. How do you cope psychologically with being called a "nigger bitch" your first day at college, with repeated anti-Asian slurs, with the assumption that your academic ability is inferior simply because your skin, hair, and eyes are of a darker hue, or with being treated with suspicion as a potentially dangerous black man on your own college campus? How can students avoid internalizing these negative messages and develop or preserve their sense of self-worth? Battling bias within their own minds thus becomes a central task of these young people.

Francesca's life has changed dramatically over the course of her college experience. At first, she truly felt like an outcast at Tufts; she retreated for a time, and then returned, to become an activist who experienced the gratification of making a difference and of working with others for something she believed in deeply. What is striking about Francesca's evolution is her ability to move from seeing herself as a victim to her recognition of her position of privilege.

Whereas Francesca's activism has focused on campus-wide issues and on advancing the rights of African Americans as well as gay men and lesbian women, Camille and Susan have focused their efforts at the University of Washington primarily on problems affecting Asian-American students. They work both within the university to improve conditions for students of Asian background and with the students themselves to enable them to feel more empowered and secure in what is often referred to as their hyphenated identities.

Marcella, who is primarily concerned about homophobia, racism, and class discrimination, has presented most clearly the dilemma of many students in dealing with their rage at overt prejudice. As she says, "To confront or not to confront. I wasn't raised to confront." Contrary to the impression left by the multitude of articles about conflict on college campuses, many students with whom I spoke were extremely reluctant to speak up when they were the recipients of prejudice, discrimination, or harassment. Marcella handles these situations by occasionally raising indirect questions about what has been said, but more often by swallowing her anger and hurt and saying nothing.

Pierre, who has had major positions of leadership throughout his college years, seems nonetheless ambivalent about the experience. He was constantly aware of the tightrope he was walking—being a major player among the elite but not really one of them. Because of his greater status and influence during his undergraduate years, he had many more opportunities to turn his back on those less fortunate, and always had to weigh where his allegiance and responsibilities lay.

Four of these five students turned their anger into direct action within the college community; the fifth, Marcella, has had to earn money in order to finance her education, and consequently has channeled her energies into working for a multidisciplinary project within the City University of New York. In this setting she has considerable responsibility and receives a great deal of respect for the high quality of her work. Nonetheless, she carries with her the hurt of being treated as an outsider, often a maligned, stigmatized outsider, and of needing to combat the feelings of depression and unworthiness that stem from these encounters.

5

Speaking Out

I will spend the rest of my life proving that I'm American.

Lisa Graham

As we have seen in chapter 4, students react quite differently when faced with overt hostility and/or discrimination based on their race, gender, class, ethnicity, religion, or sexual orientation. Some withdraw to safer ground for a period of time, as Francesca did, and may or may not reemerge to try to have an impact on events and attitudes on their campuses; others, such as Camille and Susan, react by mobilizing and working with both individuals and groups of students to combat bias within the organizations on campus that are organized along racial or ethnic lines. Still others, like Marcella, continually struggle with the problem of confrontation, sometimes choosing to remain silent, at other times feeling compelled to speak out, even when that action may not be politic. And, finally, there are students, like Pierre, who are committed to working within the student culture and the school structure to move the entire community toward greater equity. Those who choose this course may have misgivings about the speed of change, or even about being used by the college to maintain a semblance of order and relative harmony among the students, but nonetheless choose to play a broad leadership role and, for the most part, to suppress the doubt and anger that surface now and then.

Whereas the students in chapter 4 are characterized by their varied reactions to specific incidents of bias, the students in this chapter either started their college years with greater willingness to speak out in protest against perceived incidents of bias, or, because of their undergraduate experiences, have become outspoken over the course of their undergraduate years. Joanne Palmer, an assertive twenty-three-year-old African-American senior at Columbia University who speaks in a straightforward, candid manner, discusses the intersection of gender, class, and race and some of the issues she has personally faced as a poor, black woman. Joanne was only sixteen when she left her parents' home in Yonkers, New York. She says, "I did not have a good relationship with my parents. It was an abusive household and I left." She became a "nanny" at the age of seventeen and attended Hunter College for one year. One of her professors there suggested that she look into transferring to Columbia, and since she had to attend part-time for financial reasons, she started in the School of General Studies. While she was there, her adviser suggested that she consider applying to Columbia College. She did and was accepted.

Joanne has had a real struggle financially. She has survived by working part-time in a clothing store, by taking out bank loans (she currently owes over $15,000), and by receiving financial aid from the state and federal government and grants from Columbia. She is currently "fully funded," receiving money from a scholarship earmarked for minority students. Her dorm fees and meal plan are paid by her various grants but, as she points out, "I just don't have any money." She continues, "There are a lot of extremely wealthy people here. They have checkbooks and write checks all the time. But people with money aren't bad. I wish I had it."

Joanne has had such a struggle to get through her college years that she finds it difficult to relate to students who place importance on "insignificant things"—like "running out of computer paper," or "getting dumped by a guy," or getting upset because their hair doesn't look right. She also finds a generally lax attitude toward academic work among many students:

> People whose lives have gone in a straight line don't care. I know people who do no work and pull a B. It's easy to get a B here. Columbia doesn't like professors to fail students.

Joanne goes on to analyze the hierarchy of Columbia/Barnard:

> Columbia College is the most prestigious. This is the administration's view, and the students believe it. The School of Engineering does not have as much prestige but is definitely the hardest academically. Barnard is seen negatively. I was going to transfer there, but Barnard rejected me. And the School of General Studies has no prestige. It's the worst place to be.

Joanne discusses some of the problems she has had at Columbia and how she has handled them:

> Maybe it's because I'm older, but if something's not working right, I just say it. Professors will say things that are inappropriate. I have a professor now who makes the crassest, most sexist, racist statements. The other day, he talked about "popping this woman," and when he talks about drug dealers, he gives them Hispanic names. He's known for that. The students just laugh.
>
> Columbia is full of brown-noses. They do whatever they need to do to get the grade. How can you sit there listening to these vulgar remarks? This professor constantly uses vulgar expressions. I was told not to say anything. I need the class. I endured him, but I can't stand him! At the end, at the penultimate [sic] moment, they can get you through your grade and there's nothing you can do about it.

Joanne continues:

In my chemistry lab, I had a TA [teaching assistant] who kept saying things to me. Because of using the chemicals in the experiments, I was getting a rash. He said, "What's the matter, is your lover going to mind?" He terrorizes people in the section by telling them, "You're so stupid. You don't know anything." He said to me, "Why do you want to be in science? You're a woman." He always favored guys and thought women had no business in the lab.

Joanne reports that the TA commented on her clothes, asking if she wore the same clothes every day because she was poor. One day he told her to pick some papers up off the floor, and that if she didn't do it she was going to get a bad grade. She points out at this time that the TA was of Asian heritage, and suggests that some of his attitudes and behavior were due to his different cultural background. When she complained about him to the chemistry department and asked to be transferred to another section, she was advised to forget about it and, if necessary, to take an incomplete. Joanne felt it was a "class thing. The dean's office didn't do anything. But if my parents were doctors or influential, people would have done something."

Joanne feels that administrators are "frustrated" at having to deal with her when she speaks up for what she perceives as her rights. She currently has a 4.1 grade-point average (4.0 is an A average; 4.33 an A+ average). "In general, there aren't very many minority students who do as well as I do. They can't just write me off."

Joanne's outspokenness was extremely unusual among the students with whom I spoke. Most prefer to swallow their anger or hurt when professors make sexist or racist remarks. This pattern was corroborated by a group of faculty members at the State University of New York at Plattsburgh. Contrary to the view that students are actively insisting that faculty toe the politically correct line, many observers feel that students are very reluctant to confront faculty members with what is perceived as inappropriate behavior. In fact, one professor felt that many students show a surprising "acceptance of domination." Students, in general, do not want to confront professors, prefer not to file formal complaints, and, if they are willing to speak up, usually wait until after grades are handed in.

The complaints about gender bias that Joanne details are unfortunately all too common on many campuses. Though women are being educated in ever-increasing numbers and moving into professions once considered far out of reach, their objectification and debasement nonetheless persist in institutions of higher education across the country. Sexist behavior may occur among students, among faculty members, or between a faculty member and a student. At large research universities faculty members often play multiple roles—teacher, employer, mentor—and relationships with students can easily become tangled and exceedingly complex.

A 1991 survey of students in two undergraduate dormitories at the Massachusetts Institute of Technology (MIT), for example, found that 47 percent of the women had experiences of harassment—sexual or other types—which they found either upsetting or very upsetting. In an article written for *The Faculty Newsletter*, Associate Professor of History William B. Watson stated, "One must conclude from these survey results that women at MIT are forced to live and work in an environment that is much more hostile, much more demeaning, and much more dangerous than it is for men. . . . It is . . . encountered not just by a small fraction but by the majority of our women students."

Whereas many students transform the anger they feel in response to racist, sexist, and classist incidents into social and political action, others, like Joanne, focus their energies on their academic work. Still others move in and out of activism. They may begin their college years uninterested in social change, become involved in some way, and then "burn out."

Lisa Graham is a double-degree student at Tufts University and at the New England Conservatory of Music who has become politicized and increasingly outspoken over the course of her undergraduate years. A violinist, Lisa applied to both Tufts and the conservatory, was accepted at Tufts and wait-listed at the conservatory. She auditioned again during her first year and was rejected. "I wasn't prepared," she states simply. "My mind and heart were not into it." During her sophomore year she auditioned again, "played really well, had a great audition," and was accepted. It will now take Lisa six years to complete both bachelor's degrees; at the time we met and talked she had finished her work at Tufts and was spending her two final years at the conservatory.

An only child, Lisa was born in the Philippines and was brought by her mother to the United States at the age of two. At that time her mother was a teacher, but she subsequently left the field, returned to school, and is now a computer analyst. Lisa's stepfather, a Caucasian, is a lawyer.

Lisa describes herself when she started college:

I came to Tufts very white-identified. I did not identify as an Asian American at all until second semester of my freshman year. My mother is very white-identified. I grew up in a white suburban area of Hartford, Connecticut, and went to a white suburban school.

I have not been back to the Philippines since I left at the age of two. I don't know the language; my mother says it's a useless language.

When she came to Tufts at the age of eighteen, Lisa knew nothing about the history of Asians in this country. She describes herself during first year as "very detached, very selfish."

As she began to learn more about the history of Asians in the United States, she became more political, but found few students with whom she could work or identify. She believes that there are very few strong, politicized Asian Americans on the Tufts campus—partly, she says, because strongly political Asian Americans do not go to Tufts and partly because East Coast Asian Americans are far less political than their West Coast counterparts. Moreover, women, she states, are far more politically active than are men, in part because Asian-American women feel they need to struggle against their families' traditional expectations of them much more than men do, and are therefore more conscious of the problems they face in the larger society as well.

She and her friends formed their own informal Asian-American support group, or sometimes turned to the African-American community for support. When people are not accepted by their own community, they turn in some cases to another group, but, Lisa feels, this course also has its "ups and downs." Sometimes one is seen as a "wannabe." On balance, she feels she did not find all that much support from the black community: "Just because you are dealing with your own oppression doesn't mean you can understand another's oppression." During part of this period in her life, she was in a relationship with an African-American man—a relationship that was not really accepted by the black community. Sometimes she felt hostility; other times she felt "objectified, put on a pedestal."

During her most active period at Tufts, Lisa was a tour guide for prospective students and served on numerous committees and on the board of the Experimental College. Begun in the mid-1960s, the Experimental College, under the direction of Robyn Gittleman, offers nearly sixty undergraduate electives, many of which are innovative and may not be found in traditional undergraduate course offerings. During the spring of 1992, for example, the list of courses included "Literary Diamonds: An Inquiry into Baseball Literature," "Introduction to Native American Studies," and "Heresy and Religious Change in Hinduism, Buddhism and Islam." The Ex College, as it is called, also administers two academic/advising programs, seminars led by upper-level students for incoming students, and provides forums for the entire college on issues of particular concern to the academic community. The policies and programs of the Ex College are determined by a board that in 1992 was composed of five students, five Tufts faculty members, two administrators, and a staff assistant. This sharing of power through incorporating students into the administration of an undergraduate program is highly unusual in academic settings.

Lisa feels her association with the Ex College was the most fulfilling aspect of her years at Tufts. "The Ex College showed me what kind of dynamics are possible between faculty and students, and I got to know the workings of the university." But by the end of junior year, Lisa felt "burned out." She couldn't do tour guiding anymore because she felt she knew too much and "it wouldn't be fair." Prospective students and their parents "certainly don't want to hear that the school doesn't listen to me."

Lisa discusses the problem of not fulfilling people's expectations of Asian-American women. In her four years at Tufts, no Asian-American men have been interested in her. Of all of her Asian friends, not one goes out with an Asian man. "I would enjoy being in a relationship with an Asian American but not if he doesn't understand where I'm coming from. They don't want such strong women."

Lisa describes how her assertiveness leads to her breaking the usual stereotypes about Asians, particularly about Asian-American women: "I love it! I get off on it! I hate people thinking they're getting away with something because of what I look like." She discusses the amount of verbal harassment, both sexist and racist, she experiences: "I walk around with a lot of attitude, so they think I'm going to keep on walking, but I've been known to counter." She gives an example:

> One night on campus, at about seven o'clock, in the wintertime, five boys around eleven or twelve were running around turning over garbage cans. They started to follow me, verbally harass me, calling me a Jap and yelling in my ear to make me jump as I was crossing the street. I finally said to them, "If you don't fucking stop it I'm going to call the police, and if you don't think I know what each of you is wearing . . ." and I described each one of them. They took off. It was purely racial, nothing gender-specific. It was the first time I had been singled out by my race.

Most of the harassment these days, Lisa says, is "gender-based. On the train, on the bus, everywhere . . . It happens ceaselessly. But I'm harassed less these days. I carry myself stronger, straighter."

Perhaps the most disturbing observation Lisa made was that others perpetually see her as a foreigner: "People assume on sight that I'm not American. When people see African Americans, their immediate reaction is that they are citizens. But I will spend the rest of my life proving that I'm American."

Lisa's experience at Tufts—taking courses on the Asian-American experience, being actively involved with the Ex College, and interacting with other students—raised her consciousness about being Asian-American and about the historical oppression of Asians in this country. After a considerable period of activism, she will now focus her energies on her work at the conservatory. Not only does she need to focus on her music for the sake of her professional career but, as in the case of so many students, she feels burnt out. She feels she has given a great deal to the institution and made some contributions but that, for the most part, "the school doesn't listen to me." Nonetheless, Lisa remains outspoken when she must deal with personal incidents of bias, and clearly seems to have a very different understanding of who she is and her place in American society than when she arrived at Tufts.

Students do not need to be victims of racism, sexism, religious discrimination, or homophobia to feel like outsiders. When he was a first-year student at Columbia University, Scott Burgess felt like the quintessential fish out of water. The oldest of three children, Scott grew up in suburban Washington State. He was one of 350 in his graduating high-school class and recalls that though he was a good student he had not been planning to go to college at all. He had actually been thinking of going into the military, to join the Navy Seal Team, a special-forces group. But he is a track runner, and the Columbia coach saw him competing at a high-school meet, called him, and suggested he consider applying to Columbia. In response to my question about whether, like so many other athletes, he was given preference in the admissions process, he quickly states that Columbia does not have special admission procedures for athletes. Scott declares that potential athletes apply and are accepted like everyone else.

Not only was Scott not planning to go to college, but he certainly never thought about going to the East Coast. "No one thinks about going east," he says; in fact, few students from high schools like his even go out of state. Moreover, his mother was worried about his going to New York City, because to her it personifies all that is wrong with urban America. But, he states with emphasis, coming to Columbia is one of the best decisions he has ever made.

Nonetheless, he recalls with some pain and irritation the orientation meetings at the beginning of his first year:

> At the beginning of freshman year, there were mandatory meetings in the dorms around gay and lesbian issues. Students

do these presentations, and if they are done well, there is no problem; if not, there are problems. There is great unevenness in the presentations. My freshman year, the presentation was not good. I felt physically threatened, attacked. It is meant to encourage sensitivity, but they acted like it was a recruiting trip. You know, there are students here from the Midwest and from the South who have never had any contact with gays, who had a general idea about homosexuality but not like it is here.

Scott continues talking about the orientation for first-year students. It is really, he believes, an indoctrination about multiculturalism. He returns to the gay/lesbian issue and says the orientation indicated that the word "fag" was not p.c.

Back home everyone said "fag" and it didn't even mean anything. We were told, "You better not say that; you can get thrown out of school for saying that. You'd better accept it or leave." It's not true that you'd be thrown out of school, but that's what everyone thought. I can remember wanting to clam up, 'cause I was afraid of being kicked out of school. And I felt I wasn't able to claim being part of some persecuted group. I didn't have anyone in my background who was a slave, or Japanese, or affected by the Holocaust. Instead, I was responsible for these problems. What they did was old-dead-white-male bashing rather than sensitivity training. They said to persecuted groups, "Look at what these people did to you," and what I felt was resentment.

Scott describes his early years:

My background is Norwegian and German but I never thought about it until I came here. I grew up in a nearly all-white neighborhood and went to a nearly all-white school. I didn't know what a yarmulke or the Sabbath were, but I've always been very pro-Israel. My family is conservative. They are all Republicans except my stepmother, who is a liberal Democrat. Actually, her father is with the Heritage Foundation [a conservative think-tank].

Scott spent his early childhood living with his parents in a one-room shack in a rural area outside of Tacoma. His father had just graduated from engineering school; his mother, a secretary, had worked to put him through school. They lived in a half-finished house with an outhouse and spent a lot of time hunting, raising animals, and growing much of their food. Scott recalls:

> Dad used to work us really hard on the farm, picking up rocks, pouring cement, cutting down trees. We worked from early morning until dark. It was very intense, but if you're used to it, you don't think about it. When I was in the third grade, I got a job cleaning out stables at $3 an hour, and I was making almost as much as Mom.
>
> When it really got bad, we lived in a trailer. The well would go dry in the summer, and we'd have no water and no income at all. My parents didn't want to go on outside assistance. Our grandparents and uncles gave us food, but Christmas when I was in the fourth grade was hard. We were living on $50 a month.

After his parents divorced, Scott recalls, he and his brother, sister, and mother moved into a "real neighborhood." Moving to New York was "totally different—there are so many more options." Here at Columbia, Scott receives financial aid, works twenty hours a week in the gym, and is trying to get a job downtown with a law firm. He goes from registration to registration barely making it financially, but it doesn't seem so difficult, because he has a very good friend who is in exactly the same financial position—actually, he says, in an even worse one. Is class much of an issue at Columbia? Scott responds, "If someone is well-to-do, they don't want to act well-to-do. It's not in to be rich. But there are things that some people do without thinking—the ski trip, the new computer. But what really gets me is when the affluent speak as advocates of the poor!'"

Scott never thought of being a political activist before he came to Columbia, but since his sophomore year he has been extraordinarily active. During the Persian Gulf War, all of the demonstrations at Columbia were against the war; in response, Scott spearheaded a national student group, Students Mobilized Against Saddam Hussein (SMASH). Students from 150 colleges, most of them on the East Coast, participated, and Scott found himself the center of the effort, featured in the media, with interviews on television and on radio talk shows. He feels that his being at Columbia made his involvement more likely than if he had been elsewhere. There was "no counterpoint" to the protests against the war, virtually no faculty supporting the war, and he felt compelled to organize the protests. It was not an easy task, because protesting and demonstrating, he feels, don't come easily to conservative students, who tend to be quieter and often more concerned with their grade-point averages and their careers. In fact, although Scott has since become very active in the Columbia Republican Club, he too is trying to decrease and limit the amount of time he spends on politics in order to concentrate on his academic work.

In his role as conservative leader, Scott has become active in other issues on the Columbia campus. He points out that the Black Student Organization, funded at least in part by student fees, has brought in "several racially antagonistic speakers—speakers hostile to whites, to Jews, and to Asians. In response, the College Republicans printed a flyer listing several of the speakers along with particularly disturbing quotations from their speeches and questioned whether Columbia students should be fighting or funding racism. Scott questions why the BSO brings in speakers who are "offensive to most students on campus" and then provides his answer by pointing out that the speakers were brought in within one month after they made headlines, that

they therefore attract a great deal of attention to the sponsoring
student group through news coverage, and that the BSO charges
admission and therefore makes money on the speakers' notori-
ety. He feels, moreover, that there is also an element of rebellion
involved—an attitude of "This will really get their goat."

Race is a major issue at Columbia, Scott feels. It may be because the school is located in New York City, with all of its tensions, but race issues never really leave, are never resolved.
Negative attitudes about affirmative action, for example, are
not considered politically correct. Scott continues, "I have a
problem with affirmative action. For me it's a real issue. First,
it doesn't work; and, second, it is inherently condescending. It
says, 'These people are so poor and inferior. . . .' It reinforces
a sense of inferiority and self-doubt." He points out that poor
and middle-class whites will suffer, not the rich. Since he himself grew up very poor, he empathizes with other whites who
are struggling economically. He feels strongly that racially
based scholarships are unfair. Many families, he says, are having a hard time; approximately 50 percent of Columbia students are on financial aid, and Columbia has already warned of
limited financial aid during the next couple of years. Who receives financial aid and how that is determined hit very close
to home for Scott.

Gender issues at Columbia do not arouse as much tension as
race, Scott feels, though "there might have been a little during
the Clarence Thomas hearings." When he takes a course at
Barnard, he says, "I'm easy to attack—I'm a conservative and a
guy." Sometimes he chooses not to say anything, because it
would create too much tension. The professors all pay lip service to welcoming every point of view, but most really do not.
Some points of view the professors do not want brought up. "It's
a left/right thing, and most of the professors are left."

What is "politically incorrect" at Columbia?

Affirmative action, particularly around race. Being prolife (one of my friends was viciously attacked for being prolife). And certain language, particularly around gender. We have to use gender-neutral language in certain classes, even when it doesn't fit. If people disagree, they don't talk about it anymore; they are afraid to talk about it. Also, of course, homophobia.

How could Columbia deal with issues of multiculturalism and diversity more effectively? Scott responds slowly, thinking as he speaks:

> People should work on being less thin-skinned. Things get blown out of proportion. The orientation is so strong, because they are trying to root out closet racists or sexists or whatever. The message is, "You've got a problem; you've got to change, because these people cannot change." They're allowed to not change. The orientation shouldn't be done at all. People's beliefs will change as they meet different people, see different groups. They should mix up roommates. Even the multicultural events don't work. The plays they put on present stereotypes and are too intense. What you want to do is laugh, but everyone is afraid to laugh. Nobody laughs. . . .
>
> Freshman year was weird. It totally changed my entire world; not one thing was the same. I realized I would have to adjust. I don't like to fail. I never really considered leaving. I would never leave voluntarily until I had finished.

Having never concerned himself with political issues before, Scott was spurred on to become politically active by his discomfort with the first-year orientation, by the overall ideology he perceived at Columbia, and specifically by the vocal opposition to the Persian Gulf War. Robert Jackson, a senior at the University of Washington in Seattle, became politically active around the issue of an ethnic-studies requirement on that campus. An African-American psychology major in his mid-twenties, Robert

worked steadily and ceaselessly for well over two years to pass
the requirement.

Robert thinks back to what he was like when he first came to
the university:

> I was older than the average student. I had spent several years
> working, and I was looking for something else. When I first came
> here, I felt I could work with white students. I came here very
> moderate, very unsuspecting. I was called an "Uncle Tom" and
> a "house nigger," but I was just trying to be a righteous person.
> I wouldn't write someone off until I tried to work with that
> person. I wouldn't write someone off just because they were
> white.
>
> I never considered myself a student leader. I didn't want to be
> a target. When I first came here, there was a racist incident. I
> didn't go to the rally that was organized, but I wanted to help—
> you know, with the flyers. . . . Then I found I was doing the work.
> And then I was in charge.

Racist incidents on the campus of the University of Washington were the catalyst for the original recommendation by the
Task Force on Racism of the Associated Students of the University of Washington (ASUW) that students be required to take
courses on diversity and multiculturalism. According to the task
force's *Report to the University: Racism and Discrimination in
the College Environment:*

> During Spring 1988, a number of racist incidents on the Univer-
> sity of Washington campus alerted students, faculty and staff to
> the increasing problem of campus racism. These incidents in-
> cluded the scrawling of the word "n——" on the Black Student
> Commission Office door, the harassment of a Latino student in a
> racially-motivated incident, and the posting of white suprema-
> cist propaganda. These incidents are NOT isolated or unusual
> events. They are indicative of a growing societal problem.

Among the recommendations of the task force was a section entitled "Increasing Awareness Through Education." The first recommendation reads:

All University schools, colleges and departments should adopt for all undergraduates an "Ethnic/Cultural Studies Requirement" to ensure students leave the U.W. with the skills and knowledge for an increasingly pluralistic society.

After the ASUW report was submitted in the spring quarter of 1989, an Ethnicity Task Force of the College of Arts and Sciences was convened, and it too recommended required courses on racism and ethnicity. The issue was then taken up by the Faculty Council on Academic Standards, which presented a draft proposal for discussion to the Faculty Senate on February 28, 1991. That discussion, additional comments, and further deliberation by the faculty council led to their proposing a five-credit ethnic-studies requirement for students graduating from the university with a bachelor's degree. The senate amended this proposal by replacing the term "Ethnic Studies" with the term "Pluralism in American Society." The senate approved the legislation.

After the legislation was approved and "published" on May 8, 1991, over 1 percent of the faculty objected in writing, and the legislation was returned to the senate's Executive Committee, where the objections were heard and considered. The Executive Committee returned the legislation without change to the senate, where it was again approved. Within the fourteen-day time limit, however, more than 10 percent of the faculty called for a referendum of the entire voting faculty on the proposed curriculum change.

In the formal mailing from the Faculty Senate to all voting faculty members, the legislation was explained as follows:

All students graduating from the University with a Bachelor's degree would be required to have five credits of study [one course] in American Pluralism. . . .

Some students would satisfy the APR with an elective course; however, a reasonable expectation is that most students would satisfy the requirement by taking a single course which would fulfill both the APR and part of some other general education requirement (e.g., in the humanities or social sciences).

To fulfill the requirement, students could take courses on race, ethnicity, gender, religion, and disability and, as the explanation states, did not need to take an additional course but could take one that met other academic requirements as well.

On October 24, 1991, the results of the referendum were announced. The requirement was defeated 921 to 434, with 26 abstentions. Members of the faculty who had been involved in the mammoth effort to pass a pluralism requirement felt that some faculty voted against it because they thought it was part of the political-correctness hysteria; others felt it was a fad and not academically sound. Some felt the legislation threatened the very substance, the heart and structure, of the institution; others felt it did not go far enough. One faculty member who had been very active in promoting the requirement felt it was perceived by some as a threat to the Eurocentric curriculum; she personally felt, however, that it was "very moderate, very modest."

Another professor actively involved in the effort wrote to me after the vote:

I expected it to go down 80/20 but thinking about it in your head and hearing it with your ears are two different matters and it stings and bites and I don't think I can talk about it without crying so I am writing this to you. . . .

. . . a lot of last year was unbelievably painful and ugly and sometimes frightening. The pluralism requirement asked us to reaffirm the definition of a liberally educated person as one who is knowledgeable about and sensitive to a changing world—we didn't seem to be ready to do that.

This professor was particularly worried about the reactions of some of the students, especially students like Robert Jackson, who had been actively involved in this issue from the beginning, from the days of the task force of the ASUW. "We convinced them [the students] to work within the system, to take the peaceful way and they went along with that but now they must be feeling very hurt, angry and bitter. They must feel a bit sold out." Another professor who also worked on developing the requirement felt after the referendum that "the students were devastated. They had worked for years on this." When the results of the referendum were known, she saw "male students with big tears in their eyes." Robert said he could not believe the discussion that took place in the senate. "Why don't they speak the truth?" he asked. All in all, she felt that the students who took part in this effort were "very special."

When I spoke with Robert less than four months after the defeat of the pluralism requirement, he claimed he was not "very, *very* surprised" at the outcome. Nonetheless, though he allowed that it had never looked as if "it was going to be easy," he and his fellow students "didn't want to believe that we couldn't make a difference."

When asked why the requirement did not pass, Robert responds, "There are too many white men on the faculty." He states that a "system of white supremacy exists," and that education at the University of Washington perpetuates that system. Moreover, if the requirement had passed, the faculty would have been challenged to deal with their own biases and prejudices and examine the body of knowledge of people of color. Students would have been in the position of enlightening the faculty, and that would disrupt the existing hierarchy. Robert states firmly, "Authority is key here." He continues:

No one ever told me there was a system of white supremacy. Racism, yes, but not white supremacy. I called my mom [a hospital worker] and asked her, "Why didn't you tell me?," and she said, "Because you wouldn't have believed me." Do they think they are protecting us in some way? It doesn't make sense. We all got suckered into believing that the success of the sixties— the efforts to integrate schools and jobs—signified liberation. But now what we have to do is forget about the past and build on the present. I never saw myself as a victim. I still don't see myself as a victim, but all this has made me more cynical. I am very angry. I try not to express it, but sometimes it boils over. It has been a transforming experience.

Robert talks about the difficulty of mobilizing other students to work on issues like the pluralism requirement. Some of the students are "scared off" by the "intergroup conflict" involved in such an effort; others find three or more meetings a week too draining; and still others feel they cannot afford to give up so much time from their course work. They say, "My family sent me here to get a degree." So he must deal with both the university bureaucracy and with the student' fears and reluctance to get too involved.

Robert, like so many other students, is trying to play many roles. As he says, he is trying to be a student, an activist, and an employee. This is his fourth year at the university, but since he has an additional twenty-eight credits to complete, he plans to stay another year so he can "rattle their cages." He feels that those who resist change count on the fact that most students come and go every four years. After they lost the referendum, sympathetic faculty members told the students not to be discouraged, that they had laid the groundwork for others to build on. Robert felt that was "a heartening message for about a minute."

Each of these students has chosen her/his own way of speaking out about recent conflicts that continue to plague virtually all institutions of higher education. None of them started college expecting or planning to take a leadership role. Each responded to events and issues as they arose, and each found strengths and skills he/she had not known he/she possessed.

Angry and hurt at the continuing racism and sexism at Columbia, Joanne speaks out but tries to choose her moments. She is aware of the power imbalance between faculty and students and does not want to jeopardize her excellent academic record or her future opportunities, but finds she cannot passively stand by while she and others are mocked, threatened, and treated with disrespect.

Not only angry but somewhat defiant, Lisa has changed significantly during her college years. As she says, she started at Tufts "very detached," "very white-identified," and through her academic work, her involvement in college-based activities, and four additional years of life experience, she has come to a greater understanding of the place of Asian Americans and particularly Asian-American women in the United States today. Her willingness to organize other students, to speak out when she feels she must, and to express her anger and outrage sets her apart not only from many Asian Americans but from many Caucasians as well. She often finds herself in the exceedingly difficult position of having to make her own way, of not fitting in easily anywhere, of having to create her own support group.

Scott, a white male from a homogeneous background very far—in social, economic, and political terms—from Columbia and New York City, has also felt stigmatized and under attack. Policies and programs that were intended to enlighten and bring diverse groups together have served instead to frighten, breed resentment in, and alienate him. But though he first reacted by withdrawing, ultimately Scott found his voice and became a conservative leader on the Columbia campus.

The experience of Robert Jackson is perhaps the most poignant among these four students. A self-described moderate when he first went to the University of Washington, Robert became active in response to racist incidents on campus. Working collectively to create an educational experience that would give students greater understanding of the many varied groups in American society and in the world, and that would, it was hoped, counter the ethnocentrism and bigotry expressed on campus, Robert and his co-workers modified their original recommendation, broadened the pluralism requirement, opened the issue to dialogue and debate, and, finally, watched as the resolution went down to defeat. And, as he said, the experience has transformed him, at least temporarily, into a far more cynical, a far angrier, disheartened member of the community.

6

Leading Students

At that point, I realized there is more than one way to call someone
a "high-jumpin', slam-dunkin' porch monkey." Kevin Wesley

As we have seen in the previous chapter, many students
enter college expecting to study, perhaps to have an active social life, obtain a degree, and prepare themselves
for the future, but almost inadvertently they get caught up in
events on campus, in the political climate, or, in some cases, become hurt and outraged by the ways they or others like them are
stereotyped, stigmatized, and thereby excluded from real membership in the college community. To their surprise, many then
become major players within their academic settings. There is,
however, a group of students who enter college hoping to play
leadership roles—some committed to specific values and agendas, others hoping to explore actively the dilemmas of our time,
but all hoping to make a difference. Many respond to the issues
being raised on campuses today, the opportunities for activism,
and their own academic development, personal growth, and increasing self-confidence by becoming student leaders during
this turbulent time.

Kevin Wesley, an African-American senior at the University
of Wisconsin at Madison, is proud that he doesn't fit into any
easily defined niche or category. A political-science major,
Kevin most resents people who expect him to "represent the
views of my people." He wants others to understand that African

Americans hold many different political views, and that to assume otherwise is "insensitive."

The middle child of three, his mother a health administrator,
his father a skilled blue-collar worker, Kevin grew up in the
Midwest. After attending a high school that was "98-percent
white" and a church that was "all-black," he applied only to
Morehouse College, a predominantly black school in Atlanta,
and to the University of Wisconsin. He decided to go to Madison
because he had heard of the hate incidents that had taken place
there—in his words, "mock slave auctions, the disruption of
Afro-American Studies classes, defacement of the property of
greek [sic] societies composed of predominantly Jewish members, and a series of hate crimes." He explains:

> I had every intention of being active and making an impact. I
> had seen segments on the television program *20/20* and read ar-
> ticles about the racial climate here. I came and looked around
> and felt this campus is no different than the society at large. The
> world is not composed of African Americans. I'm going to have
> to learn to deal with diversity. I'm going to have to be competi-
> tive with everyone.

Kevin feels that many students at this university "don't know
how to deal with difference. Many of them can go all day without
dealing with a person of color." His first year at the university,
he met students who had never seen a black person. At a party
on campus during his first week, someone came up to him and
asked him if he was on an athletic scholarship. As he writes in
an article in one of the university newspapers, *The Badger Herald*, "At that point, I realized that there is more than one way to
call someone a 'high-jumpin', slam-dunkin' porch monkey.'" Another student asked if he could touch his hair. Yet another white
student, meeting Kevin for the first time, extended his hand and
said, "What's up, bro?" As Kevin describes the interaction, "As

I knocked his hand away, I wondered why he hadn't just called me a '70s-superfly Big-Daddy-Kane-dealin', Afro-wearin' pimp.' Well, in a sense he did."

In his book, *Bourgeois Blues: An American Memoir*, Jake Lamar, a middle-class, private-school-educated African American from New York City, describes similar incidents of the stereotyping of blacks when he attended Harvard in the early 1980s:

> Never had I felt my otherness to whites so acutely. Some white students I met seemed shocked as soon as I opened my mouth. To me, my voice sounded flat, lacking in character. To them, it sounded bizarre. I'd been talking to a white Midwesterner for about two minutes when, staring in apparent astonishment, he asked, "Where are you *from*?" A young white woman remarked, "You don't sound like a black person." Who am I supposed to sound like? I asked. Uncle Remus?

Kevin sees serving as a source of education for students who would not otherwise meet black students as his obligation. "Ever since I was this little," he says, gesturing, "I knew I was a member of a minority group, and that added responsibility and risk went along with that. My father told me at an early age that I could not afford to be lackadaisical, that I would have to demonstrate my ability and would be held to a higher standard."

Though he feels the university is "sincere in its efforts to deter racism," Kevin has opposed codes developed by the Board of Regents to limit hate speech. He believes that students must be encouraged to think independently, and for this to happen there must be a "free flow of ideas" and "absolute free speech." He also opposes an ethnic-studies requirement. He feels that it is "just another gesture on the part of the university that wants to stay in the forefront, stay a world-class university," and therefore that the administration feels it has an obligation to be concerned about these issues.

On the other hand, Kevin spoke at a demonstration following the acquittal of the police officers in the first Rodney King trial. He claims he was not shocked by the verdict, that it "fueled an internal fire that always boils." In a speech that he describes as "off-the-cuff" but nonetheless "very forceful," he stated that in this country "individuals are innocent until they are proven black."

Kevin plans to go on to law school and specialize in civil-rights law, "protecting the rights of the underrepresented peoples of the world." His final words to me were, "No matter how successful I am, I am compelled not to turn my back on other black or oppressed people."

Merrill Kirkland, a twenty-one-year-old Barnard senior, is president of the college's Student Government Association. She begins our conversations by talking about the fifty mezuzahs that were recently torn down in the Barnard dorms, about how "disturbing and disruptive" it was. (A mezuzah, considered by many Jewish people to be a sacred object, is a piece of parchment printed with a section from the Old Testament, rolled up in a wooden or metal base and attached to a door frame.) A conference on the environment was going on at the same time; it must have been someone at the conference, she says. But if someone at Barnard did it, the administration must, if possible, find out who it was. In response to a question about the existence of anti-Semitism at Barnard, Merrill responds that she does not think it exists. "I have been here for four years and nothing like this has ever happened before. But we have to assume it happened from here. But why did it happen if there aren't some people who are anti-Semitic?" A broad-based student group was formed to deal with the issue; it was important to be inclusive. Though Merrill states, "I'm not Jewish and can't really know how it feels," she immediately speaks of the "pain and violation" that the students must have felt. At a town meeting attended by approximately sixty or seventy students and perhaps twenty-five administrators, the group discussed the feelings that the incident aroused, what it was doing to the Barnard community, and what they could do about it. As Merrill speaks, she stresses that her task, like that of other student leaders, is to create both a cohesive community and one that simultaneously celebrates difference and unity—no easy feat, as she well knows.

Merrill emphasizes that problems outside of Barnard have a definite impact on the community:

> We live in the middle of New York City, with racism, anti-Semitism, homophobia, and economic turmoil all around us. Are we letting what's going on outside our community affect what goes on inside? We are a small community. If *we* can't work together and talk and prevent these kinds of problems, how can the larger community work things out? It's frightening, and it's discouraging.

The elder of two daughters, Merrill grew up in and around an old New England city. Her family is itself a microcosm of diversity—religious, economic, and ethnic. Her maternal grandparents were first-generation, working-class Italian Catholics, her paternal grandparents very wealthy Protestants. They all lived within ten minutes of one another; in fact, Merrill's maternal grandfather worked for a time at the private club of which her paternal grandfather was a member. Although her parents divorced when she was ten and her father died during her sophomore year in high school, she has remained very close to both sets of grandparents. She recalls going from one house to the other at Christmastime—from "rosary beads and doilies" to "old furniture, antiques, and portraits of ancestors from long ago."

One of the issues on campus with which Merrill has been involved is date rape, or, more generally, sexual assault and violence. She points out that when a Barnard student is raped it often means that a Columbia man was involved; because Barnard is a woman's college affiliated with Columbia, when a Barnard student is sexually assaulted, it is difficult to address the issue within the system. The student must go through the college and university bureaucracy, and students frequently have the feeling that Columbia doesn't believe Barnard students. The man often gets a second chance, and many feel the system doesn't really work. Students therefore have developed their own methods of dealing with the issue. For example, a couple of years ago, Merrill recalls, a Columbia College woman was date-raped and brought charges to the appropriate university committee. The case was dismissed, and the young woman, frustrated with the way Columbia handled the issue, went to a local shop and had stickers printed saying "————, C.C. '92, is a rapist." Merrill felt that students resort to these tactics when they see no other way to address the problem. There was considerable dialogue and debate about the tactic—some of it on the walls of the women's bathrooms—and though some felt, "How could you do this?," the majority were in support of the woman.

After the woman in question put a sticker on the accused rapist's door, he brought countercharges against her. According to Merrill, "The alleged victim [the woman] was almost put on trial and eventually put on probation. Nothing happened to the male student."

Merrill points out that most often rape on college campuses is date rape, but that date rape *is* rape.

If she says "no" and the man keeps going, that's rape. It is a time of changing norms and there is increasing discussion among men about where the line is now. When does "no" mean "no" and when does "no" mean "yes"? Norms are changing, and men better think about what they do. What's acceptable and what's not acceptable is changing.

Merrill talks about the annual Barnard "Take Back the Night" rally and speak-out: "It is an attempt to reclaim the night. The message is, 'We will stay together. Women can do it without men.' Women are working together and bringing issues about sexual abuse and violence into the open." The students march through Riverside Park, an area near Barnard that is considered dangerous for women at night, and then hold a rally on the grass in front of Barnard Hall. The rally, according to Merrill, provides students a channel to express feelings of violation and pain. No matter how many people are there, it is an intimate environment; one person after another tells about violent experiences such as incest or date rape. Some of the experiences occurred in junior-high school or in high school, but most occurred during college. After each woman speaks, the group thanks her for speaking out, and individuals hug her and tell her she's beautiful. People feel great afterward; they feel empowered, according to Merrill. Speaking out in that environment eases their tremendous burden and helps them make the transition from victim to survivor. The whole point of Take Back the Night is to say, "We are not victims; we are survivors." First there needs to be consciousness raising about the degree of violence in the society, then, she feels, we need to see women as victims, and finally as survivors.

Some observers believe that the issue of date rape has been exaggerated out of proportion to the actual incidence and that this preoccupation perpetuates women's view of themselves as victims. There has been some attempt by the Barnard administration to emphasize that women have some responsibility in these situations, and to urge caution on the part of female students. Members of the administration have suggested that there are situations in which women must think twice—perhaps not go back to a man's room, for example. Many students, however, feel this is a dangerous approach, because, "the more we emphasize women's responsibility, the more we detract from men's responsibility." But can a lack of emphasis on women's responsibility actually perpetuate the role of women as victims? How can each individual's responsibility for him/herself be balanced with holding others responsible for not inflicting pain and suffering? When does encouraging women to be appropriately cautious amount to blaming the victim?

Merrill discusses some differences in social interaction between Columbia and Barnard. She feels there isn't as much tension and friction within Barnard, which is, after all, a much smaller community. Black and Jewish students, for example, aren't as divided as they are at Columbia. She quickly says, however, that she doesn't want to make Barnard sound like an integrated community. Elected leaders mix and work well together, and there are diverse turnouts for big events, but a lot of activities are divided into clubs. Just look at dramatic groups, for example: there is a Jewish Theater Ensemble, an Asian Theater Group, and a Black Theater of Performing Arts. Merrill notes the increasing number of groups on campus and their increasing specialization, and feels that students work together less and less across racial and religious lines but that this separateness gives them the opportunity to identify more with their background and celebrate it. She talks about a relatively new group, Asian students at Barnard tutoring Asian students in the community, and wonders what these developments mean for the college community. Will it become even more fragmented, or will groups come together again to support each other? The key issues for students, she believes, are identity and community and how to balance the two.

Whereas many students at Barnard socialize within their ethnic, racial, and religious groups, class is not a significant barrier at Barnard, Merrill feels. With the tuition approaching $25,000 in the midst of the recession of the early 1990s, the "majority of this campus has to work to go to college. More than 55 percent are receiving financial aid. I am receiving financial aid. I don't know anyone who hasn't experienced financial problems." Merrill worries aloud about the consequences to Barnard and Columbia if need-blind admissions were discontinued. She feels it would become an entirely different kind of school. Today the mean yearly income of families of students receiving financial aid, she believes, is approximately $36,000. That fact, and the recent changes in the social environment, have translated into few class distinctions on campus. The presence of so many students from single-parent families has meant that more are facing financial hardship. Though she is clearly not reflecting the views of all students, Merrill feels that the Barnard life-style discourages class distinctions. Consider clothes, for example. A few basic styles of clothing are popular at Barnard. There's the "New York trendy" look—otherwise known as Barnard Black black pants and a black leather jacket, a white T-shirt or black turtleneck, a big belt, and boots. Or what she calls the "crunchy-granola" look, exemplified by sandals and socks. Or the acrobics look—spandex and sweatshirts. Or the preppy look (that's her style, she feels). There's also the "frum" look, a style worn by many orthodox Jewish students who do not wear pants—a long jeans skirt, Keds, and a sweatshirt. How much money you have just doesn't play a part in any of these styles.

In discussing the impact of political correctness on life at Barnard, Merrill notes that, though many issues are freely discussed, such as affirmative action and differentiating between the "deserving" and the "undeserving" poor, political correctness has nonetheless made a real impact on language. Students who might once have said, "Oh, that Oriental girl," will now say, "Oh, that Asian woman," and she feels that is all to the good. She feels it is unfortunate that "p.c." has taken on negative connotations; some of the changes that have been made are important and positive. She points out that her fellow students are eighteen to twenty-two years old and, for the most part, say what they think; they are not reluctant to express their opinions even if those opinions run against the current grain. The students' perceptions of their professors' political views, however, might indeed affect what they say, whether in class or on exams and papers. They might well, Merrill says, "go along and stifle their opinions in order to get a better grade."

Merrill connects the issues of "political correctness" and the need for a diverse student body:

> Students are aware of how few black students there are on this campus and of the need for diversity. They have come to see the link between education and a diverse student body, to have an appreciation of socioeconomic, racial, and ethnic diversity. In fact, the negative connotations of political correctness threaten to detract from an appreciation of diversity and from sensitivity to different people.

I wondered how Merrill came to have these beliefs and values. What in her background made her so passionate about such issues? She believes that a lot of her commitment is due to the impact of Barnard on her. "I came here wanting to be thinking about these issues and wanting to express myself about them. I wanted to form opinions, and this environment facilitated that." Merrill feels her mother has also had a "big impact on who I am. She wants my sister and me to do whatever we want. We're outspoken, and she's not threatened. She's been very supportive." Speaking slowly as she thinks out loud, she says that her experiences before college led to her open-mindedness, and that Barnard fit right in with her mind-set. Merrill believes that the fact that the people closest to her were so different—both her parents and grandparents having different backgrounds and different politics—facilitated her open-mindedness. "I could take what I wanted from them. I was close to all of them and could take what I respected from each one and make it my own." She has worked particularly hard on her relationship with her paternal grandfather. She had a lot of anger toward him, because of problems between her father and his father, but she has been able to verbalize these feelings and forge a closeness. She describes her grandfather as someone who has trouble expressing his feelings. Over the phone she would always say to him, "We love you, Pops," and he could never respond. Now he can tell her that he loves her too. No matter what problems or tensions were present within the family, "there was always a lot of love."

Merrill plans to work for a year, perhaps abroad, and then go to law school. Eventually she would like to run for public office. She is not sure at what level she'll start: "It depends on the political dynamics and what I feel comfortable with, but that's where I personally feel I can make the most difference. There are so many issues I care about; I want to be in a position to address these issues."

Whereas Kevin and Merrill consciously want to test out their ideas and play leadership roles on their campuses, Magdilene Ryan did not see herself in a position of leadership during her first two years at Vassar, but as she acquired knowledge, questioned her assumptions, and was affected by the political events on campus, she emerged as an active, forceful, self-confident leader.

Maggie (as she is known) is an African-American woman who grew up in the suburbs of Atlanta. The youngest of three children, she and her siblings attended a Catholic elementary school where most of her classmates were also African-American. "My parents felt they would lose control if we attended public school," she states quietly. "My father dropped me off on his way to work [he is a scientist], and my mother picked me up on her way home from her government job."

She describes her high-school years:

> When I was in the eighth grade, a family friend called to tell us about Project Match, a group that was trying to place students of color in boarding-school settings. I took a week off and visited several schools—Miss Porter's, St. George's, Groton. I got in everywhere and decided to go to Groton. I wanted a coed school, and it seemed the most prestigious.
>
> While I was there, not very much fazed me. I knew there was institutional sexism and racism—there was only one faculty person of color, very few women teachers, and a Eurocentric curriculum—but it worked for me. At thirteen and fourteen, I was very confident; I felt very intelligent and very capable. My mother always told me, if I put my mind to something, I could do it. I knew I belonged there.
>
> At Groton, we were always told, "You're the cream of the crop; you're the elite." We were all intelligent, all the same level. I made all kinds of friends. I learned academic discipline. But at the same time, I was forgoing the social experience I would have had in high school—the coming-out parties, the debutante balls, all of the embellishments of the black upper-middle class. The white dresses, the long white gloves, the limos, the whole nine yards. But, as my parents said, there are always opportunity costs, and twenty years from now all that won't mean much. By junior year, I knew I belonged at Groton. I wasn't there to fill a quota; I was there to get an education. I was doing it for myself and for my family.

When Maggie started the college-selection process, she knew that Groton put her in a different pool. Her first choice was Brown, then Vassar, Columbia, and Barnard. She didn't get into Brown ("They are going to want me to speak there in twenty years!") or Barnard, but did get into Columbia and Vassar. She visited Vassar in the fall of her senior year for an interview and

a tour and loved it. She and Vassar fit "like a hand to a glove."
It was not so regimented; there were more women teachers and
more faculty of color. And she was "accustomed to the social
system."

> I had grown up in the white world and knew the codes. I knew
> what is socially acceptable and what is not. I knew the lan-
> guage, the dress codes, what the leisure weekend activities were.
> Groton socialized me to the white upper-middle-class world.
> And I knew how to play the name game—who do you know in
> the Atlanta, Washington, and New York circles? Everyone knows
> everyone, and it was important being able to fit in.

At Groton, she often felt she was denying her cultural heritage:
she was using different language, adopting different forms of behavior, and even adapting to "acceptable" ways of expressing anger. These adjustments were not only part of moving from a
predominantly black world to a predominantly white world, but
were also the product of the norms and mores of the extraordinarily privileged world of Groton. Because of her assimilation into
that world, she felt she was "playing a tightrope." When she went
home, her friends told her, "You now sound like a white girl." By
the time Maggie was in her junior year at Groton, she had many
fewer friends at home—actually, only one good friend—and her
two best friends were at boarding school with her.

In *Black Ice*, a moving memoir about her years at St.
Paul's—a formerly male, virtually all-white prep school in New
Hampshire—Lorene Cary talks about the enormous sense of responsibility she felt in 1971 as she entered the foreign, white
world of the upper and upper-middle class: "Wasn't it time for
me to play my part in that mammoth enterprise—the integration, the moral transformation, no less, of America?" She understood that she was at St. Paul's not simply as an individual but
as part of a long, tortuous process: "I was there because of sit-

ins and marches and riots. I was there—and this I felt with extraordinary and bitter certainty—as a sort of liberal-minded experiment. And, hey, I did not intend to fail." She not only had to
succeed for the sake of "the moral transformation . . . of America," for the sake of her parents and grandparents ("*My* duty was
to compete in St. Paul's classrooms. I had no option but to succeed, and no doubt that I could will my success"), but also for
the generations that had gone before: "If we could succeed
here—earn high marks, respect, awards; learn these people,
study them, be in their world but not of it—we would fulfill the
prayers of our ancestors."

"Be in their world but not of it." Is this the dual consciousness W. E. B. DuBois wrote about? What a difficult feat for these
young people—to be, in the words of Patricia Hill Collins, professor of Afro-American studies at the University of Cincinnati,
the "outsider within," part of the world of white power, a seduc-
tive world glittering with promises, but not quite of it. Cary recalls a visit to St. Paul's by Vernon Jordan, then president of the
National Urban League, and his words to her: "You've got to get
as much as you can here, be the *best* that you can, so that when
you come out, you'll be ready. But you cannot forget where
you've come from."

During her sophomore year, Maggie feels, Vassar helped her
to "come into my own—to understand where I've come from and
where I'm going." She feels she did "a lot of reconciling about
my privileged life, a privileged life most young black women are
not going to have. How come I was the lucky one? How come I
was more deserving?" She feels, however, that she now understands the dual discrimination faced by black women. She recognizes that she had not yet reached this level of consciousness
when she was at Groton, and feels that, if she had known then
what she knows now, she would have been a lot more frustrated.
Now she has the "theories and bibliographies to go along with
the experience. Knowledge now gives me energy. When I was

younger, it would have made me angry; when you're older, you teach others."

Nonetheless, sophomore year at Vassar was not easy for Maggie. During the fall of 1989, a Ku Klux Klan member was stopped and searched in the Poughkeepsie area, and ammunition was found in his car. Later it became known that the Klan was planning to march in Poughkeepsie, and some on campus received threats from Klan members. On one Saturday in October, five hundred students marched through Poughkeepsie protesting the Klan. According to Maggie, "It was a fairly scary situation." The following February, the incident with Senator Moynihan occurred, leading to the takeover of Vassar's Main Building.

During that time, Maggie says, she was "pegged [as] an assimilationist," as someone who was "mainstream." She feels that the expectations of faculty and students, particularly black juniors and seniors, are that first- and second-year students will "have it all together." They are expected to be "ten times better, ten times more clued in, ten times more aware, and if they are not, they are seen as lesser individuals. The numbers of people of color are so small that, if one person does something different, it has impact on the entire group."

Moreover, one is often the only woman of color in many classes, and is expected to represent all black women or the black point of view. A professor will turn to the black student and ask, "So, what's the black perspective?" Maggie shares Francesca's and many other students' concerns about professors relying on students because they, the professors, have a lack of information or feel uncomfortable with a certain body of information. They "depend on the student to guide them." She feels that students should not have to educate professors. "Many students of color," she says, "recognize this as a necessary evil, but ideally you should not feel you have to do it. You try to say, 'This is *my* opinion, *my* perspective.' You are not the authority in the classroom—that's not my role here—so you try to shift it." It got to be too much. According to Maggie, "Many get to the point that they don't feel they are getting out of Vassar what they are giving."

By the end of sophomore year, Maggie said she was not feeling "affirmed" at Vassar. "I was not feeling very intelligent. I did not feel I had a grasp on what was going on academically. I did not feel I had something to contribute to the process, and I didn't feel anyone cared."

During this time, she started to "process" her Groton experience, in which conformity and assimilation were stressed.

> You have to get along; it's a matter of survival. You have your friends; the faculty likes you; you play on teams. Everyone else is in that mode. There was a feeling of optimism. There was no recession, no deficit. The world still seemed to be an O.K. place; we felt we could change things.

During the second semester of her junior year, Maggie had what was to prove to be a very positive experience. She took graduate courses at the Bank Street College of Education in New York City and taught at a school in East Harlem. She was part of a group of nine students, the only African American in the group. At Bank Street, she felt she had something to contribute; she wasn't just a representative of a group: "My thoughts and feelings had validity." And her student teaching was rewarding as well. This was the first time her students had ever had an African-American woman as a student teacher; she felt she was giving something back to the community.

> It meant a great deal. I was not there on a missionary trip or to save the poor helpless masses. I was there because I wanted to be. I had been given the tools to play the game. Unless you receive the tools, you're clueless. There has to be mentoring in some form; there has to be mentoring in *every* form.

When Maggie returned to Vassar in the fall of her senior year, she became active in the Black Commencement Committee. The previous year, the three black members of the Senior Class Commencement Committee had resigned, according to *The New York Times*, because "the committee was not addressing the social and cultural needs of black seniors." The black-student committee members felt their suggestions for graduation were not being seriously considered.

The history of many colleges can be seen as periods of conflict and confrontation alternating with periods of consolidation and relative calm. In November 1990, during Maggie's junior year, twenty-six black members of the Vassar senior class signed a statement expressing their dissatisfaction with the commencement committee's "consistent neglect" of black concerns. Traditionally, the commencement committee plans activities for one hundred days and nights prior to graduation. According to one Vassar professor, many of the activities were to be at a local tavern that plays country-and-Western music, a place where local residents whom some have referred to as "rednecks" go to drink. The black women on the committee kept saying they would not feel comfortable going to the tavern; some said they would not feel safe there. The response by the committee was that graduating seniors *always* went to the tavern. When the African-American students suggested doing something other than drinking—going to an amusement park, for example—the response was that going to an amusement park was a "black thing" to do. According to one professor, the black students were "stunned." The black students formed their own commencement committee, which was recognized by the college, received funding from the Vassar Student Association, and planned activities prior to commencement. Before 1969, the baccalaureate service at Vassar had been a worship service; in 1991, this event became the vehicle for black students to express their feelings concerning commencement activities. The 1991 baccalaureate service featured two gospel choirs, and the Reverend Jesse Jackson as the keynote speaker. The chapel was packed to overflowing, and the service had to be piped into another auditorium. Contrary to many press reports, however, there was only one, unified, commencement.

While there was considerable discussion on the Vassar campus during the spring of 1991 about separatist moves threatening the unity of the senior class, there was also considerable support for diverse activities in celebration of graduation. According to one black student, "This college wasn't made for us, but we're here now, and provisions have to be made." Another student, a history major, stated, "Commencement is a totally cultural affair. The very hats worn during the ceremony are out of sixteenth-century France and England. Everything stems from Western culture. If you feel your culture isn't being represented, you should represent it."

Throughout the following year, Maggie and others worked with the Black Commencement Committee in planning the baccalaureate service. On May 23, 1992, a warm, sunny Saturday afternoon, the day before commencement, two gospel choirs, one an integrated group from Vassar and the other the Abyssinian Baptist Church choir from Harlem, sang in the Vassar chapel before a racially diverse, standing-room-only audience. Calvin O. Butts III, pastor of the Abyssinian Baptist Church, gave the baccalaureate address. In a moving speech, Butts declared that America is a nation gone mad, prostrate before the god of materialism, and that we are suffering from "an erosion of values." He exhorted the students, whom he repeatedly referred to as "beloved," to remember the words of W. E. B. DuBois, who wrote that education should first strengthen character, then should increase knowledge, and only lastly should enable us to earn a living. Butts ended by reminding those present that we must learn how to live with one another and truly make the United States the "land of the free and the home of the brave."

Far from being divisive or "separatist," the 1992 baccalaureate service, with Maggie's leadership, was a celebration of the roots and culture of these African-American students, of their educational coming of age as Vassar students, and of Vassar's recognition of the importance of celebrating diversity.

Maggie acknowledges that this year, her senior year, has been a special one for black students at Vassar: both the student-government president and the senior-class president have been African-American. What about the issue of separatism? On many campuses—indeed, in many high schools as well—the phenomenon of student groups organized by race and religion and of groups sitting together in the cafeteria has been noted and criticized.

Blacks and other minority groups have been particularly singled out for criticism for separating themselves from the majority of students on college campuses. Jake Lamar discusses this phenomenon at Harvard during the early 1980s and places the so-called separatism of black students into a broader context:

> I'd found Harvard to be a dull, cold, segregated place where, in the first several weeks of school, students scrambled to join the appropriate clique. Walking into the freshman dining hall for the first time and seeing, along one wall, three tables filled exclusively with black students, I felt that my social place had been preassigned. The young people at the "black tables" were no different from other Harvard students who found solace in sameness. There were Asian tables, Wasp tables, Jewish tables, jock tables, gay tables, nerd tables; every undergraduate tribe imaginable staked out its turf in the Freshman Union.

When asked about this phenomenon, Maggie says that it is "comforting being surrounded by people like you. It gives you the opportunity to regroup, like when you go back to your family and sit around the table and talk family business. Many of us are well integrated in the college community; time together is valuable time for us." Maggie's closest friends at Vassar are five women of color—four African Americans and one Asian American. All are from upper-middle-class backgrounds, since their parents are largely professionals, and they attended predominantly white high schools.

During her senior year, Maggie, an urban-studies major with an education focus, did eight weeks of student teaching in a middle school in Poughkeepsie, right up the street from Vassar. She taught U.S. history and social studies to 155 eighth-grade students. Five were students of color. It was not an easy experience for her. Part of the problem, she feels, was being a Vassar student—the usual split between town and gown. "They think Vassar students are full of themselves, elite, and excessively liberal. Also incredibly wealthy and, you know, vacationing in France." Maggie felt that being a woman, and particularly an African-American woman, made it even harder for her. She describes the school as "male-run," with faculty members who are clearly "sexist, racist, and homophobic." One day early in her stint there, while she was in the faculty room preparing a lesson plan, a teacher described an African-American boy on the wrestling team by saying, "He's an animal, just like all the rest of them." During her first week or two, a student said, "I don't want any nigger teaching here." Many of the students "throw around the 'n' word" but Maggie felt, "Some things you let go by."

Other things, however, she clearly did not let go by. When one student made homophobic comments about another student, comments that Maggie considered "straight harassment," she took him out of the classroom and told him that she was not going to tolerate such behavior in her classroom. The student responded mildly and meekly, "O.K., O.K., Ms. Ryan." The comments stopped.

Maggie describes these eight weeks as a terrible and wonderful experience.

They [both students and faculty] were waiting for me to fuck up. I planned my own units, gave homework, implemented multicultural education. And I was really a hard-ass. When they were rowdy and rude, I kept whole classes for detention. Some were unruly, called out, were disruptive; some didn't have their homework, weren't prepared, didn't even have a pen and a notebook. Eventually they figured out that, the more they talked, the more homework they got. It was like being under a microscope. I had to be very, very careful—about what I did, what I said, what I wore, my makeup, my hair. But I loved the reality of it—getting up at six, leaving at seven, every day. I had to be there. No one else could do what I was doing. And I liked the feeling of being really tired at the end of the day.

Maggie sees herself as having moved through "different levels of consciousness" from her first year through the end of senior year:

Now I know I'm an African-American woman in this country, and I know where they stand on the totem pole. I'm always going to have to work against that reality. Before this, I knew it but I didn't really accept it. We all like to live in fantasyland as long as possible, but you have to prepare yourself for the world. The first two years here, I had a boarding-school mentality—that I was very special, the crème de la crème. But then you have to wake up and not be so self-centered. The individualistic mentality, the pull-yourself-up-by-your-bootstraps-Horatio-Alger mentality, doesn't work for the African-American community. You need to go with the community and have a collective sense of self. No one does anything by oneself in this world.

Nina Hsu, a twenty-one-year-old junior who grew up in Hawaii, gives yet another picture of a student leader who is also struggling to understand her own identity. The elder of two daughters, Nina attended an all-girl Episcopal school through the fifth grade and then went to a coeducational prep school.

Her father, a government employee, and her mother, a social worker, had wanted her to go to one of the California state schools, but Nina didn't even apply to any of them. Like so many other students whom I interviewed, Nina bypassed a closer, more familiar college environment and opted for a distant, more challenging experience. She applied to a variety of schools, including to Barnard and during the Open House weekend at Barnard, she stayed with a student from Hawaii and "we really clicked. Barnard was definitely my first choice." At Barnard, Nina has been very active, particularly in the student-government organization and in the Chinese Student Club.

She discusses the differences in how she viewed herself in Hawaii and after she came to Barnard:

> When I was in Hawaii, I never thought of myself as Asian. Here you need to identify yourself as Chinese or Korean or whatever. My dad is fifth-generation Chinese, and my mom is Korean. They don't speak either language. Once I came to college, I became more identified with my heritage and wanted to study Chinese history.

Even though Nina studied Chinese for two years in high school and two more years in college, she thinks Chinese students on the East Coast feel that she is not quite Chinese enough. She joined the Chinese Student Club because it was easier—her last name is Chinese, and the Korean students would not have accepted her as easily. Clearly identifying more as Hawaiian than as members of a specific Asian subgroup, her friends at Berkeley and at other West Coast universities join Hawaii clubs rather than clubs designated by nationality.

She illustrates the changes that often take place in young people's attitudes when they leave the more homogeneous environment in which they were raised and suddenly feel like an outsider, like a member of a minority group within a majority culture. She describes a cousin of hers who she states was "definitely an assimilationist. He would never want to eat Korean foods like kim chee or kalbi; he would only eat pizza and hamburgers!" Now he is at Andover and has founded the Korean Student Association there.

In discussing the issue of the "model minority," Nina states that her parents would like her to study something more concrete like medicine or engineering, because it is safer, more secure than politics or policy-making. She is studying economics, however, and has just received a major, prestigious scholarship which will provide her with a summer internship in the public sector in Washington, D.C., and a substantial amount of money toward graduate school. But it has not been easy for her to reach this point. She feels she was taught to be quiet, not to be articulate, that she lacked many social skills, such as speaking up in class and voicing her opinions. But being at Barnard has really changed her. The environment has fostered her speaking up and becoming successful. Being active in student government has also helped, because she has learned from other students who are strong advocates. She states, "What Barnard teaches you, you can keep and take into the real world."

Having moved from Hawaii to the East Coast, Nina often feels she doesn't quite identify with either environment:

> I need to live in a big city. People in Hawaii are so relaxed; that's why I couldn't stand to stay there. There are no theaters, no anything. Not necessarily New York, maybe D.C. I just don't feel as close to Hawaii. My parents can't understand why I don't want to go home. A lot of time, I don't identify with people born on the East Coast, but I don't relate to people in Hawaii either. The West Coast is closer to home, but I wanted more. When I came here, I really fit in.

Asians and Asian Americans are not only diverse in terms of their countries of origin and the geographical areas in the

United States where they grew up, but also in terms of when they or their families immigrated to this country. Nina talks about the ABCs, American-born Chinese, and those who are newer arrivals. ABCs at Barnard, whom she characterizes as "more sophisticated," are likely to belong to the Chinese Student Club, a group that sponsors parties and a popular, well-attended dinner and fashion show that features Asian designers. Recent immigrants, who often speak Chinese among themselves, are more likely to join the other Barnard Chinese club, Sounds of China. Nina sums up the hierarchical nature of these distinctions by saying, "My parents would be extremely concerned if I married a recent immigrant."

What forces propel students into positions of leadership on college campuses, particularly during an era riddled with conflict? Surely personality plays a major part—drive, commitment to specific values and/or issues, perhaps a desire to stand out, to be noticed. The interplay, on the one hand, between personal experience within the family unit, in prior schooling, and within a community, and, on the other hand, major issues and events in the college context, has a significant impact on which students come forward to lead.

Kevin Wesley, having grown up in both the black and the white worlds, chose a large, overwhelmingly white institution in part because he felt it reflected the American society in which he would have to live and compete the rest of his life, and in part because he wanted to make a difference on a campus already struggling with racial conflict. Kevin exemplifies the complexity of responses within most individuals and groups on campuses today. Though it is generally assumed—indeed, is a central component of our overgeneralized, stereotypic thinking—that virtually all black students support affirmative action, are likely to support speech codes that limit racist speech, and generally support the black student groups on campus, many of the students interviewed for this book, particularly Kevin Wesley, point out the fallacies of such generalizations. Although Kevin feels keenly the discrimination and stereotypic thinking that are widespread on the University of Wisconsin campus, he nevertheless thinks through every major issue for himself, taking an independent stand whenever he feels he must, and joining with other black students when he agrees in his own mind. He has forged an independent role for himself and speaks out frequently and forcefully.

Merrill Kirkland attempts to lead by bringing people together. The product of a complex family marked by religious and class difference, Merrill spent part of her childhood and adolescence trying to bridge the gulfs among family members, was actively involved in leadership positions in her small, all-female high school, was encouraged by her mother to be a strong, independent woman, and entered Barnard hoping to participate actively and think through some of the issues of our time.

Maggie too seems to have been destined for leadership. Armed with the experience of attending an elite boarding school where, as Maggie says, she learned the codes of the elite white world, and gradually recognizing the oppression of African Americans, particularly African-American women, within that white world, she can almost be called a natural leader in the Vassar setting. In a larger, more hostile collegiate environment, Maggie might have withdrawn, but in that relatively small, responsive community, she could flourish, bringing to bear her ability to function effectively within the black community and also within the larger white community, and her almost nononsense way of sorting out what is important from what is peripheral. Maggie's ongoing experiences in the wider society—at the Bank Street College of Education and in her two student-teaching experiences—also helped to give her self-confidence and to ground her in the real world. It is important to note that though Vassar played a key role in her development, Maggie at one point felt she needed to get away from Vassar, arranged to do so, and consequently enriched her educational experience; perhaps most important, she had opportunities to stretch and test her own abilities. When she returned to Vassar, she then brought to her leadership work there the maturity, skills, and understanding she had gained.

Nina has become a leader at Barnard in the broad-based student-government organization at least in part by overcoming her early socialization, becoming more assertive, putting her own interests and desires for success before her parents' wishes. She differentiates between the attitudes of Asian Americans who have lived in the United States for generations and those who have recently immigrated, recognizing that recent immigrants often feel more closely identified with their country of origin, its language and customs, than do those whose families are fourth- and fifth-generation Americans. Though she recognizes these differences and the tensions they cause, and attempts, as both an Asian American and a Barnard leader, to relate to both groups, she acknowledges the gulf between the new arrivals and those who have been here for generations when she says that her family would be very disappointed if she were to marry a recent immigrant. Nina is very much aware of the dilemma of trying to balance loyalty to one's parents and adherence to the norms of one's culture, and one's own desires and dreams, which have often been fostered by the undergraduate experience. Chapter 7 will explore these conflicts in greater depth.

7

Walking in Two Worlds

*I feel as though I'm inside but not inside—you know, inside but
outside.*   Tanya Robinson

A s Merrill stated in chapter 6, one of the central issues
during undergraduate years is balancing identity and
community. Many students struggle to understand
and come to terms with their complex, multifaceted identities,
and simultaneously to remain part of the many and varied communities to which they belong. Today, in an era in which assimilation is seen as naïve at best and traitorous at worst, young
people often seek to understand the history, culture, language,
and even the oppression of their ancestors, while living from day
to day in the dominant culture. The strains placed on many of
these students—of needing to relate to and satisfy the hopes and
dreams of their parents and grandparents while being continually exposed in college to very different norms, values, and
goals—are at times intense. We have already seen Nina move
from a Hawaii-based, Asian-American environment to the very
different world of the East Coast. And Maggie, who took on the
speech patterns and social customs of her peers while living and
studying in an elite, overwhelmingly white boarding school. And
the young woman at Tufts who was ostracized by some of the
African-American students there because she wasn't "bilingual"—that is, she didn't speak the urban black dialect in addition to standard white English. But these students not only need
to balance multiple identities and identifications. Like many of

the others, they must also try to resist internalizing the disparaging attitudes of many around them and protect a core of self-worth. Once again, their battle against bias is often both personal and public, individual and collective.

As it has taken other students time to begin to feel comfortable at college, it took Simeen Ahmad until her sophomore year to begin to come to terms with being an Asian American, and to begin her active involvement in Vassar's Asian Student Alliance. Simeen, whose parents came to the United States from India, went to Vassar, she says, "by default." She originally wanted to go to Columbia, but she wasn't accepted. After a "very sheltered" childhood and a "wonderful experience" in a private Catholic high school, Simeen describes her first year at Vassar as "hell." She had been a "shy and introverted" person who didn't deal with social issues. During her first semester at Vassar, she was not only acutely miserable but did not do well academically. Consequently, she took the second semester off, lived at home, and took classes near her home on Long Island.

When she returned to Vassar for her sophomore year, she was "very nervous" about how she would fit in. During her first year, she hadn't joined any groups. Early in her second year, Simeen went to a meeting of the Asian Student Alliance; she feels that that was a major turning point in her life. "A lot of anger came out. I had spent most of my life denying that anger—anger that the fact that I'm Indian is the first thing people see about me, that my Indian background made people look down on me."

Simeen's parents are both professionals who were born, raised, and educated in India. The oldest of four children, Simeen plans to go to medical school, perhaps to work in the field of international health. She describes her home as a "semiprogressive Indian home" in which "philosophy is more important than ritual." Her parents, like other Asian parents, are struggling with issues of integration and assimilation. She has seen Asian parents renounce their Asianness, because they felt it was the only way to be accepted; in fact, she comments that many Indians do not identify as Indian for the same reason. Several months after we first met, she tells me a revealing and poignant story of her first day at college. She and her mother had driven to Vassar together, and although her mother often wears Western clothing, that day she wore a sari. Simeen was upset at her mother's choice and asked her to change before they arrived. Her mother refused, but then also refused to get out of the car the entire time she was there. As a senior, Simeen looks back on that incident and realizes how much she must have hurt her mother, and how she was trying to deny her heritage. Echoing Maggie's words, Simeen now feels that at that time she was an "assimilationist." She recalls how she always wanted to blend into the society—actually, how she always wanted to wear subdued colors, so that she wouldn't be noticed at all.

Originally she felt very rejected by the Indian community. She believes that she was looked down upon as an "oddity" because she was able to transcend her background and work within the white world, that she was seen as someone who "really doesn't care." As her interest in and awareness of the Asian experience in the United States grew, she became increasingly active in Asian issues at college. At the end of her sophomore year, she ran against a Japanese-American woman for president of the Asian Student Alliance (ASA). She lost that year—she feels she was perceived as not really Asian—but at the end of her junior year, she ran again and was elected.

According to Simeen, over 10 percent of all students at Vassar are Asian-American. In her opinion, the more progressive, "artsy" Asians come to Vassar. Analyzing the representation of Asians in the media, and addressing the fact that there is no Asian-studies department at Vassar—only an Asian Studies Program—are two of the issues the alliance is dealing with this year. Simeen also hopes to work with other groups at the college.

She feels, however, that the members of the Black Student Union do not want to work with other groups. Their attitude is, "Oh, do you people face problems too?" She echoes the concerns of other Asian activists when she says that there is a hierarchy of victims and Asians are perceived to be at the bottom of that hierarchy—that is, to be the most privileged of the minority groups. Part of the problem is that Asians are perceived as the "model minority," an image as disturbing to Simeen as it is to other Asian students. She believes the stereotype sets up standards they cannot possibly live up to.

Simeen echoes Maggie's concerns as she expresses her discomfort—and the discomfort of other students—at being the "token minority" in class:

> I will speak from an Asian perspective, but don't make me the spokesperson. If an issue dealing with minorities comes up, the minority person would be singled out. How do I handle it? It makes me angry and it's frightening. Assumptions are made that a minority person should be able to speak for all minority people. But there isn't one single answer, and that's what education is all about—expressing many different viewpoints.

As her senior year progresses, Simeen has mixed feelings about the efforts of the ASA. On the political front, she feels not enough has been accomplished. A task force on a multicultural curriculum has been meeting, but Simeen believes it "hasn't gotton very far." They are still grappling with the basic issues." Some of the faculty fear "losing the classics," and there is, she feels, real resistance to fundamental change.

The student groups—the Black Student Union, Poder Latino, and the ASA—have not worked together as she had hoped. At first they met together to discuss problems and to plan strategy, but, as she sees it, the BSU has been resistant, feeling that their situation is the worst, so they deserve the most attention. More recently, conflict has erupted over the plans for an intercultural center. The center is primarily for Asian, Black, and Latino students, but the question of sharing the space with BIGALA, the bisexual, gay, and lesbian students' group, has surfaced. A current plan is for this group to have space in the basement of the center. That is unacceptable, Simeen states: "They might as well be in the closet." She feels that minority students' groups should make extra effort to reach out to BIGALA and is saddened that all the groups do not agree. She echoes Francesca's concerns at Tufts when she describes a split between the black community and the gay community, with black men sometimes taunting gay men. This kind of intergroup fighting about which group is going to get resources, attention, and sympathy takes too much time and divides groups one from another. At the beginning of the year, she recalls wistfully, "I had visions of everybody coming together," but a combination of "personal politics and racial politics" make that dream difficult to realize. The Asian student group therefore "ended up doing our thing."

From a personal perspective, Simeen feels she has learned a great deal through her college experience "about my own ethnicity, about subtle forms of racism." As she talks, she elaborates on both themes, interweaving them:

> I look at this country in a different way now. As a citizen I am disturbed by the Japan bashing I see. I often wonder if people in this country really respect human beings. I walk down the street and wonder what people are thinking. By this time, I should not feel alien. I used to be ashamed about being darker; I'm proud of my heritage now. But the process of learning more and becoming so active has made me cynical. I hear people who say, "I'm not racist; I have an Asian friend." I walk around [outside of Vassar] and hear racial slurs. I've been harassed by white males who call out, "Go back to India." It's very frightening. We all have enough to put up with; why should people carry that extra burden?

"The Vassar experience has changed me completely," Simeen states. When I ask what part of the experience had the most impact on her, she immediately responds that her friends and the discussions they have had were key. "I am hesitant about leaving, because I have such a strong friendship group, such a strong support group here." Most of Simeen's friends at Vassar are white. Their respect for her as she found the courage to speak out gave her still greater courage and self-confidence. In addition, Simeen credits her greater insight and self-awareness to courses she has taken (she is doing her senior thesis, for example, on respresentations of women in Indian cinema) and to her involvement in the ASA.

But Simeen acknowledges that her friends at Vassar have difficulty understanding her priorities. They feel one acts for individual reasons, for the self. But she feels one acts for one's parents as well as for oneself. In India, for example, you marry the person your parents want you to marry. Her parents don't know much about dating. They want to choose or have final approval over her husband. In fact, she thinks they are currently looking for someone for her to marry. "They want to make a pre-emptive strike"—that is, find someone for her before she becomes seriously involved with someone on her own.

Simeen is clearly torn about this issue. On the one hand, she is uncomfortable and somewhat embarrassed by the idea of an arranged marriage; on the other hand, she says it is very important to her to "make my parents happy. I don't want to antagonize them. I depend on them emotionally. Even when I'm down, they're there. If I could walk away, I would." When I ask what would happen if she married someone non-Indian, she says simply, "I would be disowned." After a moment, she expresses both sides of her dilemma: "Here I was taught to assert my independence, but is it possible, given my current state of consciousness, to marry someone who is not Asian-American?" What Simeen doesn't articulate is the other side of her dilemma: given the increased sense of independence developed during her undergraduate years, is it possible for her to accept an arranged marriage?

These cultural and psychological conflicts are also discussed by Hi Lim Sun, a nineteen-year-old Korean-American sophomore. She says that her parents would "freak out" if she married someone who wasn't Korean. She herself doesn't feel that way. She has dated outside of the group. While she was in high school, her closest friend was a non-Korean who was a Dartmouth student. But she doesn't want to marry anyone too Americanized either. After thinking a few minutes, she states quietly that her parents' marriage was arranged. "I hope they don't do that to me. Maybe they could just introduce me to someone. . . ."

Janet Greenleaf, a twenty-two-year-old junior at the University of Wisconsin in Madison, provides another example of students straddling two cultures. A member of the Oneida tribe, Janet was born in Nebraska and did not move to the Oneida reservation until she was ten years old. She says, "Me and my sister never had a rough life, ever." Janet describes her father as "extremely successful. He had the opportunity to go to school and took it from there." Her father has a law degree and is currently the attorney for their tribe; her mother has a master's degree in early-childhood education. Janet's older sister also attended and graduated from the University of Wisconsin.

Janet began college in the late 1980s and remembers the racial incidents of that period. Though she says that she has not experienced "racial stuff" personally, she recalls "outsiders disrupting Afro-American classes, a black girl getting beat up," incidents with fraternities, and she remembers at one point not feeling too safe. "If they're doing it to one group, they can do it to another." At one point she recalls walking with an African-American man and woman as a group yelled "Niggers!" at her companions. "Today things are not as bad as they used to be," she says. "Students are more aware. Or maybe they are just quieter and don't say things. People get along even if they don't want to. Madison tries to live off its liberal image, but I see more conservative attitudes."

"Most kids," Janet feels, "are ignorant about minority groups. They're trying to promote that everyone's the same; they want minority groups to go along with the flow. But groups are identifying with their heritage with pride."

Janet is somewhat active in the university's multicultural center. All groups are welcome, and each "does its own thing." Even though she says she doesn't really enjoy that sort of thing, she attends meetings, because she likes to know what is going on. The main function of the various groups is for students

> to have someone around who is like you in case you get that lonely feeling. Many Native Americans come here directly off the reservations, and they may not have interacted at all with whites. On such a big campus, and with so few Native Americans, if there were no special meetings and programs planned, you might never see other Indians.

In addition, Janet believes campus-based organizations are necessary for recruitment purposes. Knowing that the group is a presence on campus helps Native American students to be more willing to leave home, helps them to be more secure with their identity.

Janet discusses her own primary and secondary education. Many reservations have their own tribal schools, where students learn their culture and their language, but since she did not live on a reservation when she was very young, she attended a regular public school. Consequently, she says, "I was ashamed to be what I was." She remembers that, when she was in fifth grade, and everyone chose up sides for games, Indians and whites were on different teams but she was always chosen to be on the team with the white kids. If anyone questioned why, someone would say, "She's not like them." She acknowledges that in many ways she was different—her father made "a lot of money," she didn't drop out of school, she didn't get pregnant at age seventeen, she took higher-level courses—but she says with feeling, "When you rip on the rest of them, you're still cutting on me."

In high school, her counselor advised her either to go to vocational school or to stay home. Despite her background and her parents' expectations, she "almost kind of believed it," but finally switched counselors and took the college-preparatory course.

During her sophomore year at the university, Janet was chosen Miss Oneida by her tribe's beauty pageant. Besides looks, the contestant's knowledge about her cultural background, her poise, personality, composure, speaking ability, and talent all play a part in the selection process. She took a semester off at the beginning of sophomore year, because once she was chosen locally she needed to compete in national pageants. As she traveled to various pageants, as an "ambassador of goodwill," her mother traveled with her as a chaperone and "kept me together." She was not selected to be the national Miss Oneida, and returned to Madison for another year before taking time out again, this time because her grades had "dipped."

Since she has returned, her friends tend to be Indian students. Before she "dropped out," she socialized more with African-American students. She has noticed, as she has gotten older, that she is "geared more toward Native Americans." On the one hand, she says, "I can't identify with white people; I can't identify with Indian people either. I don't feel I fit in." On the other hand, she feels she is "learning to overcome separateness." She is "learning to blow off whites who don't like you—as long as they don't bother me." She gives an example of the discrimination that occurs routinely: she and some friends were recently in a restaurant with other Native Americans and, though the restaurant was not very busy, no one waited on them for forty minutes. But, she says, "You try not to get geared in that mode of thinking; it can get real negative." At athletic events, people scream, "Fuck the Buckeyes! Fuck the Redskins!" She wonders, "Where did that come from?," but at the same time does not want to jump to conclusions. Above all, she doesn't want "to be dealing with the anger." It is so easy, she points out, to look at a few people and assume everyone thinks like that.

> Whites see a drunk Indian and say all Indians are drunks. I don't want to hate a whole group of people. During a recent anti-Columbus march, I could hear the hatred toward white people. They are doing exactly what they are screaming others are doing to them. Friends forget I'm Oneida and say, "Those fuckin' Oneida." Just because I don't sit around and preach about it doesn't mean I don't care. I'll always be attached to them. Others ask me what I wear when I go home, or if I live in a teepee. And other minority groups don't go out of their way to understand either. They think they're the only group being discriminated against. Don't they know? I don't think so. . . .

Janet continues:

> I feel I am walking in two worlds. We have to keep the traditions alive, but we have to make money to survive in society. We can't blame everything on the past. People get caught as victims. We've got to get out of that.
>
> We must learn to cope with both worlds. Some will say, Once you step into the other world, you can never come back. They stress that we should get an education and afterward come back to help our people but then they are hesitant to let you back. Someone who has been gone has new ideas and they don't necessarily want new ideas. They lose some type of trust in you once

you've left. Now they think you think like a white person. And you're trying to balance both worlds without losing yourself.

Janet plans to get a master's degree to prepare her to plan and run museum programs for children. She is currently planning not to return to her tribe after she completes her education: "I'll go where I need to go; I can always go back to the tribe."

Feeling conflict around identity, feeling like an outsider, and seeking some way to belong are experiences described by many of the students I interviewed; students from very different class backgrounds are another group who often feel like quintessential outsiders and must learn to function in a very different world from the one they previously knew. Tanya Robinson, a poor, African-American woman, must simultaneously deal with difference around race, class, and gender.

Just a few years ago, Tanya was homeless and begging for money in front of a supermarket in New York City. Today she is a student in her next-to-last year of the five-year Higher Educational Opportunity Program (HEOP) at the Columbia University School of General Studies. How did Tanya, a twenty-seven-year-old welfare recipient, the mother of a five-year-old, get to Columbia? Tanya describes her early life:

> I was a prison baby. I was born while my mother was in prison—for forgery, I think. When I was six months old, my father brought me to live with two older women who were sisters [but not related to her father], and they adopted me. My father was black and my mother was German. Her parents would not accept me because I was too dark, and my father thought I was too light. He would say I was "that baby-shit color."
>
> It was awkward having two elderly parents. One was senile, and I thought they were both crazy. They were obsessed with making a lady out of me. Even though they were poor, they sent me to ballet school and charm school, where we were taught how

to walk, how to sit, how to eat. They tried to give me the best they could. They were both past retirement, and one of the sisters, Dorothy, even though she had lost an arm above the elbow due to medical negligence while she was hospitalized, went back to work at a local college doing custodial work just to have a little more money. They taught me to cook and sew and clean so I could get a man.

Everything was O.K. until I was twelve, when there were significant changes in Dorothy. She started forgetting where she put things and would then accuse me of stealing. One time, she couldn't find some money. She called her son over to the house, and I got the beating of my life. They said no one wanted me and that they could send me back where I belonged—in the trash. I loved and respected them, but I hated the hell out of them. I hated them with a passion, and I'm glad they're dead!

Part of the trouble was that I was very ugly. I didn't develop on time and always looked like an oddball. My parents [the sisters] used to have their clothes cut down for me, and they got me a wig, 'cause my hair wouldn't grow. Sometimes, if I got into fights with kids at school, the wig would come off and I was left standing there feeling like crap. I had a lot of emotional problems, but really just wanted to be normal. When I was fifteen, I met a white girl from the other side of Chicago and discovered a whole world outside my neighborhood. I discovered other kinds of music and other kinds of people. I adopted a sense of humor, 'cause, if I hadn't been laughing, I would have been crying.

At sixteen, I was still very thin, unattractive, and underdeveloped. I was the only girl in my neighborhood who was still a virgin, so I had sex to get rid of that. He didn't care about me and I didn't care about him. Later I met a guy from the Middle East who was older than I was. He was mannerly, nice, and polite, and we became boyfriend and girlfriend. Then I wished I had waited.

Around this time, one of the sisters died, and Tanya's father came up for the funeral. Although she had met him only once before, when she was nine, she moved back to Pennsylvania to live with him, his wife, and their kids. She didn't know that he was an "alcoholic and a drug user as well as a wife beater."

> Everyone hated him. People felt, "Oh, you're his kid, you've got to be trash like him." My father was beating me. I had bruises and a swollen lip. Everyone knew my business. Parents didn't want their kids to be with me. So I ran away, and eventually my father put me out. He said, "Go back where you came from." He painted me a tramp, a drug user, one who walked over elderly women.

Tanya remained in Pennsylvania but went to live in a runaway shelter and then in a group home. She says that, though the group home was not a bad place, she was the only black person there and felt that the town was very racist. "I got beat up, spit on, my stuff was thrown out the windows. I made a fool of myself trying to make friends, but it just didn't work."

When Tanya was eighteen, she came to New York, essentially on her own, "to be anonymous and to finish my senior year in high school." She didn't consider college at that time, partly because she couldn't afford it. As she says, "Poor people go to work; rich people go to college. But I loved school. I was addicted to books. I can see myself in school forever." After high school, Tanya had a series of jobs, including one as a topless dancer in a "cruddy bar," which she left because there were just too many drugs. In 1985, she met her future ex-husband and married him.

> I was looking for someone to love me. He's a wannabe from an Italian middle-class family in Massachusetts. One year later, my husband, who was on drugs, walked out and took all of our savings, $9,000. I was pregnant at the time. I was homeless and had to beg for money. I slept in the bus terminal, because I didn't have anyplace to go. I went to Georgia—that didn't work. I went

to San Francisco, and after sleeping on a bench for the first two nights, I finally got into a shelter sponsored by Mother Teresa. I ate at the soup kitchen they ran feeding people with the scraps that others don't eat. Eventually I returned to New York, the toilet bowl of America, and got work as a temporary office worker.

During this period, Tanya was making little money and had no health insurance. She saw that everyone around her had a college degree, realized there were "things I wanted to do with my mind," and decided to go back to school. When she told this plan to an acquaintance, he said, "Why don't you save the application fees and just take a typing course?" Her response was to stop by Columbia to find out about applying. She states calmly, quietly, "I knew I was cut out for more than scrubbing floors and welfare."

Tanya started at Columbia in 1988. It hasn't been easy for her. She speaks with great warmth about the director of Columbia's HEOP, the person she credits with making it possible for her to attend Columbia and helping her to get this far. Nevertheless, Tanya states flatly, early in our conversation, that there is one group at Columbia that doesn't have a voice—low-income students. Frequently these are students on welfare or students who must work; many are people with kids who must go home at the end of the day and never get to participate in Columbia activities. They are students, according to Tanya, who "don't fit the Columbia College mode. We can't afford to live around here; we can't afford to socialize. A lot of students are alienated; a lot feel stigmatized, especially black women." Tanya and her daughter live in the Bedford Stuyvesant section of Brooklyn, where they dodge bullets and gangs. She tells of a friend who was beaten to death. "I grew up in a ghetto in Detroit, but it was nothing like this."

Tanya continues by describing her peers in the School of General Studies: "Most of the students in GS are older—over

twenty-five, many in their thirties, and even in their forties—
and we're treated differently, we're not taken seriously. Everything is separate—Columbia College and General Studies."
Tanya points out how crucial education is for students in GS:
"*Our* college education is going to directly affect our future.
Many of *them* are the daughters of so-and-so or the sons of so-
and-so, who are going to make it anyway. Columbia is real quick
to invest in what they see as the young, bright future leaders of
the world."

Though Tanya is very proud, even thrilled, that she is a student at Columbia and grateful for the opportunity, she clearly
has some negative feelings about the experience as well: "I
don't belong here; I don't really belong here. It hasn't kicked in
yet—that I'm going to an Ivy League college." Nonetheless,
Tanya states emphatically that the institution is "guilty—guilty
of racism, sexism, classism, and homophobia." She ascribes
much of her feeling of not belonging to class differences rather
than to race. She points out how expensive it is to eat in the Columbia area; she generally brings food with her from home. She
points out the enormous expense of books (in one Barnard
course alone, the books cost approximately $200) and wonders
what she would do if it were not for HEOP. She looks around the
Barnard cafeteria, where we are sitting, pauses, and says wistfully:

> I'd love to be like some of these girls with their little conversa-
> tions. They don't have to worry about heat, rent, rats, taking care
> of little girls. I envy them. They're right here. Everything is at
> their fingertips. I love the Barnard campus. When I came here,
> I didn't know Columbia was Ivy League. I haven't assimilated
> that yet. I feel as though I'm inside but not inside—you know,
> inside but outside. I thought it was because I'm older, but it's
> not—it's the class/race thing. They're not discriminating. It's
> more subtle than that.

I ask whether it's how she is treated or how she feels, and she responds that it's a combination. She and her classmates are unsure how to talk to one another. "You talk in class, and then you go your separate ways." Within the School of General Studies there is a very mixed population, Tanya states, and everyone hangs out with everyone else. But between GS students and Columbia College students there is much less mixing, and she thinks it is due to class differences. She recalls a time when she brought her daughter to class, because she had nowhere else to leave her. Her professor questioned her and asked, "How serious can you be if you do this?" She felt that professors saw it as a tactic to gain sympathy, that she was trying to "get over." Those reactions, she feels, are due to both class and racial bias.

The curriculum at the School of General Studies is, moreover, significantly different from that at Columbia College. According to Tanya, Columbia College students must take a core curriculum that includes Plato and Chaucer. "They get a foundation in classics that we don't; they get a foundation in English literature that we don't. We're just thrown into the pool. In writing classes, it is assumed that students have already read the classics of English, American, and world literature. They have, but we have not. And while Columbia College students can take GS courses, GS students cannot take core-curriculum courses." Tanya feels GS students are constantly "playing catch-up"—in math; in foreign languages, which Columbia students have often had in high school and GS students generally have not; in writing; and even in grammar, which core-curriculum students had "drummed into them" in junior high school and high school and she never had at all. The conjugation of verbs, she states flatly, is all new to her. "I have to learn the principles of grammar and Italian all at once; it's twice as much work."

Tanya talks about being African-American at Columbia: "The Black Student Organization [BSO] is really the Bullshit Organization. They think they know everything. I think their Afrocentrism is just another excuse for anger and violence." Tanya points out how difficult it is for a "black kid" coming to college:

> They are pressured to stay with their own kind, because the blacks on campus feel they need to be strong and united to help their own people. But the BSO is divided among themselves. Some are staunch racists; some are trying to make a difference on the campus. It can really be alienating. You're seen as either for them or against them.

Tanya believes that the BSO and their supporters overplay the issue of blacks as victims: "It may be so, but we have to get off that shit. You can't live that way. The BSO is split over focusing on blacks as victims. Some of them are angry kids who go around wearing Malcolm T-shirts. Some of it is a fad, and a lot of it is anger." (This conversation took place long before Spike Lee made Malcolm X T-shirts widely popular.) But she and many others don't want to "wear Malcolm T-shirts and beat the drum." In part, she feels, it is a matter of age. Some of these kids are young—only eighteen, nineteen, twenty. One day, they will need to recognize that they will

> go out and get a job and probably be paid by a white man, will live next to a white man, and need to know how to live in that world. Sure, sometimes I'm angry, but it doesn't help me to wear my blackness on my shoulder; it will only make me feel more alienated. If I wear the race thing, it is going to hurt me a lot. You have to work within the system.

What about sexism, particularly in the classroom? Sometimes, Tanya states, echoing Joanne's complaints, professors use language that is offensive, and some courses, like one theoretical course in sociology, are structured as though women don't exist. "But," she quickly explains, "I never say anything to a professor. I don't want to take the chance of pissin' them off.

That's my grade that's at stake." Some classes, she says enthusiastically, have been great—like her "Feminist Theory" class, in which there was a lot of discussion.

> In that class, people talked to me, not about, at, or around me. But I try to get along with everybody. When I walk into a room, I'm a person first. Others say, "No, you're a black first, and a black woman next." A lot of people knock me for that. People say, "That's because you've lived with them for so long; you've gotten to be like them." Others don't trust "them." I don't walk around with that chip. They say, "Oh, you're sleeping with the enemy." [Tanya is at present in a serious relationship with a white man who is, interestingly, from Germany, the country her mother came from.]
>
> To me, the enemy is not race-based. I don't have to prove anything by wearing a bone in my nose or an African headdress. Yes, I have a white boyfriend and a half-white child. Do I need to go to Howard? Do I need a black boyfriend? Do I need to live in Harlem? Or do I need to be in touch with myself?

Tanya's experience is particularly poignant. She has worked incredibly hard to get this far. She commutes from Brooklyn, she cares for her daughter, and she works in the library to help pay her way. In addition, she must study many extra hours to compensate for the deficits in her earlier education. She constantly feels unprepared for the level of the courses she must take. Her latest concern is biology. She must take a science requirement, and even though it is a science course for nonscientists, she feels lost in the class. She is afraid to drop it, because she doesn't want to extend her time at Columbia for fear that HEOP will not continue to help her financially. Moreover, there has been talk of a cutback of HEOP; without it she could not possibly manage.

Another serious question is the welfare department. Recipients of Aid to Families with Dependent Children are only supposed to attend two-year colleges; in any case, Tanya's daughter is in kindergarten, and she is afraid the welfare department, as part of "welfare reform," will at any time force her to quit school and go to work. Her welfare worker has already questioned why she is attending Columbia rather than the City University. Tanya is clearly juggling several worlds and attempting to make sense of all of them. The pressures of moving back and forth between such difficult roles are severe, and the stakes are high. If Tanya can graduate, she has the opportunity to transform both her life and her daughter's life. If she does not succeed in overcoming the multiple barriers, she will have to live with that social and economic reality, as well as with her profound disappointment.

Gay and lesbian students are yet another group who are, in Janet's words, "walking in two worlds." Many think that at college they can finally acknowledge their sexual orientation without repercussions but quickly learn that even the academic community is not sufficiently accepting of difference to make many of them feel truly welcome. Craig Atkinson knew that he would "come out" when he went to college. Originally from Rochester, Craig applied and was accepted to both Cornell and Tufts. He saw Cornell as a "partying school," so he decided on Tufts, which he says had a "more progressive reputation." Craig describes what happened shortly after he arrived at Tufts:

> I came out within the first month. I was very excited about it. I was so happy that I told a friend from home, and he told everyone. His parents told my parents, who are divorced. I hadn't told them. My mother was disturbed at first but said she sort of knew. Over time, she has become very supportive. My father and I do not speak.

Craig describes his initial reactions to Tufts:

When I was first here, I thought Tufts was wonderful. I thought
there were no problems. I came out to my roommate. I went to
meetings. It was an exhilarating experience.

During the second semester of his first year, Craig became involved in AIDS education on campus. He did presentations in
the dorms for all of the students, both gay and straight. There
was, he feels, a lot of resistance to the information. "Students do
not really think it affects them; there was low turnout, denial all
over the place." He and others who did the presentations were
trying to be inclusive. They tried to talk in "neutral terms," used
the term "partner," and tried to incorporate "gay material" so as
not to turn off straight people.

It was at that time that Craig began to realize that "the students at Tufts are more conservative than the administration,"
that they were resistant not only to AIDS education but to the
first-year orientation about diversity as well. They thought, Craig
observes, that the administration was "trying to ram diversity
down their throats." He feels that Tufts students are largely
"upper-middle-class white students," most of them "preprofes-
sional and concerned with making lots of money." Some are "a
little liberal," but "there are a lot of very conservative students
here."

During Craig's sophomore year, he felt Tufts was "not a great
place. There was a lot of discrimination toward gay people, and
others as well. People wouldn't say things directly to me, but I
would hear from others the very homophobic things they would
say about me." During his junior year, Craig lived off campus
and became involved with the AIDS Action Committee, a group
of gay and bisexual men at Tufts and other schools including
Harvard, MIT, Northeastern, and Boston University who gave
workshops about AIDS for gay men, with the goal of helping
them to alter their sexual behavior.

Craig moved back into the dorm his senior year and during

the first semester was the victim of two separate but connected hate incidents. He had pinned some material on the outside of his door; when he returned to his room one day, he saw a group of international students stopping to read what was on the door. The instant they saw him, they pointed at him and moved toward him menacingly; at this point, he felt he needed to leave for his own safety: "I felt chased out of the dorm." Two or three weeks later, friends of this group called him a "faggot" and threatened to kill him. He contacted the university police, who informed him that the incident was a reportable FBI hate crime and that, if the students did anything physical to him, they would be expelled.

Craig feels the incidents colored all of his senior year. He was "always a bit afraid to go back to the dorm." There should be a "gay house," Craig says with feeling. "It's a safety issue; we need a safe space. A gay house would be wonderful!" The administration offered a couple of apartments, but the students did not accept the offer, preferring instead to hold out for a gay house. They will, however, be getting a new center, and that is a good start, he believes.

Craig has been feeling his way as a gay male in an overwhelming straight world. There are, he estimates, from eighty to a hundred gay students on campus but only about twenty activists. And even within this small group there are tensions—between gay men and lesbians, between those who see sexism as the main issue and those who see racism as central. Nonetheless, he is, all in all, glad he went to Tufts. He has found supportive faculty and administrators; he has found, in his words, "my own place. If I had been in an environment that was too cushy, I might not have had the chance to strengthen my arguments and myself. The world at large is not an easy environment. At Tufts, I did not lose touch with reality."

Other students, while constantly feeling the pressure of hostility and homophobia, have been nonetheless extremely successful during their college years. Karen Morris, student-body president at the University of Oregon at Eugene, talks about the election three years ago for the job she later held:

> Three years ago, an out gay man ran for student-body president. He was very loud and boisterous about being gay, and he lost. During the election, there were posters showing him making love to an ape, there were death threats, bricks thrown through windows. It was very ugly.

When I interviewed her, Karen was, in her words, the first "out lesbian president, after a stressful and hard battle." During the intervening years there have been serious homophobic incidents: attacks on gay and lesbian students and faculty; death threats telephoned into the office of the Lesbian Gay Bisexual Alliance; "fag and dyke bashing," often using violent language, by fraternity members; and efforts by the ultraright to pass a referendum making homosexuality illegal.

According to Karen, it is far easier for lesbians to be politically active on campus than for gay men, because they are far less threatening to straight white men. When gay men run for office, the fraternities run "all-out" against them. Moreover, women in general are more active on campus than men. They vote more, are more likely to be leaders.

At many colleges across the country, gay and lesbian students are taking leadership positions and being recognized for their academic excellence and their contributions to college life. At an academic convocation at Ohio State University in June 1993, twenty-one-year-old Rebecca Woods was recognized for being an honors student, an athlete, and a campus-government leader, and was also cited for her work with the Bisexual, Gay and Lesbian Alliance. Ms. Woods, a women's-studies major, "daydreams" about becoming a Supreme Court justice. But, though more students are taking and being recognized for their leadership roles, others still suffer ostracism and self-doubt. When another twenty-one-year-old Ohio State student, an African-American woman, told her grandparents, who until this revelation had been extremely proud of her accomplishments, that she was in love with a woman, they did not speak to her for a week. When she asked them, "Would you rather I be with a man and be unhappy?," her grandmother responded, "Yes, I'd rather you be with a man who violently abused you."

Karen points out the counterpoint between the atmosphere in Eugene and the often violent attitudes toward minorities:

> Eugene is Mecca. The weather, the climate, the environment is beautiful. It is called "North Berkeley." California is known as refined; Oregon is rugged and refined. And this is a pretty active campus, with many lesbian and gay leaders.

And yet Karen, raised in an Orthodox Jewish family herself, points out that, during the previous year, a Jewish professor was yelled at and insulted, skinheads have moved into the West Campus area, and swastikas have appeared on campus, and there have been death threats to the leaders of Jewish organizations. "Everyone assumes everyone is Christian," Karen states. Recently, a black student was taunted and beaten and, in yet another incident, six men beat an African student. There is ongoing violence against women—a student was recently molested, and five women were assaulted and raped in two days.

She describes what she terms "horizontal hostility" on the campus—that within each subgroup there is considerable hostility toward other groups. But she also sees "interlinking circles of oppression." She asks, for example, "How can gays and lesbians be free if women aren't free?" She feels her task is to work as an out lesbian with many different groups—with the "Greek leadership," with older students, with a wide variety of groups on campus—on a variety of issues.

—

All of these students are struggling to sort out who they are and what their place is in American society. Many must grapple with varying levels of hostility and bias within the larger society, and some must cope with discrimination and exclusion on their campuses. Others are fortunate to find supportive faculty, administrators, and fellow students. Whatever their specific circumstances, none of these particular young people walk in lock-step with the groups that purport to represent them on campus or, for that matter, with their families. Though students, particularly minority students, are often pictured by some academic analysts and the media as the epitome of political correctness, these young people clearly attempt to think issues through for themselves.

Simeen's college years were very much occupied with exploring her own identity and, in the context of the Asian Student Alliance, helping other students to explore and define their identity. Her experience points out the extreme difficulty of building coalitions among groups of "others," and the divisive nature of claiming victim status. It also points out the close connections between rifts among groups in the wider society and rifts among student groups in the college world. The competition for scarce resources, the hierarchy of minority groups, and, above all, the suspicion and difficulty in communication are all replicated from the larger environment to the far more protected space of the college community. And Simeen's experience highlights the extent to which many students, particularly those who come from a subgroup within the culture, must simultaneously move into the broader society with increasing independence, sense of autonomy, and acculturation, and yet maintain their identity and affiliation with their parents' culture. When these identities conflict, as they so often do, the experience is particularly painful, and the resolution particularly problematic. Perhaps one of the mothers in *The Joy Luck Club*, herself the victim as a young girl of an arranged marriage in China, expresses the conflict best: "I wanted my children to have the best combination: American circumstance and Chinese character. How could I know these two things do not mix?"

Janet illustrates the complexity of moving between two worlds. As she says, she does not quite fit in on the reservation but does not feel she really belongs in the white world either. Moreover, she poignantly explores the Catch-22 many students feel when they are encouraged to obtain an education and then viewed with suspicion because they have of necessity acquired new ideas. In a society profoundly divided by race and ethnicity, these contradictions can leave many young people uprooted, feeling a part of no group within American society.

Tanya, a poor, single mother, finds herself walking in many worlds—from Bedford Stuyvesant to the Upper West Side of Manhattan, from caring for her young daughter to debating feminist theory with Barnard students, as an African-American woman who thinks independently about race in a predominantly white school often divided by race. Tanya insists on moving in many circles and, above all, on thinking for herself. Despite feeling outside the mainstream and frustrated at being so poorly prepared for college work, Tanya perseveres.

The experience of Craig and Karen indicate both the level of hostility that persists toward gay men and lesbian women even on so-called progressive campuses, and also that, although the group may be vilifed by some, certain individuals can find a place for themselves, can use the experience to understand more fully the nature of homophobia in American society; a few can even rise to significant positions of leadership. Karen's experience, in particular, demonstrates the need of the "other" to walk in many worlds. Karen, as an "out lesbian," recognizes the linked circles of oppression at the University of Oregon and understands the necessity of entering those circles in order to work with a wide spectrum of groups on campus.

Finally, what of those students who have moved from relatively homogeneous worlds to the more diverse college world, and in so doing have been fundamentally changed by the experience? Chapter 8 will explore the ways in which several students, over the course of their undergraduate years, have crossed boundaries and consequently altered their thinking and their perceptions of themselves and others, and have moved their lives in very different directions.

8

Facing Diversity

I have met so many people here; I have so many more ideas. I am
much more open-minded and less judgmental than if I had gone
to a more homogeneous school. I always knew who I was, but
my experience of living with other kinds of people opens
your eyes to different ways of life.   Rebecca Taub

While many of the students whom I interviewed have
gone through difficult, often wrenching experiences
during their college years, virtually all of them have
been significantly changed by their undergraduate experience.
Moving, as many of them have, from relatively insulated, homogeneous environments to far more diverse communities has in
itself stretched their minds, their sensibilities, their understanding of themselves and of others. Moreover, entering a relatively
closed, intense environment in which issues of race, religion,
gender, sexual orientation, and class have high visibility has
forced many of these students to face some of the conflicts and
contradictions in American society. In certain instances, merely
interacting with a variety of people, often for the first time, has
stimulated a somewhat different world-view, and even a different view of oneself.

Angela Marino, a junior at Hunter College, grew up in an Italian Catholic family on Staten Island. After attending a parochial
elementary school attached to her parish church, she went to a
small, all-girl Catholic high school where most of the students
were of Italian or Irish descent and "everyone knew one an-

other." Many of the students went around in cliques and were what Angela describes as "glitterchicks":

> They wear lots of jewelry, pay special attention to their hair and nails, have the latest jeans, and always look great. Even when they're smart, they're stupid, twirling their hair and cracking their gum. We all had to wear uniforms, but the "glitterchicks" rolled their skirts up, wore lots of gold jewelry, and had their hair frosted. Almost everyone was middle-class and white (you could count the number of black people at school) and grew up with the same values.

Angela's decision to go to Hunter was an impulsive one, she recalls. The College of Staten Island "didn't have a good reputation"; Wagner College, also on Staten Island, specializes in Math and Science; and St. John's, a local Catholic university, seemed too similar to high school. At the time she was considering colleges, she was working at a store in a local mall, and the boss's daughter was a student at Hunter. One day, Angela went into Manhattan to visit Hunter; since she didn't want to stay on Staten Island and thought Hunter would be "an experience," she applied, was accepted, and decided to attend. She thought it would give her a "broader view, more social awareness." She assumed Hunter was a "more liberal school and more tolerant of different people's views" than the environment in which she had spent her childhood.

Angela describes what it was like going from her small, homogeneous, Catholic high school to Hunter College, a school in the middle of Manhattan with over eighteen thousand students:

> Hunter is so huge, all you have is yourself. There are no cliques; you have different friends in each class. At first, I was scared I was going to miss my subway stop! The teachers didn't know me. Everything was my decision. I was like incognito. But I accepted

that and I liked it. I didn't want to go to school with the same glitterchicks. I was tired of that scene.

Angela talks about realizing suddenly that at Hunter she, "an Italian from Staten Island," was a member of a minority group:

> By the end of first semester, it was hitting me that most of the people who come to this school are minorities. When that hits you, it's really something. I'm not used to that. It's strange. It's not the norm for me; it's not what I'm used to. In the past, I've been mostly with white people. I've never been made to feel less than anybody; I've never been made to feel wrong. I've never experienced discrimination. On Staten Island, I used to notice a black person. Now I don't notice at all.
>
> I thought it might be more difficult to find friends and be part of a group. I wondered, Who's going to be my friend now? I was not worried for my well-being; I was not worried that I was going to get mugged. It was more to do with having friends. And I've found I have had friends of color.

Angela sees Hunter as a "very liberal college"—liberal with regard to racism, sexism, oppression, particularly women's oppression and black women's oppression. She feels that, if you're conservative in any way, you have to be very careful of what you say, you might not want to voice your opinion, because you would be pounced on—by students, not by professors.

> If I have a different opinion, I just don't say it. What I believe is often not mainstream, but I have a gift for being able to see others' viewpoints. About abortion, for example. People assume I'm prochoice; I'm not but I won't speak on the prolife side. It's not worth the argument. People have tried to show them the other side before I came along.

The youngest of three children, Angela comes from what she characterizes as a very conservative family. Her father, a contractor, and her mother, a clerical worker, have been separated for five years. One brother, ten years older, dropped out of college six months before graduation and now works for their father. Her other brother, eight years older, never graduated from high school and works as an electrician for the housing authority. Angela notes with some pride that she will be the first in her family to graduate from college:

> I feel good about that. I'm proud of myself. I've managed to be an educated person in a family that is not too educated. It separates me from my brothers. I am more liberated and more liberal. When you're educated, you're different from those who aren't. It gives us nothing in common.

Angela lives at home with her mother. She calls their relationship "a blessing. We have each other. She is very open, very supportive of me, very proud of me." She describes her father in quite different terms:

> He is prejudiced toward minorities—particularly black people. He feels colleges lower standards so black people can pass, that black students, particularly those on football scholarships, graduate from college without knowing anything. He recognizes that some black people make something of themselves, but he feels it isn't the norm. He feels blacks are lazy and stupid and don't work like the rest of us.

Angela talks about how her views about society have changed. She's not sure if it's the education she's received at Hunter or simply the experience of being there.

> I am much more liberal now. I am much more aware of oppression and racism now, more socially aware, more into doing things to help people. I now feel that people who have power

should use that power to help others. I am now geared to helping others who have less.

But there are things I still don't quite understand. It is so hard—I'm not black and haven't gone through those years of oppression, of racism. I'm still not sure what black people are fighting for, what they want. I also don't understand the thing about roots. They walk around in strange clothes and yet want to be equal. I don't walk around squashing grapes. At some point, people need to assimilate. But, maybe because society hasn't let them develop roots here, hasn't let them belong, they need to reach back to other roots. We're not letting them assimilate, but I still can't understand why you would accentuate differences and want to be treated differently.

Angela has moved from a conservative, homogeneous—by race, religion, and class—section of New York City into an extraordinarily heterogeneous academic environment and has been significantly changed by the experience. It is not only the mix of students and the opportunity to know them that have changed her; the relationships she has developed with members of the faculty, her interactions with them, the exchange of views, both in and out of class, have opened Angela to alternative ways of perceiving the world.

She recognizes that she still has substantial ideological differences with many students and faculty members but does not seem unduly discomfited by these differences. It is, rather, her family with whom she is now sometimes uncomfortable. When she is with her father and her brothers, she is acutely aware of how much her attitudes have changed and how little they now have in common.

Leslie Gilbert, a twenty-two-year-old senior at the University of Wisconsin, grew up in a small Wisconsin community that she characterizes as "pretty conservative, not a lot of multiculturalism or diversity." Leslie's mother is a public-health nurse, her father a blue-collar worker. An interior-design major, she originally wanted to go to the Art Institute of Chicago but could not manage the out-of-state tuition. Her brother and sister are also studying at the university in Madison, and with the three of them in college at the same time, she can really use scholarships to pay her $5,000 to $6,000 annual tuition.

> Leslie describes her first reaction to the huge campus: At first I was really scared. The university is so big, and you're moving out of the safety of your home. The issue of women's safety is of real concern here. The campus is very aware of the dangers. Women don't walk alone at night; they are also concerned about date rape.
> I had a wonderful house and resident adviser as a freshman. I made friends right away, and they are the friends I still have today. The size of the campus is intimidating but it is also exciting. It prepares you for the real world.

Leslie talks about how being at the university has changed her:

> I've come in contact with everything. I've become so much more open-minded. I have friends from Puerto Rico, Central and South America, African-American and Asian-American friends. There are a lot of Asian Americans here; not a lot of African Americans. I've dated a guy from El Salvador. I have a friend who's from India, and I forget she's from India. You learn so much more about yourself. You become so much more independent.

Whereas Leslie's sister shares many of her ideas and is even more active on campus than she is, Leslie characterizes her brother, who she says has been influenced by the "traditional" attitudes of extended family members, as "a bit homophobic" but "not really a racist." As an engineering student, he comes in contact with many Asian Americans who are excelling academically, so Leslie feels he tends to stereotype all Asian Americans.

Leslie spent a semester in Italy, outside of Florence, studying Italian culture, language, and art renovations. When she returned to the campus, she became an RA (resident adviser) in an all-woman dormitory, an experience that was to prove extremely stressful. There were two women in the dorm who were, in her words, "insinuating they were lesbians." They would "hug a lot, laugh a lot, and pinch each other a lot." When it came time for her performance as an RA to be evaluated by the dorm residents, she received many complaints from other students, including anonymous notes, about the young women's behavior. About one-fourth of the evaluations mentioned incidents in the shower between the two women which the other students clearly found disturbing, but no one would openly confront the issue. When she tried to talk with the two young women directly, they denied having a lesbian relationship and asked Leslie to try to keep the entire matter "subdued." She sent out a newsletter to all of the students in the dorm, not specifically mentioning this problem but asking anyone who had any concerns to "please come talk with me"; no one did. She stopped receiving notes about the women; no one was willing to talk openly about the issue, and the two students in question "isolated themselves a lot." Leslie was mystified by the behavior on all sides:

> On this campus, homosexuality is pretty open. Once people decide to come out of the closet, it is pretty easy to do here. There is a lot of support—more than on other campuses. Everyone might not accept it—some have been thrown into a new environment and are faced with something they never thought they would be faced with—but usually people just ignore it.

Leslie never did resolve the issue in the dorm. When she reached out, the young women were "sometimes nice—if they needed me," and "sometimes rude," leaving notes on her door, for example, that read, "Oh, you're never around, bitch." She felt that one of them wanted to talk with her but the other one did not. As she tried to deal with the situation, one of her concerns was, "I don't want to be known as homophobic."

Leslie discusses some of the dominant values among her fellow students:

> To most people on this campus, money is a big thing. Their goals are to find a good job and be happy, have a family and be happy. But happiness is more important than money. If you can just live comfortably—you don't have to have everything to be happy. Some are not quite as materialistic—what with the economy. Some are starting to realize that, just because you go to college, it doesn't mean you're going to get a great job.

After graduation, Leslie hopes to join an architectural firm, but she is planning to go to Hungary to work with Habitat for Humanity over the summer following graduation. She has also considered joining the Peace Corps, but isn't sure if she wants to "give up two years of my life."

Leslie sums up some of her concerns about the Madison campus:

> I wish there was some way to promote awareness. I wish men would take women's-studies classes. I wish a man could feel the way a woman does walking down the street at night. I wish people would be more active. I wish people would focus less on making money.

Leslie traces her concerns over her college years: "I started out with only academic problems; then, as an RA, I had to deal with other people's problems; and now I have to deal with life's problems—with the question of how do I want to spend the rest of my life."

As we have seen, Angela moved into a far more diverse environment and suddenly saw herself in that setting as a member of
a minority group; because of this experience, she is now able to
relate far more empathetically to those who are always seen as
outsiders. By choosing a more diverse academic environment
than the homogeneous community in which she was raised,
Leslie has had close relationships with a wide variety of friends
but did find herself frustrated at being unable to cope with a difficult interpersonal situation during her final year.

Rebecca Taub, a Barnard senior, sees herself simultaneously
as an individual with her own unique personality, values, and
future goals, as a committed member of a subgroup, and as a devoted member of the Barnard community. Rebecca was brought
up in what she describes as a modern Orthodox Jewish family in
suburban New Jersey. The middle child of three, she attended a
private Jewish high school and then studied for one year in Israel before attending Barnard. She applied to Stern College, the
women's undergraduate division of Yeshiva University; Queens
College, which is part of the City University of New York; and
Barnard; although she received a scholarship to Stern, she chose
to attend Barnard.

Rebecca talks about her family and how her attitudes were
formed: "We were always taught not to judge anyone, to be
open-minded. My dad was very liberal, very democratic; now
he's more conservative." Rebecca's paternal grandparents were
poor. Her grandmother "scrubbed floors," and her father grew
up on New York's Lower East Side of New York City. Her mother,
however, was considered "well off." Her maternal grandparents
came to this country at the time of the Second World War and
worked "in diamonds." After attending City College, her father
went on to law school with the help of loans and scholarships;
today he practices and teaches law. Her mother taught originally, was home while the children were growing up, and today
teaches English as a second language to recent Russian immi-

grants. Rebecca feels her family is an example of the American Dream but is quick to say that she feels a "certain amount of guilt" about the $22,000 that the Barnard tuition costs her father annually. "It definitely affects the vacations they can take, but I wouldn't do it differently. I made the right decision."

During Rebecca's first year, she felt isolated at Barnard. She wasn't happy and wondered if she had made the right decision. But by junior year, she really felt comfortable; it was "the best year yet." Now she's sad that she is a senior; she doesn't really want it to end.

Recently, however, a series of incidents have occurred at both Barnard and Columbia that have highlighted and exacerbated tensions between African-American and Jewish students and have caused Rebecca real pain. First the Columbia University Black Student Organization invited the Reverend Al Sharpton to speak, and Rebecca and many of her friends felt he was hostile to Jews. Then they invited Leonard Jeffries, a professor of African-American studies from City College who had recently given a speech that was widely perceived to be anti-Semitic. According to Rebecca, Jeffries spoke for three hours straight and answered no questions. In his speech, he said that the white man is the cause of all evil. He spoke about joining a Jewish fraternity when he himself was a student at City College. According to Rebecca, he did allow that the Jewish fraternity was the only one that would admit him, and that he eventually became its president. What offended her particularly was his saying that he became the "king of the Jews for two years." Rebecca and many other Jewish students attended his lecture and held up signs saying "Jeffries offends me." It is interesting that the Jewish students chose this particular way to phrase their concerns. They did not use angry, hostile slogans; they did not try to prevent him from speaking. Their signs emphasized, rather, that Barnard/Columbia is a community, and that groups need to be sensitive about the feelings and sensibilities of other groups on campus.

Rebecca recognizes that there is a freedom-of-speech issue involved but cannot understand why the BSO invited Jeffries in the first place. She states vehemently:

> I hate this man! I hate him because he hates me. He states that everything originated in black culture. I consider myself very Jewish, but I try not to hate anyone. Most Jews here pay full tuition, and we're hated. Al Sharpton also hates us. My grandparents were survivors of the Holocaust, and I've never felt this before in my life. My best friend, who lived next door while I was growing up, was not Jewish, but she never made me feel different. It took until junior year for me to feel that I'm different and people hate me for it.

Rebecca points out that the Jewish group at Barnard/Columbia never invited Meir Kahane or anyone from the Jewish Defense League to speak.

> I can get caught up in what they are saying, but I know that some of them can be offensive. We're careful. I think they are careful too, but it's been such a rude awakening for me. Of course, up until now, I've led a very sheltered life and haven't paid much attention to anti-Semitism.

Rebecca describes the same incident that Merrill discussed— the removal of fifty or sixty mezuzahs from students' doors.

> When mine was pulled down, I said that I really didn't think it was anti-Semitic. My friend said, "What, are you crazy? Why pull mezuzahs off of doors?" Barnard has been great about it. They handled the situation beautifully. We went around knocking on people's doors with a petition and then went to the dean of students. A meeting was organized, and the deans and Pres-

ident Futter were there. And not only Jewish students showed up, not only Jewish students felt betrayed; lots of other students were there. And when we went around with the petition, the only person who wouldn't sign was an Orthodox girl.

I don't know who took the mezuzahs off the doors. I don't know if it was people inside or outside the school. I don't know why Jews were singled out. Maybe we're too visible. It's a sacred document. It has God's name; it contains very holy articles. Some students kiss their mezuzah when they go out. Whoever did it probably didn't even realize how holy it is—but maybe I'm being naïve.

Though Rebecca recognizes the hostility between blacks and Jews, particularly at Columbia, she does not feel that there is an undercurrent of hostility toward students of color at Barnard. People do not suggest that students of color are here because of affirmative action. Still, she is not sure exactly how she feels about affirmative action. She does think it is sometimes reverse discrimination but wonders how else people will move up. She wouldn't want people admitted to Barnard who are not up to standard; however, if the admissions officer thinks they haven't had a chance and can excel, that's fine. She doesn't believe a company or a college should just check off that they hired "a minority," but if that person is equally qualified or able to do the job, then that person should be hired. She herself does not test well. She only scored an 1150 on her SATs, yet her grade-point average this semester is either 3.75 or 3.8.

I'm at a disadvantage too. I would want people to look not only at my test scores but at my entire application. Maybe a minority student has not had the same opportunities. There must be some way to balance everything. It's not an easy thing. . . . It's a very hard decision. . . . You cannot know someone until she is in the environment. It is always a little bit of a gamble. . . .

Rebecca analyzes how she feels at Barnard today:

I feel like an insider here. I feel very comfortable walking around. I feel like it's my school. I'm very lucky. My religion gives me a strong commitment; it gives me someplace to go to. Even freshman year, when I felt like an outsider, it gave me a place to belong. Religion gives me something very concrete, tangible. Right away when I came here, I fit in.

There is a particularly large and cohesive group [of religious Jews] here at Columbia, and it's a great advantage to be part of a subgroup. We're a large group, and we're a real group, because many of us came in knowing each other, and we might seem overwhelming to some. It's like an identity. It doesn't need to be religious—it can be the student council or the track team. I have a friend who is on the crew team. He says, "These are my friends. These are the people I want to be with. These are the people I go out with in the evenings and have breakfast with in the mornings." Jews at Columbia are automatically insiders; other groups have to work harder. It doesn't have to be religious or ethnic—it can be the people on your hallway freshman year—but it's very important to have a group.

Rebecca summarizes her Barnard experience:

I have met so many people here; I have so many more ideas. I am much more open-minded and less judgmental than if I had gone to a more homogeneous school. I always knew who I was, but my experience of living with other kinds of people opens your eyes to different ways of life. I don't want to graduate. Maybe I'll stay in an academic setting. I'm so glad I chose this school; I'm so glad I didn't go to a Jewish school. I would have been happy there, but this experience cannot be duplicated.

Rebecca's experience at Barnard has, in many ways, been typical of the experiences of many members of minority groups on college campuses today. In a diverse and sometimes threatening environment, her bonds to the group have been reinforced, her feelings of solidarity strengthened. Belonging to a subgroup has helped her to feel she belonged at Barnard, whereas she felt isolated within the larger community; being an Orthodox Jew in a diverse community gave her a reference group, a group identity. But the very size and power of this group of students have also bred hostility.

Moreover, the fact that Rebecca chose a college in New York City has meant that she, as well as the other students, are constantly buffeted by the complex crosscurrents of racial, ethnic, and religious conflict, as well as the political posturing that is ever-present in the city. Are the student groups at Barnard and Columbia acting out their own agendas, the agendas of the city's major players, or, what is most likely, a combination of both? And when Rebecca comes into contact with these conflicts, she experiences anti-Semitism directly for the first time; for the first time she feels like the "other," like the despised outsider. It is important to note that Rebecca's feeling of belonging to a subgroup has been key to her ability to withstand the hostility, even the hatred, that she felt. Without that group identity, that support and solidarity, Rebecca might well not have felt, in the spring of her senior year, "so glad" that she chose Barnard College.

Steven Shulman, a senior at Vassar College and the editor-in-chief of the *Vassar Spectator,* which is subtitled *The Journal of Neglected Ideas,* also moved from a relatively homogeneous milieu to one in which he has rethought some of his fundamental beliefs. The elder of two sons of two Bronx schoolteachers, Steven grew up on Long Island. He characterizes himself as "basically a middle-class Jew, a kid from New York." He characterizes many students at Vassar as "a lot of rich kids" who were born with "silver spoons in their mouths" and stresses that he and his friends were a "pretty middle-class bunch, not so prosperous." His high-school friends' fathers were blue-collar and white-collar workers, and many attended community colleges or state schools. "The big thing was to go to Michigan."

Why did he come to Vassar? "It's convenient, close to home," he replies. Moreover, he's very interested in geography and economic development, and Vassar is known to have a very good geography department. He continues, "I had a great interview, there are no frats, people are accepting, there's an open, relaxed climate, and it's so beautiful in the fall."

Steven feels that prior to Vassar he always had strong opinions but had never been political. Though he feels he reflects his family's politics—he's a "radical prochoicer" ("My mother would never vote prolife!") and vehemently anti–affirmative action ("My parents are definitely not for it!")—he claims they never talked politics at home, at the dinner table or anywhere else.

Originally Steven wrote for a school paper, *Left of Center.* Then, in 1988, when he was still a first-year student, an incident occurred on campus that seems to have been a turning point for him. The Vassar Conservative Society and the *Spectator* hosted a reception for a speaker from the "Nicaraguan resistance." At the reception after his speech, according to Steven, a black student disrupted the meeting, threatened white students with violence, and shouted anti-Semitic slurs at Jewish students attending the event. According to Steven, the administration did nothing about this incident. The *Spectator* then published a picture of the student under which it recounted the incident and named the student. At the bottom of the article, the *Spectator* set up a tear-off poll to be sent to the journal's box number. It asked students to judge whether the African-American student was a racist or not. If respondents wished to answer in the negative, they could check off the box that said, "No! I hate Jews too. He's not a racist (in my book at least!)."

For this action, which Steven claims stemmed from the editor's frustration because of the administration's double standard and inaction following the outburst of the black student, the *Spectator* was banned from the campus for a year and a half, and all of its campus-related money was taken away. It continued to be supported financially by some Vassar alumni and by outside conservative groups. Steven characterizes the *Spectator* during his senior year as "pretty well funded."

Steven thinks the key issue at Vassar is fairness, equity. "Vassar is looking for a new dean of student life. There is talk of a black, a Hispanic, a homosexual." He wonders, "How about the best person?" The previous June, he felt there was no need for the Black Commencement Committee to break away and form their own group.

> There is no need for them to feel so isolated and miserable. Vassar goes out of its way to attract minority students. The student government is comprised of affluent, upper-middle-class kids who listen to the blacks and feel guilty. It's white guilt. When some black students said the bar seniors traditionally patronize during graduation festivities was a redneck bar, that was rude, but nobody said a word. People are afraid to call tit for tat.

Steven contrasts himself with the affluent students who, he says, are afraid to say when blacks are wrong:

> My dad worked two jobs, sixteen-hour days, to put himself through college. He worked from six in the morning to ten at night. Now they have two teachers' incomes and we barely qualify for financial aid. You know, it's very hard for a Jewish teacher to become a principal in the New York City system. But we've lived very well off of the sweat of my dad's brow.
>
> Those who come from a rough, rough background and make it to Vassar, I applaud them. If they make it from Taft High School [in New York City], they should get help. If their father is a top executive from IBM, I'm opposed to their getting help. I really

believe in merit. In recruiting students to Vassar, I think they should take the most qualified, but I would take socioeconomic status into consideration—not race.

Steven sums up by saying he's glad he came to Vassar. He is now fluent in Spanish and Portuguese. His professors took an interest in his work, and he has had opportunities here that he "never dreamt of." He has spent time working in Brazil and in Mexico, and may eventually go on for a Ph.D. "Vassar has rewarded me very well for hard work."

The conflict between African-American and Jewish students on the Vassar campus was a significant catalyst to Steven's ideological swing to the right and his markedly increased activism. In contrast, it took several different factors and a year or more of unhappiness for Jeffrey Goldin to carve out an active role for himself at Tufts and in the larger community.

Jeff is a twenty-one-year-old senior at Tufts University who is majoring in anthropology and minoring in African studies. He is also working toward a Peace and Justice Studies certificate around gender equality in Tufts' Experimental College. The younger of two children, Jeff grew up on the Upper West Side of New York City. After his father, a "businessman," and his mother, a psychologist, divorced, he lived with his father and attended the Bronx High School of Science. He applied to Stanford, Brown, and Tufts, and was accepted at Tufts. He talks about his initial experience there:

> For a year and a half, I didn't like it. I thought it was a country club. It wasn't real life. The previous summer, I had worked in an office on 43rd Street [in New York]. That was real life. I was frustrated at Tufts. There were problems around diversity, and no one did anything about them. I felt it was an artificial environment; I didn't feel comfortable. It was like a big bubble in the

world. I wanted to leave after first semester. I felt it was like thir-
teenth, fourteenth, fifteenth, and sixteenth grade, but I stayed.

Now, in his senior year, Jeff feels staying was definitely the
right decision. What turned his Tufts experience around? During his sophomore year, he took an English course, "Conformity
and Rebellion," that he feels helped him to "think things out."
Then he took an anthropology course in the Experimental College, taught by a formerly battered woman, on the social construction of reality. That course, he believes, politicized him,
particularly a paper he wrote on privilege in which he dealt with
privilege as it relates to "money and college" and to issues
around gender. Before this, he describes himself as "the liberal"
who used to say somewhat simplistically, "Everyone is equal;
everyone should be equal." He continues, "In high school, I
went with the flow. I saw everything as isolated incidents. I felt,
I'm not a racist, racism's over. I didn't see how it is part of the
structure of society."

By the end of the year, he had joined a men's group that had
emerged from "Violence Against Women" week and was trying
to "rethink reality." He relates the following incident as an example of how superficial his understanding was during this early
period. During his sophomore year, a friend of his "came out as
being gay," and Jeff's response was, "Oh, good! Great! I'm glad
for you! I'm happy for you!" He feels that he didn't really deal
with it—that he couldn't really deal with it. But in retrospect, he
feels that the combination of the courses he took and his emerg-
ing activism made this second semester of his sophomore year a
"big semester, a big turning point."

During his junior year, as part of his work in Peace and Justice Studies, Jeff needed to do an internship at a "social-change
organization." When he went to choose an organization, he
found he was not as attached to the issue of the environment as
he had thought, or as attached to issues of nuclear disarmament

or hunger. He was attracted to working with young people in the inner city of Boston, but is glad now that he didn't take that route either. What he did choose was to work with a Cambridge-based organization that counsels battered women. For the first couple of weeks, he observed a group of men who batter women and was shocked at what he heard—their "minimizing and denial" of their behavior. Eventually Jeff took a course in counseling men who batter, and has since become very active in MESA, an organization of Men to End Sexual Assault. The experience has oriented him to working with perpetrators, not just with victims. He feels he can more appropriately and more effectively deal with what men are doing, with those who are responsible for the battering.

During his senior year, Jeff is expanding his activities. He speaks to high-school kids about the culture of rape, including sexual harassment, violence, and pornography. He is attempting, he says, to "dispel myths." He is also actively working on campus around the issues of rape and gay and lesbian rights. The shift in Jeff's priorities and level of activism completely changed his activities and his friends on campus. He describes his first year as "drinking beer," his sophomore year as talking about issues, and the time since then as being actively involved in "pushing for change."

This profound switch in Jeff's outlook and activities took place in part, he believes, because of a course he took in Yiddish literature—"Yid Lit," as it is called. Jeff describes himself as a "Jewish New York kid who went to Hebrew school." He feels the comparisons of other people's experience to the Jewish experience "tapped into something real in me. It made me feel vulnerable and drew links to other, parallel kinds of oppression and prejudice."

Jeff's experience at Tufts is particularly revealing. Originally dissatisfied and somewhat disheartened by his perception of the college, Jeff became empowered to alter his own behavior through courses that opened his eyes to new ways of understanding society. He then worked in the community, learned concrete skills, and found that he could be part of a process of change. Finally, he took a course that tapped into his own heritage and helped him make the connection between the oppression Jewish people have felt over the centuries and the oppression other groups have experienced and are currently experiencing today. Jeff has been literally transformed from a somewhat passive, alienated first-year student into an optimistic activist exploring his own beliefs and abilities and seeing that he can truly make a difference.

Each of these last three students, all Jewish young people from the New York area, has reacted very differently to his/her undergraduate experiences. Rebecca, the most religious, has been faced with anti-Semitism, and though she has reacted with hurt and anger, she has tried to focus her anger on specific public spokespersons rather than allowing her feelings to spill over to include an entire group on campus. She has appreciated being part of a more diverse community but recognizes that one of the reasons her years at Barnard were so rewarding was her membership in and allegiance to a tight, homogeneous group on campus. Steven has also experienced anti-Semitism and has moved from a relatively liberal political philosophy to activism within Vassar's small conservative community. And Jeff, through a variety of factors including his own dissatisfaction during his early years at Tufts, has become the most active, finding issues about which he cares passionately, and discovering a level of empathy and ability within himself that he never knew he possessed.

The ideology and attitudes of each of these young people also reflect, to some extent, their families' economic and political positions. Both Rebecca and Jeff come from upper-middle-class backgrounds; their parents are relatively successful financially and are, in all likelihood, not in direct competition with members of minority groups. Steven's parents, however, feel that their race and religion have been a real hindrance to their rising within the teaching profession in the Bronx. They are, like Steven, vehemently opposed to affirmative action. As we have observed with so many other students, these young people's values, attitudes, and agendas for change are a complex amalgam of their childhood experiences, their families' attitudes, and their own experiences as they have moved away from the environment of their early years. Each of these students, when faced with diversity and the mixed messages that are transmitted within a complex, heterogeneous environment, has been challenged by the experience and has, over the course of their undergraduate years, found meaningful ways to interact with the larger community and to feel positive about her/himself and her/his educational experience. Each of these young people is leaving college a substantially different person from when she/he arrived.

Part Three

What can the experiences of the students presented in part II teach us about the nature of recent events on college campuses, the impact of these events on individual students, and, more broadly, about the tensions and conflicts within American society around the issues of race, class, gender, and sexual orientation? As we have seen, the bias facing many of our young people in the United States is both deep-seated and wide-ranging. They live in a society that promises equal opportunity but instead is characterized by an increasingly unequal distribution of wealth and income and a massive structural inequality of resources and services. Over the past thirty years, many women and members of minority groups have been the beneficiaries of increased social, political, and economic opportunity; but many more members of these groups continue to live in or near poverty, receive inadequate, inferior education, and are both covertly and overtly discriminated against in virtually all aspects of their lives. Thus it is clear that the young people of this country are beginning their sprint to the future from very different starting lines, and that the animosity, the denigration, and the conflict that we have seen on college campuses constitute a microcosm of the animosity, denigration, and conflict we see daily in the country at large.

These deep-seated divisions within the United States at the end of the twentieth century, and the rage and powerlessness they often engender, are present in virtually all aspects of our national life—in our political life, in our work lives, in our res-

227

idential patterns, in our criminal behavior and our criminal-justice system, in our military services, and in our popular culture. It should therefore come as no surprise that our institutions of higher education have been beset by bias incidents that reflect the tensions within the larger society.

How have the students interviewed for this book responded to these issues during their undergraduate years? It must be stressed that they have acted and reacted in a wide variety of ways. One of the real dangers of the recent discussion of events at colleges and universities has been the simplistic nature of many of the analyses: the stories about minority groups segregating themselves, with little exploration of the factors that may have led to this so-called separatism; the articles about students aggressively attempting to root out purported faculty insensitivity around race, gender, and sexual orientation within college classrooms without discussion of the ambivalence many students feel about confronting members of the faculty; the focus on anger and conflict to the exclusion of the efforts of many students to bring people together. As part II has stressed, student responses to their college experience are complex and multifaceted and have been determined in great part by their earlier experiences, their personalities, their cultural background, by events and attitudes in the broader society, and by the campus environment and specific events they experience once they enter their undergraduate years.

Part III will attempt to summarize these students' actions and reactions, and to highlight what we can learn from their experiences. It will, in addition, raise questions about directions for the academic community—and, indeed, for the larger society—as we struggle to move toward greater equality and a stronger sense of community in the twenty-first century.

9

A Matter of Survival

As communities dedicated to intellectual inquiry, universities should
give the broadest protection to free speech. But, having protected
everyone's right to speak, university communities need not
and should not be silent when faced with racist, anti-Semitic,
or other disrespectable speech. Members of academic communities—
faculty, students, and administrators—can use our right to free
speech to denounce disrespectable speech by exposing it for
what it is, flagrant disregard for the interests of other people,
rationalization of self interest or group interest, prejudice, or sheer
hatred of humanity.   Charles Taylor et al.,
                                Multiculturalism
                                and "The Politics of Recognition"

Talking directly with students about their undergraduate
years enables us to examine recent developments on
college campuses through their voices, their perspectives, and the nuances of their personal experiences. As the debate about diversity, multiculturalism, political correctness,
hate incidents, and the role of the university has become more
and more heated during recent years, students have often been
portrayed one-dimensionally—as single-minded activists on the
left or right, as victims or aggressors, as race-obsessed separat-
ists or self-absorbed careerists. It is noteworthy that none of the
students interviewed for this book fits neatly into these or other
equally simplistic categories. Virtually all of them see their academic institutions as complex social worlds with competing
pressures and multiple tasks and goals. They understand, more-

over, the difficulties of moving large, multilayered bureaucracies in new directions and the delicate task of working with extraordinarily heterogeneous groups of students. Many of them have come to understand both the necessity and the complexity of bringing various groups together. Though several of the young people in part II are angry about recent events on their campuses or about perceived injustice in the wider society, most have struggled to keep their anger under control and have searched for ways of working effectively to bring about change.

The majority of the students in part II emphasize activism, but many others, of course, spend their undergraduate years studying, partying, working to help pay for their education, and in some instances dealing with complex family matters. As we have seen, some, like Kevin at the University of Wisconsin and Merrill at Barnard, go to college intending to make a difference; a far more common pattern, however, is for students to move through what can best be described as an arc of activism. During their first years, many, such as Francesca and Jeff at Tufts, Pierre and Simeen at Vassar, or Scott at Columbia, feel out of place, fear they have made a mistake in their choice of school; some even leave college for a period of time. During their sophomore and junior years, many feel their way toward active participation in one or more facets of college life. During senior year, the students I interviewed tend to fall into two groups: those who go on to still greater activism and become significant leaders on their campuses, and those who, in the words of several students, "burn out." Examples of student leaders who continue to make a genuine impact on their college communities include Karen at the University of Oregon, Robert at the University of Washington, Merrill at Barnard, and Maggie at Vassar. Examples of those who retreat from activism include Lisa at Tufts and, to some extent, Leslie at the University of Wisconsin.

Within this arc of activism, many styles emerge. Several of

the students practice what has come to be known as "identity politics," focusing primarily on issues involving specific groups on campus: Craig at Tufts working on gay rights and AIDS; Francesca, also at Tufts, working on scholarships for black students and gay and lesbian rights; and Camille and Susan at the University of Washington, both working for the most part on issues affecting Asian-American students. Other leaders are active in both identity-based and campus-wide groups—for example, Robert at the University of Washington, who has been active both in the Black Student Union and in the broad-based effort to establish a multicultural requirement; Karen at the University of Oregon, who has been concerned with gay and lesbian rights and worked with a variety of groups as president of the student-government organization; and Nina at Barnard, who was a member of a Chinese student group but concentrated most of her efforts on college-wide issues and organizations. Yet another group of students work primarily within broad-based student groups on their campus; Merrill at Barnard focused her efforts, for the most part, in the student-government organization and other groups that represent all the students.

Another pattern that emerges is that of students battling bias in individual ways—Marcella at Hunter, speaking out when she musters the courage against individual instances of prejudice and discrimination; Joanne at Columbia, protesting sexist and racist attitudes of the faculty despite her anxiety that such assertiveness might harm her academically; and Rebecca at Barnard/Columbia, silently protesting speakers whom she considers anti-Semitic. Even students who do not speak out are often battling bias within themselves—Angela, who has been profoundly changed by attending a multicultural school; and Janet, who struggles to control her antiwhite anger precipitated by the prejudice and discrimination directed toward Native Americans and other people of color at the University of Wisconsin.

Several of these students stress the difficulty of their roles within the classroom. Often the token minority, they frequently feel, in Francesca's words, "the burden of going to a white school," particularly being singled out to represent the perspective of the entire subgroup of which they are but a single member, and often being in the exceedingly difficult position of teaching the teachers about multicultural issues. Other students discussed the loneliness and isolation of the activist role: Francesca, talking about eighteen-hour days with little time for socializing and, perhaps even more important, being stigmatized—falsely, she believes—as a "militant black activist, a separatist"; and Lisa, describing how her activism has led to the absence of relationships with Asian-American men, and the need to find support among other minority groups at Tufts.

For all the discomfort and pain that their activism has caused some of these students, Francesca succinctly sums up the experience of many of them when she says that she sees her activism as "a matter of survival—my survival, my community's survival." Perhaps Francesca most vividly illustrates this when she explains that she "transferred" her addiction "from coke to activism." Over her last three years of college, political action became her way of life. Developing a "voice," learning how to make sure that Tufts would "deal" with her voice, and moving the institution in directions she considers important have literally become her work, her mission. Simeen found a place for herself at Vassar and started to come to terms with being of Indian background in a largely white environment through her work within the Asian Student Alliance. Because of his support of the Persian Gulf War and his subsequent activity with the Columbia Republican Club, Scott, after an alienating first year, found his niche at Columbia and formulated opinions and developed skills he never knew he possessed. Indeed, activism has enabled these students to turn hurt and anger into action and connection with others—connection with students and faculty alike, with members of their own subgroup and, in some cases, with members of the broader college community and even the wider society who share their point of view—and to achieve new levels of competence and maturity. Coming together with others around issues bigger than self and, in many instances, broader than the interests of their subgroup, has enabled them to connect with others and realize the power of that connection.

Moreover, becoming politically active on the campus has enabled many of these students to overcome, to a considerable degree, feeling like victims. One of the profound dangers of coming face to face with *ad hominem* prejudice and discrimination is that many students, some for the first time, realize the fear, the hatred, the contempt with which their subgroup is viewed by some in the dominant culture, and begin to explore ways in which they and others are victims of a racist, sexist, and/ or homophobic society. It may well be necessary to understand intellectually as well as emotionally the history of that oppression, and the exact nature of current discrimination, but danger lies in the passivity and feelings of powerlessness that can accompany the awareness of the depth of prejudice and discrimination toward one's group in American society. As Cornel West has stated, the fundamental danger for African Americans and for many other groups is a "profound sense of psychological depression, personal worthlessness, and social despair. . . ."

Charles Taylor, professor of philosophy and political science at McGill University, analyzes the ways human identity is affected by our interaction with others:

> . . . our identity is partly shaped by recognition or its absence, often by the *mis*recognition of others, and so a person or group of people can suffer real damage, real distortion, if the people or society around them mirror back to them a confining or demeaning or contemptible picture of themselves. Nonrecognition or misrecognition can inflict harm, can be a form of oppression,

imprisoning someone in a false, distorted, and reduced mode of being.

Arthur Ashe has poignantly described the impact of racism, more specifically of segregation, even on one who achieved great success and personal fulfillment:

> I do not want to be misunderstood. I do not mean to appear fatalistic, self-pitying, cynical, or maudlin. . . . In some respects, I am a prisoner of the past. A long time ago, I made peace with the state of Virginia and the South. . . . But segregation had achieved by that time what it was intended to achieve: It left me a marked man, forever aware of a shadow of contempt that lays [sic] across my identity and my sense of self-esteem. . . . The mere memory of it darkens my most sunny days. I believe that the same is true for almost every African American of the slightest sensitivity and intelligence. Again, I don't want to overstate the case. I think of myself, and others think of me, as supremely self-confident. . . . Still, I also know that the shadow is always there; only death will free me, and blacks like me, from its pall.

Many of the students described in part II have come to realize that joining with others in political action to fight injustice is a powerful method of combating that shadow, the contempt, the depression, the sense of worthlessness and despair endemic among so many individuals and groups that have suffered from denigration and dehumanization in American society. In a very real sense, activism has truly become "a matter of survival," a way of overcoming self-doubt and self-hatred, a way of connecting with others, a way of replacing passivity with action, despair with hope. Whereas denigrated and isolated individuals may feel angry and impotent, joining with others who share similar characteristics and points of view not only strengthens the individual but permits a celebration of the very characteristics others disparage. Celebrating blackness and black culture defies negative stereotyping and affirms the worth of the individual and the group. Celebrating Asian languages, culture, and food provides individuals with positive feelings to balance the slurs and insults. Celebrating sexual freedom gives gays and lesbians courage to see themselves as human while so many around them seek to deny their humanity.

Troy Duster, professor of sociology and director of Berkeley's Institute for the Study of Social Change, analyzes what he terms "hyphenated identification":

> In such a diverse nation as this, such identification can provide a sense of belonging to a recognizable collectivity. It allows a sense of uniqueness, while paradoxically giving a sense of belonging— of being one with others like self—that helps to overcome the isolation of modern life.

But there are limits to what these groups can achieve, and, indeed, there are negative consequences for students working exclusively within their particular orbit.

In a recent article entitled "The Rise of 'Identity Politics': An Examination and a Critique," Berkeley sociologist Todd Gitlin states, "Identity politics is a form of self-understanding, an orientation toward the world. . . . Identity politics presents itself as—and many young people experience it as—the most compelling remedy for anonymity in an impersonal world." He continues by pointing out that identity politics "is a search for comfort, an approach to community." In fact, many of the students interviewed for this book have participated in and experienced identity politics—belonging to groups that are organized by race, gender, religion, or sexual orientation—and have experienced the increased understanding of self and the self-validation as well as the knowledge, self-confidence, and understanding that can accompany working with others of similar backgrounds to effect change. But, as Gitlin points out, there are negative aspects of identity politics as well: the establishment of a "self-enclosed world," a "turning inward," and, in some cases, a "grim and hermetic bravado celebrating victimization and stylized marginality." Yet another criticism of identity politics is that individuals can become so entrenched within their group and within the group's perspective that they may perpetuate the very outsider identity and status that they were originally protesting and seeking to overcome. Moreover, it is important to note, as Gitlin states, that "Identity politics is intensified when antagonistic identities are fighting for their places amid shrinking resources," a phenomenon often seen on college campuses in recent years.

Contrary to most reports, large numbers of students on college campuses today who are members of minority groups reject total immersion in identity politics—indeed, some reject it completely. As Tanya states, "To me, the enemy is not race-based." She criticizes some of the activists in the Black Student Union at Columbia for overplaying the issue of blacks as victims; she speaks of the necessity of learning to live in a country dominated by whites and questions in a mocking way how "black" one has to act in order to be accepted by the group. Kevin explicitly rejects the need for uniformity of attitudes among African Americans and sets out to discover and act on his own values and opinions. Whereas many African-American activists at the University of Wisconsin favored some sort of speech code to deter hate speech, he opposed such regulations; whereas many black activists on the Madison campus might be seen as left of center, Kevin wrote extensively for the conservative student newspaper. Francesca, while actively involved in issues concerned with the well-being of black students at Tufts, was nonetheless critical of the attitudes of many African Americans regarding gay and lesbian rights and did not hesitate to express her views. And Janet, although she clearly identified as a Native American at the University of Wisconsin, nonetheless remained on the periphery of the organized groups and consciously resisted internalizing the widespread feelings of anger toward whites. These students think issues through for themselves and resist automatic affiliation with the dominant politics of their subgroup.

One of the central problems in organizing across the traditional lines of identity politics is the phenomenon of minority groups vying for the status of "most victimized." The issue of whose past history and present circumstances are most oppressed divides groups and breeds resentment among those who might otherwise perceive their common concerns and work together to improve conditions for all who share experiences of oppression. Many students—particularly those of Asian background, whose claim to victim status was most often questioned—discussed the phenomenon with considerable irritation. They are once again mirroring a similar debate within the broader society. The comparison of slavery and the Holocaust, of the treatment of gays and lesbians in the United States with the treatment of blacks, the likening of present and historical discrimination against Asians and Asian Americans with that of other maligned groups, often arouses strong reaction and prevents members of these groups from recognizing their common experiences and circumstances. Moreover, groups on college campuses often vie for increasingly scarce campus resources—financial aid, physical space, seats on key committees, or, most basic of all, admission to the college or university—and one group's success can easily mean fewer resources and less status for another.

Not only do groups on campus compete for status and resources, but virtually all groups and individuals as well are also vying for protection of their basic rights. One of the most thorny and polarizing controversies that have developed during the recent years of campus turmoil has been the protection of some students from denigration and harassment, on the one hand,

and, on the other, the protection of the right to free speech as guaranteed by the First Amendment. In parts I and II, we have seen numerous instances of open disparagement of individuals—from the mockery of blacks in *The Dartmouth Review* to the violent homophobic messages on T-shirts sold by a fraternity at Syracuse University, from vicious antifemale lyrics sung by students at the U.S. Naval Academy and UCLA to anti-Semitic views expounded by both faculty members and guest lecturers at institutions as disparate as City College of the City University of New York and Columbia. Among the students interviewed specifically for this book, we have seen many examples of open hostility and discrimination: Francesca called a "nigger bitch" her first day at Tufts, Pierre repeatedly "carded" simply because he is black, Asian Americans the victims of anti-Asian gibes, Joanne taunted by a teaching assistant because she is a poor, black woman, and Rebecca the recipient of hostility because she is Jewish. Considerable controversy has been created between those who seek to protect the rights of the victimized and those who hold that the right of free speech is inviolate.

Jonathan Rauch, author of *Kindly Inquisitors: The New Attacks on Free Thought*, states forcefully that words are not violence, but I suggest that denigrating language—particularly hostile, demeaning language—that focuses on characteristics over which individuals have no choice is indeed a form of assault. Racial epithets, ethnic slurs, antifemale abuse, and homophobic comments are intended to diminish, to dehumanize, to isolate, and to undermine the confidence of the recipient. They are, in Taylor's terms, a form of "*mis*recognition . . . mirror[ing] back to . . . [individuals] a confining or demeaning or contemptible picture of themselves." Such slurs state clearly that the individual involved, simply because of membership in a despised group, does not deserve the same respect as those of the dominant group, is fair game for open hostility and ridicule, and ultimately, of course, does not really belong.

It is, moreover, my view that the hate incidents we have seen on campuses in recent years are yet another manifestation of the violence—most often committed against people of color and the poorest among us—that has been permeating American society: the all-too-frequent drug-related shoot-outs on the streets of our inner cities that put an end to the lives of innocent people, including children; the excessive violence increasingly employed by police officers, reported in cities across the nation and most vividly exemplified by the vicious beating of Rodney King; the ubiquitous availability of guns and their increasing use to settle all manner of disputes even among the youngest of our citizens; the increasing violence in professional sports; and, of course, the violence that pervades American popular culture, particularly television and films. In an extraordinarily disturbing article in the Arts & Leisure section of *The New York Times,* Jeff Silverman details American movies' "long romance with guns." He points out the symbolic and highly erotic way guns are used and viewed today:

> Of course, guns in movies (and on television) don't surprise us anymore; they just get larger, sleeker, more powerful and more destructive. Cameras caress them from every angle. By size and design, they are there to draw attention to themselves. In some cases, they are the stars. They have become more than just characters; they've become sex symbols—for both men and women.

In a society obsessed with violence, where sex has been replaced by murder and other forms of sadism as the ultimate high, it is no wonder that violence has erupted on college campuses. That the assault is usually expressed verbally rather than physically is also not surprising, since the very nature of higher education is to stress verbal expression. But we must recognize that attempting to destroy the worth of another person, both in that person's eyes and in the eyes of others, is indeed a form of violence. Verbal abuse is clearly a less lethal form of assault than murder, rape, and other forms of physical violence but it is nonetheless a form of assault.

A recent controversy at Wellesley College clearly illustrates the debate between protecting the rights of individual students and groups and protecting free speech. The controversy involved a book, *The Secret Relationship Between Blacks and Jews*, that was used by Professor Anthony Martin in an African-American-history course at Wellesley. According to Nannerl Keohane, then president of Wellesley, "This book has been adjudged to be anti-Semitic by many people who have read it, including the Chair of Professor Martin's own department, Professor Selwyn Cudjoe, and many other members of the Wellesley faculty." She points out that, though she and two deans have "publicly condemned the tone, temper, and dubious scholarship of the book," they at the same time recognize that, "within the usual definition of academic freedom," Professor Martin has a right to "teach the book in his course." She states further that the Wellesley Board of Trustees "has gone on record as both supporting free speech and condemning intolerance." Perhaps this statement is the clearest expression of the stand colleges and universities must take—both supporting free speech and simultaneously condemning intolerance.

Yet another example of the need to protect free speech is illustrated by the destruction, during the spring semester of 1993, of copies of student newspapers by some African-American students at both Penn and Dartmouth. These particular publications contained articles that were felt by the students involved to be offensive to the black community, but destruction of the written word is just as objectionable as interfering with a person's right to speak. What recourse, then, do students have who have been maligned and reviled because of their group membership? Each person's First Amendment rights must be protected, but academic communities can certainly try to use moral suasion to encourage individuals in their midst to treat one another with respect and civility. Even if some might mockingly call this effort "political correctness," it seems to me that the least students can expect from others in their college community is not to be harassed or ridiculed because of their race or gender or sexual orientation. In addition to moral leadership, colleges and universities should, I believe, establish standing committees (as many already have) made up of faculty, administrators, and students available to hear cases of possible harassment— racial, sexual, or any other type that might occur—and, depending on the nature of the offense, to recommend disciplinary measures. What, then, is the difference between an individual exercising his/her right to free speech and harassing others? It might be established, for example, that a single episode is protected by the First Amendment but a pattern of abuse might be viewed as harassment. Schools should establish explicit definitions of what behavior is considered harassment and publicize guidelines and regulations making the definitions clear. We must indeed protect the rights of all in our midst, neither ignoring genuine assaults, even if they are verbal, nor depriving individuals of their constitutional rights.

Critics of speech codes and so-called political correctness have often ridiculed the reactions of victims of hate incidents. They have been accused of being excessively thin-skinned, of inventing the incidents, exaggerating them, or using them for political gain. Moreover, far more attention has been paid to the measures taken by colleges to counter hate speech than to the impact of these incidents on the victims. Perhaps Dinesh D'Souza, author of the widely read *Illiberal Education: The Politics of Race and Sex on Campus,* most harshly criticizes the role of minority students on campuses over the past few years:

With the encouragement of the university administration and activist faculty, many minority students begin to think of themselves as victims. Indeed, they aspire to victim status. They do
not yearn to be oppressed, of course; rather, they seek the moral
capital of victimhood. . . . Everybody races to seize the lowest
rung of the ladder. . . . Ultimately, victimhood becomes a
truncheon with which minority activists may intimidate nonmi-
norities—thus the victim becomes a victimizer while continuing
to enjoy superior moral credentials.

But, of course, many members of minority groups are indeed
victims—victims of racist policies in the broader society, victims of poverty, victims of inferior primary and secondary education, and, indeed, once they arrive at college or university,
frequently victims of hate incidents there. And then they are
critized by writers such as Dinesh D'Souza—hardly an impartial
observer, since he was editor of the ultraconservative *Dartmouth
Review* when that paper published an interview with a former
leader of the Ku Klux Klan, illustrating it with a staged photograph of a black man hanging from a tree on the Dartmouth campus. During his tenure there, the paper also published an article
on affirmative action that was written in what was meant to be a
parody of black speech ("Now we be comin' to Dartmut and be up
over our 'fros in studies, but we still be not graduatin' Phi Beta
Kappa"). How would D'Souza and other critics prefer that students
who have been vilified react? As though nothing were happening?
As though they were not being ridiculed and demeaned? And
then, when students who have been lumped together and reviled
because of their skin color, gender, or sexual orientation organize
along these lines, they are once again reviled.

Though limitations to identity politics are real and have been
discussed earlier in this chapter, making an asset out of the very
characteristics that cause students to be reviled may well be a

necessary stage in developing a positive identity and in combating the depression and despair of which Cornel West and Arthur Ashe speak. Arthur Schlesinger, Jr., criticizes identity politics by stating, "The cult of ethnicity exaggerates differences, intensifies resentments and antagonisms, drives even deeper the awful wedges between races and nationalities." Did Francesca "exaggerate differences" when she was called a "nigger bitch" her first day at college? Did Marcella "intensify resentments" when an adviser discouraged her from entering a graduate program in English because she looks as though she is a member of a minority group? Did Craig "intensify antagonisms" when he was threatened in his dormitory by other students merely because he is gay? Did Robert Jackson, who worked within the multiracial student-faculty coalition at the University of Washington for over two years to establish a one-course multicultural requirement, drive "even deeper the awful wedges between races and nationalities"? I suggest, rather, that these students are truly trying to bring people together, and that it is those who perpetrate hate incidents who are driving people apart. How has it happened that the victims are blamed for their victimization and for the deep divisions in American society?

As Troy Duster points out, so-called separatism—or "Balkanization," as it has come to be called—was practiced by all-white, all-Christian fraternities at Yale, Michigan, Harvard, and Berkeley well into the mid-1970s, and, as a consequence of widespread exclusion, all-Jewish fraternities were "a common phenomenon as late as the 1960's." Moreover, the Hillel and Newman foundations have played important roles for Jewish and Catholic students during much of the twentieth century. No "national campaign" was launched against these forms of "separatism." Duster goes on to point out that the national debate over political correctness, quotas, and diversity is, in reality, "a struggle over who gets to define the idea of America."

Are we essentially a nation with a common, or at least dominant culture to which immigrants and "minorities" must adapt? Or is this a land in which ethnicity and difference are affirmed as part of the lived experience, in which we try to pursue a common heritage?

These questions are at the heart of the ongoing debate about the nature of higher education today and the course both academic institutions and the broader society must take in the future.

In addition to the barriers of race and ethnicity, several students in part II discussed the economic barriers to attending college: Joanne describes her constant efforts to stay afloat financially while attending Columbia and her sharp awareness of the gap between her financial situation and that of many other Columbia students; Tanya, a welfare recipient and mother of a five-year-old, struggles both to pay the bills and to keep up academically. Marcella pieces together money from a job, some financial aid, and occasional academic awards. Scott, having grown up in a family whose finances ranged from below the poverty line to a working-class income, must also constantly worry about getting, as he puts it, from registration to registration. And Steven, though certainly not poor, nonetheless is keenly aware of the financial limitations of being the son of limited-income schoolteachers in the Bronx. Both he and Scott resent not the wealthiest of their college classmates, not the students, in Joanne's words, who "write checks all the time," or, in Scott's words, those who "without thinking" go on "the ski trip" or buy "the new computer"; like the white residents of Canarsie whom Jonathan Rieder describes so memorably, these students resent students of color, who they feel are getting too much attention, too much money, too much overall assistance from college administrators.

Despite the resentment of many students and the rage that frequently spills over, as academic institutions struggle to protect the rights of individuals and groups of students, so must they, and the larger society, enable the broadest range of students to participate in higher education. But as we call for greater efforts to make higher education available to a broad range of students, it must be clear that all students who face significant barriers must be included—white students of limited financial means as well as students of color and members of other minority groups.

Part I delineated both the economic necessity for postsecondary education in this era of high technology and specialized knowledge, as well as the political necessity for the vast majority of citizens in a democracy to be knowledgeable about the major, highly complex issues of our time. Though millions of Americans do indeed seek out some kind of post–high-school education, numerous barriers to higher education remain: the quality of primary and secondary education, academic achievement, financial considerations (both the cost of continuing one's education and the loss of immediate income to students and their families from replacing full-time work with part-time or full-time study), and the not insignificant barrier of an unfamiliar and sometimes intimidating academic environment.

The problem of grossly inequitable primary and secondary education is particularly complex in a society in which education is largely financed by local taxation. The inequality of financial resources of school districts has been a major issue all over the country. Annual spending per pupil ranges from less than $3,000 in Utah to over $7,000 in New York and other Northeastern states. Many states are struggling to find an acceptable solution to the wide disparity between wealthy school districts and poor ones; as of May 1993, school-financing lawsuits were pending in nearly half the states. Other inequities plague American education. A judge has ruled, for example, that Alabama's schools violate the state constitution by failing to provide an adequate education, and Philadelphia's schools are being sued because of continuing segregation.

In Connecticut, a lawsuit seeks to integrate Hartford's schools with those of the neighboring suburbs. According to a recent study prominently cited in the suit, Hartford's children, for the most part poor, economically and racially segregated, and socially isolated, achieve significantly lower scores in reading, writing, and math and are far less likely to go on to four-year colleges than are suburban children. The Connecticut suit advocates breaking up the concentration of poor minority students in Hartford through a desegregation plan covering the city and twenty-one surrounding towns. Stating clearly that the students' poor academic performance is due to the problems brought on by intense poverty, serious health deficiencies, parental unemployment, and a variety of other debilitating social problems, the suit seeks to redistribute resources for Hartford's children based on a 1984 definition of equal educational opportunity by the Connecticut Board of Education: "Equity . . . does not mean an equal distribution of resources; rather it implies that those who need more must receive more." This definition might indeed provide a framework for evaluating schools all over the country.

Higher education is, of course, important for increasing the student's knowledge and understanding of the world, but that is only one of its functions. A bachelor's degree often enables students to raise their social class status, to learn the social codes of higher-ranked social classes, to become credentialed (particularly important in this era of credential worship), to achieve the prestige and instant patina that some institutions confer, and to be able to participate in that network of contacts still important in our society. John Gregory Dunne provides a vivid portrayal of the social and economic benefits of attending Princeton in the 1950s:

Time was a glorious place to work in the years that I was there, from 1959 to 1964. I was twenty-seven when I was hired, and an ignoramus, vintage Princeton '54, with a degree in history. . . . I got my job because a woman I was seeing on the sly, Vassar '57, was also seeing George J. W. Goodman, Harvard '52, a writer in *Time's* business section who was later to become the author and PBS economics guru "Adam Smith." Goodman, I was informed by Vassar '57, was leaving *Time* for *Fortune*, which meant that if I moved fast there was probably a job open. I applied to *Time's* personnel man, a friend, Yale '49, and was in due course interviewed by Otto Fuerbringer, Harvard '32, and *Time's* managing editor. The cut of my orange and black jib seemed to satisfy him, and the $7,700 a year I was offered more than satisfied me, and so a few weeks later I went to work as a writer in the business section, although I was not altogether certain of the difference between a stock and a bond, and had no idea what "over the counter" meant.

Lest we think that this vignette is simply an amusing anecdote from a bygone era, Jake Lamar describes how he got his job with *Time* in the late 1980s:

During my first week on the job, a jocular man with bushy eye brows and a thick Southern accent introduced himself to me as the affirmative action recruiter for the writing staff. "Where did you come from?" he asked, looking bewildered.
"College," I said. "I just graduated a couple of weeks ago."
"From where?"
"Harvard."
"Hmm. And how did you wind up at *Time?*"
"A professor of mine introduced me to a senior writer here and he passed my clips on to the editors."
"Ah, the old-boy network."
"I guess."

Considering the importance of a university education in today's world, particularly the importance of an elite university education, what is the responsibility of higher education in a democratic society characterized by gross inequality? Clearly, colleges and universities cannot completely compensate for the class, race, and gender inequity in American society. Until the wider society redistributes resources to ensure that all children truly have equal opportunity, students will continue to compete on an unequal basis for the scarce resources of admission to university, financial aid, status within the college community, and, ultimately, the significant benefits higher education confers. The benefits of undergraduate education, of course, include the possibility of going on to graduate or professional school—the level often necessary to achieving any significant degree of economic security, power, prestige, and upper-middle-class status in American society.

Although higher education cannot alone redress the injustice within American society, many steps can be and have been taken by colleges and universities to make higher education more accessible to a broad range of students. To start with, elite institutions might consider closer scrutiny of the admission of children of alumni. In admitting the class of 1997, for example, Princeton sent acceptance letters to 15.4 percent of its total applicants; the same year, Princeton accepted 43 percent of its applicants who were alumni children. Are those "legacies," as they are called, as genuinely qualified as the other applicants? Might a closer scrutiny of legacies yield spaces for students who may be qualified but less well placed in terms of family background?

Furthermore, as part of the admissions process, schools need to search out with even greater zeal students who have traditionally been underrepresented, qualified candidates of color and students whose financial background might preclude their even considering a four-year college or university. It must be stressed that, though African Americans, for instance, constitute approximately 12 percent of the U.S. population, they constitute only 5 to 6 percent of the students at Ivy League universities.

Colleges and universities are often located in or near communities in which significant numbers of low-income and/or people of color live, but admissions offices all too frequently overlook these areas in their search for appropriate candidates. Many students at Vassar felt the Office of Admissions could and should focus more on students of color in the Poughkeepsie area. Does UCLA reach out sufficiently to underrepresented students in Los Angeles? Does Princeton make special efforts to recruit in the nearby cities of Camden, Newark, and Trenton? Perhaps colleges need to make connections and long-term relationships with high schools attended by low-income students and students from underrepresented groups in the same way they have developed connections and relationships with elite private and public schools across the country, so that able, achieving students, early in their high-school years (or even in junior-high school), can know that a Yale or a Carleton or an Oberlin or a Fairleigh Dickinson is seeking them out and is willing and able to smooth the way and welcome them. Many schools have used some of these techniques—in some cases with great success, in others with less success. Some students from educationally and economically disadvantaged backgrounds have not been able to keep up academically; others have felt their outsider status so keenly that they return to the cities in which they grew up and may enroll in public, commuter schools there.

One of the most important reasons for the small percentage of low-income and minority students at many schools is clearly the inferior quality of their secondary-school education, but to wait until the United States decides to equalize educational opportunity at the primary- and secondary-school levels will almost surely mean the sacrifice of at least another generation of children. Colleges and universities must seek out students who they feel can eventually do college-level work and provide more in the way of compensatory courses—during the summer before the first year as well as during the regular college year. Some of these programs have been found to be effective, others less so, but every effort must nevertheless be taken to give our young people a chance for gratifying, productive lives.

In addition, many students are taking longer than four years to complete their undergraduate education. Some observers have frowned at the use of additional years to complete what has been seen traditionally as a four-year experience, but, after all, what is sacred about four years? Students who begin their college years by taking remedial courses, those who must work while studying, or students who must actively care for family members are among those who may well need to take longer to achieve their degree. Stretching out undergraduate education to more than four years has sometimes been seen as weakness or failure, on the part of students or on the part of colleges. (A student beset by serious illness during her first and second years recently told me that her parents should be proud because she completed her baccalaureate degree within four years. How much additional stress did she place on herself because of her—and perhaps her parents'—desire for her to finish college in the traditional four years?) If we hope to encourage the matriculation of nontraditional students, we must give them and academic institutions flexibility while encouraging creative educational efforts. Many schools already provide compensatory education, but money is scarce, programs are underfunded, and many programs are being cut back. Again, higher education cannot wait until there is a substantial pool of disadvantaged students who measure up to the standards set for the more affluent and privileged in our society; that policy will only serve to perpetuate existing inequalities. Rather, colleges and universities must take an active role in helping students from underrepresented groups to improve their academic skills so that they can move on and succeed within higher education.

When students and others object to searching out and establishing special compensatory programs for those traditionally excluded from higher education, perhaps we should puncture the myth of individual achievement and "merit" and tell our students the truth—that few of us succeed simply on the basis of individual effort. Perhaps we should tell them that, though each student brings unique characteristics and talents to the collegiate community, many are members of the first-year class at least in part because they were fortunate to have been born to affluent parents who could assure that they attended first-rate schools and benefited from cultural enrichment, travel, or perhaps after-school and summer opportunities. Others may be accepted to the coveted place in the college of their choice in part because they provide the geographical diversity sought by admissions committees, still others because they come from foreign countries and give the college the prestige of internationalism. Some students receive the prized letter of acceptance because they have special interests and talents— athletic, musical, linguistic—which they may have honed over the years, but such talents often run in families and are cultivated by attentive parents. The clearest examples of getting "a leg up" in the often Byzantine process of college admissions, of course, are the legacy students. It must be noted that, whereas students of color have been stigmatized because of affirmative action, legacy children seem to have suffered little if any disparagement as a result of their special consideration. Perhaps, when the individuals receiving special consideration belong to the more affluent and powerful among us, we accept their privilege as though it is their due.

Part of the mission of all schools—public and private, urban, suburban, and rural, elite and not so elite—must be to demystify higher education, truly to reach out to poor and working-class people, to older students, to potential applicants who never thought they had a chance to continue their education, thanks to poor academic preparation, recent arrival in the U.S., economic problems, or family responsibilities. Some of this outreach needs to be individual in nature—admissions offices and alumni recruiters seeking out students, one by one, across the country—but other, more institutionally based ways must be found to help talented people make the leap to higher education and ultimately make the most of their abilities. Such an effort was undertaken by Vassar in the early 1980s.

With funding in the early 1980s from the Andrew W. Mellon Foundation, the Association of American Colleges encouraged the establishment of partnerships between two- and four-year colleges. The goal was to increase the number of community-college students who continue their education at four-year colleges and ultimately receive a bachelor's degree. Vassar received one of the AAC-Mellon grants and joined with LaGuardia Community College in Queens, New York, a two-year school that is part of the City University of New York, to form a partnership that came to be called Exploring Transfer—ET.

Exploring Transfer is intended for students who traditionally have been closed out of admission to private colleges: older students, minority students, people from poor and working-class backgrounds, women with young children, and "second-chance" students—women and men who did poorly in high school and may even have dropped out, but later earned equivalency degrees and went on to study at two-year colleges. Nearly three hundred students have participated in ET since its inception in 1985. The program brings students from LaGuardia and other community colleges in the area to the Vassar campus for an intensive, rigorous five-week academic program at no cost to the students. The idea, according to one program organizer, was to go beyond "skimming" the "best and the brightest" off the top and to really try to change people's lives by encouraging them to seriously consider studying at a four-year college.

Willa Panvini, an ET student from LaGuardia who graduated from Vassar in June 1992, had no idea what or where Vassar was before her five weeks there. She describes her arrival at the campus:

> We were all stunned by the June beauty of upstate New York. We drove down Raymond Avenue and admired what we thought was a lavish country club on the left. Then we slowed. Our mouths dropped as we turned into Main Gate. . . . The squirrels and huge trees seemed to number in the billions; the grass was so green it seemed to flavor the air.

Panvini goes on to describe her group:

> We were eighteen to sixty; we were West African, South African, East African, African American, Japanese, West Indian, Puerto Rican, Greek, Italian, German, Irish, Lebanese, Chinese, Korean, Indian, Brazilian, Bolivian, and more. . . . We spoke Spanish, French, Chinese, Korean, Japanese, Portuguese, English, German, and native tongues I'd never heard of. We were "ET"

She describes having so many books to read, papers to write, and class discussions that went on for hours as "swimming in a tidal wave of knowledge." Discussions of "racism, homophobia, feminism, class, social construction of gender, power and political policy, United States foreign policy, Richard Wright, the media, Toni Morrison, David Leavitt, the Holocaust, [and] global economics" filled the air. At the end of the five weeks, the students cried and laughed, danced and sang, and, above all, wondered, "Now what?'

Gail Green, a professor in the English department at LaGuardia who has taught in the ET program at Vassar, described her five weeks there as "my most pleasurable teaching experience." Each course is interdisciplinary and team-taught by one professor from Vassar and one from LaGuardia. The course Green co-taught was "Landscape as Text / Text as Landscape." This five-week course used seven books, including fiction such as Margaret Atwood's *The Handmaid's Tale* and Gloria Naylor's *The Women of Brewster Place,* along with readings in cultural geography and other social sciences. The course explored how authors perceive the landscapes around them, both urban and rural, North American and Third World, and how they use them in their writing. It also involved field study in the Poughkeepsie area, and assignments required both collaborative and individual work.

Professor Green talks about how the campus "oozes Vassar atmosphere," even though very few regular Vassar students were around; how anxious many of the students were at the beginning, but how the anxiety eased by the middle of the second week; how "respectful and generous" the students were in listening to one another; and, echoing Willa Panvini, how the real question became, "So now what happens to the rest of your life?"

More than thirty ET students have since continued their education at Vassar, many graduating with honors and several with election to Phi Beta Kappa. Willa Panvini reports that nearly all of her fellow ET students have gone on to four-year schools, many to first-rate liberal-arts colleges such as Vassar, Barnard, Colgate, Middlebury, and Cornell. A high percentage of graduates complete their undergraduate education, and some go on to earn master's and Ph.D. degrees.

This effort, replicated in five other partnerships between four-year and community colleges in different parts of the country, goes beyond the usual scenario of individual colleges seeking out nontraditional students one by one, to a collaborative effort identifying appropriate students, providing them with a challenging academic experience, and, in so doing, giving them some real choices in their lives.

ET is clearly an expensive, experimental program, one that, if replicated, would need in all likelihood to be collaboratively funded by the schools involved, by foundations, and by government. Such efforts are costly, but unused talent, underemployment, and unfulfilled potential are even more costly. The ET students learned far more than course content. They learned that they could deal with demanding academic material; that a magnificent campus that at first looked like a "lavish country club" could become home to them, albeit for only five weeks; and above all, that they might succeed if they dared continue with their education. Even though many of the students were given some help around future opportunities, the most important issue ET explored, according to Professor Green, was: what does it take for people to see opportunity in their lives?

Once nontraditional students matriculate at what are often still quite traditional institutions, care must be taken that they be truly accepted. It is clear that open hostility, such as the myriad incidents documented in this book and elsewhere, often undermine the confidence of students who may enter institutions of higher education with severe misgivings about how they will fit in. But the open expression of prejudice in relatively close communities harms not only the recipient; it also harms the perpetrators and the community as a whole. The categorizing of people in terms of their differences and the denigration of the "other" provide a simplistic analysis of the social and political world that serves to bolster the self-image of the perpetrator at the expense of the recipient. Such expression of bias, often stemming from deep feelings of powerlessness and rage about conditions in the broader society and fear for the future, diminishes the capacity for public discussion so essential in any community. As Ralph Potter, professor of social ethics at the Harvard Divinity School, has stated, "The peace and vitality of the community require the preservation of our ability to discuss lively and potentially explosive issues together. That requires, in each new generation, a renewal of civility in public life." Potter continues:

"Civility" is the treatment that citizens owe to one another simply as fellow citizens. We may have other duties and obligations
toward one another as friends, neighbors, parents, employers,
co-religionists, lodge members or whatever. But conscientious
effort to keep open the channels for the most inclusive and con-
siderate public discussion is the primordial obligation assumed
in taking up residence in a community.

While colleges and universities attempt to educate and sensitize students about the culture, history, values, and daily lives of
the myriad groups that make up the United States and the world,
attention must be paid to the feelings of the majority as well as
the minority. White, middle-income students, for example, come
from a variety of backgrounds, and themselves often face substantial culture shock when they arrive at college. As Scott has
movingly pointed out, he came from a homogeneous suburb in
Washington State and virtually entered another world when he
started his first year at Columbia. He had had essentially no
contact with either Jewish people or people of color, and his attitudes toward gays were, he feels, attacked aggressively. He recalls feeling acutely uncomfortable during orientation meetings
and, indeed, frightened of being expelled if he were to use language deemed politically incorrect. Orientation sessions and
other methods of encouraging students to respect one another
and to live together amicably must, in the social-work idiom,
start where the students are. Attitudes are far more likely to be
modified when all the students involved are treated with respect
and when ideas are introduced gradually and with care.

In order to promote greater understanding of the diverse
groups that make up the United States, and in order to promote
civility, many colleges and universities have adopted multicultural requirements. None, perhaps, is more inclusive than the
requirements at Hunter College. Beginning in September 1993,

all students are required to take a total of twelve hours of classes, four courses, in four categories: non-European cultures, American minorities, women's studies and sexual orientation, and traditional European studies. Students may, of course, fulfill these requirements through classes they are taking in the usual curriculum of their undergraduate years.

It is hoped that, through such multicultural requirements and through wider use of readings by women, people of color, and thinkers from the developing world that students will develop greater understanding and respect for the philosophy, literature, and points of view of peoples outside of the Western tradition. But merely adding readings and a course here and there will not suffice. As several students pointed out in part II, professors also need to become familiar with traditions outside Western civilization. Many students described how their teachers relied on them to communicate a particular minority perspective to their classmates and the awkwardness of the position in which they were placed. Marcella's recommendation is particularly noteworthy: that professors, including those who are tenured, be required to participate in workshops to bring their knowledge up to date, particularly with regard to multiculturalism. As she stated, issues such as racism and multiculturalism need to be worked on like a marriage, continually.

Finally, how do people who have been victimized move beyond victim status? Cornel West suggests that self-love and the love of others is the only real way to "generate a sense of agency among a downtrodden people," to combat the nihilism that characterizes so many sectors of American society. To encourage self-love and the love of others, institutions of higher education must themselves promote dialogue and open discussion, must affirm the dignity and worth of all citizens, and must discourage the spewing forth of hatred on all sides. This does not mean negating the First Amendment right to free speech of any citizen but, rather, upholding the right of free speech, condemning intolerance, and encouraging dialogue as an alternative to confrontation.

Many colleges are struggling with all of these issues and have been for some time. As they strive to affirm the value and worth of the citizens of their communities, administrators, faculty members, and students alike must join together to speak out against injustice, within academia and the broader society as well. While they work within their own institutions, within higher education, and within secondary education to redress some of the inequities of American society, they must also state clearly and repeatedly that the problems plaguing college campuses cannot ultimately be solved until the inequities in the larger society are addressed; that, until all of our children receive a decent primary and secondary education, until there are adequate, productive jobs for those who wish to work, until people's basic human needs are met, the politics of scarcity will ensure that intergroup distrust and hostility will continue to be played out in the country at large and on our campuses.

Perhaps we can learn from the students themselves who understand that activism on college campuses is indeed a matter of survival. Many of the students understand that they must go beyond identity politics and work together with those who share their point of view (and even, in some instances, with those who do not), whatever their race, ethnicity, religion, economic background, gender, or sexual orientation. Todd Gitlin refers to this as "commonality politics," a "frame of understanding and action that understands 'difference' against the background of what is *not* different, what is shared among groups." Many of the students have spoken about the important connection developed among students who share a commitment—whether that commitment is political action and social change, a passion for athletics, or theater, or activism around AIDS. Perhaps Eddie

Olivera-Robles, a Princeton senior originally from Puerto Rico, says it best. Though he feels that Princeton, despite its diversity, "is still very much an upperclass, racially homogeneous institution" in which "the campus culture . . . isolates not just minorities, but people from a lower-income background," he found a way of breaking through that isolation and separateness. He cofounded a salsa band, La Junta del Son. The band, all Princeton students, included a Puerto Rican piano player from New York who was the music director, a Jewish student from Minnesota who did the musical arrangements of all their favorite salsa songs, "two conga players of European descent," a Brazilian guitarist, a Jewish piano-and-trumpet player, two other trumpet players who are white, and a white bass player. Eddie states, "But the funny thing is, we don't even think in racial terms." He goes on to sum up the importance of an activity such as the band: "La Junta has taught me that a common love for something can be made into a bond between people."

During several conversations at Barnard, Merrill Kirkland told me it was her belief that the fundamental issues with which students are dealing are identity and community. In my view, these concepts include personal identity as well as group identity and membership in their specific subgroup, in the college community as well as membership in the broader society. Often on college campuses today, these issues seem to conflict: the search for identity can preclude identification with the larger community; some students' struggles to understand their identity can disrupt whatever semblance of community seemed to exist, however tenuously; or one group's expression of their point of view—their identity, if you will—can call into question another's fundamental sense of worth and well-being. As delicate and explosive as these issues are, they will not be resolved within our academic communities or within the broader society until we as a nation recognize the need to move toward greater respect for one another, greater caring for one another, and greater equality. As we move into the twenty-first century, let us learn from our young people and recognize that working together for a more humane society is truly a way of bringing people together, and indeed may be a matter of survival.

Notes

Introduction

page

7 "hate incidents": Howard J. Ehrlich, Ph D. *Campus Ethnoviolence and the Policy Options* (Baltimore: National Institute Against Prejudice and Violence, 1990), p. 3.

8 "total institutions": Erving Goffman, *Asylums: Essays on the Social Situation of Mental Patients and Other Inmates* (New York: Doubleday, 1961).

10 our identity . . . an intricate web: Nancy A. Hewitt, "Multiple Truths: The Personal, the Political, and the Postmodernist in Contemporary Feminist Scholarship," Center for Research on Women, Memphis State University, Memphis, Tenn., Working Paper 5, January 1992.

Chapter 1. Who Shall Learn?

19 "We are living . . .": Robert B. Reich, *The Work of Nations* (New York: Vintage, 1992), p. 3.

19 ". . . joke on history": Jonathan Kozol, *Savage Inequalities: Children in America's Schools* (New York: HarperCollins, 1992), p. 35.

20 American commitment to mass education: Ian Robertson, *Society: A Brief Introduction* (New York: Worth, 1989), p. 278.

21 "As recently as the 1950's . . .": Felicity Barringer, "As American as Apple Pie, Dim Sum or Burritos," *New York Times*, May 31, 1992.

22 15 percent of the total population: Kelvin Pollard, "Faster Growth, More Diversity in U.S. Projections," *Population Today*, February 1993, pp. 3, 10.

22 speakers of Asian languages: Felicity Barringer, "For 32 Million Americans, English is a 2d Language," *New York Times*, April 28, 1993.

23 ". . . officials can pinpoint . . .": Karen DeWitt, "Large Increase Is Predicted in Minorities in U.S. Schools," *New York Times,* September 13, 1991.

23 One economist suggests: in Joseph Berger, "Schools Cope with Influx of Immigrants," *New York Times,* April 15, 1992.

24 Low Anglo in-migration: David E. Hayes-Bautista et al., *No Longer a Minority: Latinos and Social Policy in California* (Los Angeles: University of California/Los Angeles Chicano Studies Research Center, 1992), pp. 7–8.

24 In his book: Victor R. Fuchs, *Who Shall Live?: Health, Economics and Social Choice* (New York: Basic Books, 1974).

25 ". . . of 'earning' respect": Andrew Ross, *No Respect: Intellectuals & Popular Culture* (New York: Routledge, 1989), p. 6.

25 Robert Reich has pointed out: Reich, *Work of Nations,* p. 7.

26 incredible $127 million: "Executive Pay: The Party Ain't Over Yet," *Business Week,* April 26, 1993.

26 "the income disparity . . .": Reich, *Work of Nations,* p. 7.

26 Data from the 1990 census: "Statistical Portrait of the Nation: Education and Income," *New York Times,* January 28, 1993.

28 ". . . persisted almost everywhere": Kozol, *Savage Inequalities,* p. 2.

28 "The dual society . . .": ibid., p. 4.

28 "If a kid . . .": ibid., p. 52.

29 "direct and swift": ibid., pp. 57–58.

29 "Our goal . . .": ibid., p. 65.

30 "humming with excitement"; "reasoning and logic": ibid., p. 95.

30 "People on the outside . . .": ibid., p. 104.

30 "So long as . . .": ibid., p. 155.

31 "I don't see how . . .": ibid., p. 128.

31 "The absence of attention to girls . . .": *How Schools Shortchange Girls: A Study of Major Findings on Girls and Education,* commissioned by the American Association of University Women Educational Foundation; researched by the Wellesley College Center for Research on Women, a joint publication of the AAUW Educational Foundation and National Education Association, 1992, p. 2.

32 "much less apt to pursue . . .": ibid., p. 16.

32 boys outnumbered girls in every state: "Boys Predominate in a Contest, Fueling Complaint of Test Bias," *New York Times,* May 26, 1993.

32 "... 'gender gap' ...": *How Schools Shortchange Girls*, p. 16.

32 "cyclical nature ...": ibid., p. 65.

32 "... than do females": ibid., p. 68.

33 "On school playgrounds ...": Barrie Thorne, *Gender Play: Girls and Boys in School* (New Brunswick, N.J.: Rutgers University Press, 1993), pp. 83, 159.

33 A 1993 study: Felicity Barringer, "School Hallways as Gantlets of Sexual Taunts," *New York Times*, June 2, 1993.

34 "... patterns of power ...": Lynn S. Chancer, *Sadomasochism in Everyday Life: The Dynamics of Power and Powerlessness* (New Brunswick, N.J.: Rutgers University Press, 1992), pp. 125–26.

34 "... other, weaker boys": *How Schools Shortchange Girls*, p. 73.

34 Examples are ubiquitous: Jane Gross, "Schools Are Newest Arenas for Sex-Harassment Issues," *New York Times*, March 11, 1992.

34 harassed by the band director: Nan D. Stein, "It Happens Here, Too: Sexual Harassment in the Schools," *Education Week*, November 27, 1991.

35 "It's negative ..."; "... and boys lie": Gross, "Schools Are Newest Arenas."

35 to 2.58 million in 1990: William Celis, 3d, "Campuses Find New Ways to Recruit as Fight for Good Students Gets Fierce," *New York Times*, April 15, 1992.

36 "... to keep even": ibid.

37 black students are choosing to go elsewhere: Fox Butterfield, "Colleges Luring Black Students with Incentives," *New York Times*, February 28, 1993.

37 A survey ... in 1990: Robin Wilson, "Colleges Scramble to Fill Openings in Freshman Classes," *Chronicle of Higher Education*, June 20, 1990.

37 high-school counselors have observed: ibid.

38 could not find jobs: "Slump Plays Role in Picking College," *New York Times*, January 13, 1992.

38 eighteen-to-twenty-four-year-olds: Michele N.-K. Collison, "More Traditional-Age Students Consider Community Colleges," *Chronicle of Higher Education*, April 10, 1991.

39 "... California higher education": Louis Freedberg, "State University Course Offerings to Be Slashed," *San Francisco Chronicle*, June 11, 1992.

39 Public-college tuition: William Celis, 3d, "Colleges Increase Student Fees Again, But at Lowest Percentage in Decades," *New York Times*, April 7, 1993.

39 ". . . some disadvantaged students": Jean Evangelauf, "Sharp Rise Reported in Public-College Tuition; Rate of Increase Drops at Private Institutions," *Chronicle of Higher Education*, October 23, 1991.

40 " 'all other things being equal' "; "given preference . . .": Henry Rosovsky, *The University: An Owner's Manual* (New York: W. W. Norton, 1990), p. 64.

40 15.6 percent of all applicants: Mark Muro, "Class Privilege," *Boston Globe*, September 18, 1991.

40 "Private universities depend . . .": Rosovsky, *University*, pp. 64–65.

40 Cornell University raised: "Pulse: Colleges," *New York Times*, April 27, 1992; "Colorado Attorney and Civic Leader to Chair Wellesley College Board of Trustees," Wellesley College News Release, April 2, 1993.

41 completion rate of 52.1 percent: Deborah J. Carter and Reginald Wilson, *Minorities in Higher Education: 1992 Eleventh Annual Status Report* (Washington, D.C.: American Council on Education, 1993), p. 4.

41 62.9 percent in 1985: Deborah J. Carter and Reginald Wilson, *Minorities in Higher Education: 1991 Tenth Annual Status Report* (Washington, D.C.: American Council on Education, 1992), p. 37.

42 28.1 percent in 1988: ibid., pp. 36–37.

42 ". . . major regression": "Mid- and Low-Income Minorities in Decline on College Rolls," *New York Times*, January 14, 1992.

42 By 1991: Carter and Wilson, 1993, pp. 6–7.

43 ". . . this is my chance": William Celis, 3d, "Colleges Battle Culture and Poverty to Swell Hispanic Enrollments," *New York Times*, February 24, 1993.

43 number of foreign students: Susan Dodge, "Surge of Students from Asia and Eastern Europe Lifts Foreign Enrollments in U.S. to Record 407,500," *Chronicle of Higher Education*, October 23, 1991.

44 statistics . . . at Ivy League schools: "1991 Enrollment by Race at 3,100 Institutions of Higher Education," *Chronicle of Higher Education*, March 3, 1993.

45 "African-Americans do better . . .": Karen DeWitt, "Rise in Number of Black Ph.D.'s Is Reported," *New York Times*, May 5, 1992.

45 "At the heart of it . . .": Anthony DePalma, "Drop in Black Ph.D.'s Brings Debate on Aid for Foreigners," *New York Times*, April 21, 1992.

46 "an irrational fear . . .": ibid.

46 Dr. Israel Tribble, Jr.: ibid.

47 ". . . old-stock Protestants": E. Digby Baltzell, *The Protestant Establishment: Aristocracy and Caste in America* (New Haven, Conn.: Yale University Press, 1987), p. 336.

48 ". . . 43 Prospect Avenue . . .": Geoffrey Wolff, *The Final Club* (New York: Vintage, 1991), p. 96.

48 "Because if you don't . . .": ibid., p. 74.

Chapter 2. The Societal Context

51 "Historically, the middle classes . . .": Jonathan Rieder, *Canarsie: The Jews and Italians of Brooklyn Against Liberalism* (Cambridge, Mass.: Harvard University Press, 1985), p. 99.

52 headlines of the early 1990s: Michael Winerip, "Economic Trend for the 90's: Fear," *New York Times*, November 5, 1991; Constance L. Hays, "Middle-Class and Jobless, They Share Sorrows," *New York Times*, December 14, 1991; Michael deCourcey Hinds, "Graduates Facing Worst Prospect in Last 2 Decades," *New York Times*, May 12, 1992; Jane Gross, "Graduates March Down Aisle into Job Nightmare," *New York Times*, January 9, 1992; Louis Uchitelle, "Pay of College Graduates Is Outpaced by Inflation," *New York Times*, May 14, 1992.

52 In June 1992: Steven Greenhouse, "Unemployment Up Sharply, Prompting Federal Reserve to Cut Its Key Lending Rate," *New York Times*, July 3, 1992.

52 Job prospects . . . in 1992: Hinds, "Worst Prospect in 2 Decades."

53 "If we're not the best . . .": Anthony DePalma, "In Uncertain Times, College Students See a Bleak Future After Graduation," *New York Times*, December 25, 1991.

54 Today more Americans: Louis Uchitelle, "Stanching the Loss of Good Jobs," *New York Times*, January 31, 1993.

54 planned . . . medical school: Peter T. Kilborn, "Top Graduates in Science Also Put Dreams on Hold," *New York Times*, June 6, 1993.

54 specter of General Motors: Hays, "They Share Sorrows."

54 support groups . . . in Connecticut: Winerip, "Economic Trend."

54 pay . . . in 1990 . . . 1973: Louis Uchitelle, "U.S. Wages: Not Getting Ahead? Better Get Used to It," *New York Times,* December 16, 1990.

55 "a jump in inequality . . .": Sylvia Nasar, "Fed Gives New Evidence of 80's Gains by Richest," *New York Times,* April 21, 1992.

55 rags-to-riches: Sylvia Nasar, "Rich and Poor Likely to Remain So," *New York Times,* May 18, 1992.

56 "To study race . . .": Michael Omi and Howard Winant, *Racial Formation in the United States: From the 1960s to the 1980s* (New York: Routledge, 1986), p. xiii.

57 The number of hate groups jumped: "Klanwatch Reports Record Rise in Hate Groups," *SPLC Report* (a publication of the Southern Poverty Law Center), April 1992.

57 rise of neo-Nazi skinheads: "Skinheads Target the Schools: An ADL Special Report," Anti-Defamation League of B'nai B'rith, New York, 1989.

59 "We're going to be beating . . .": Joseph Berger, "Forum for Bigotry? Fringe Groups on TV," *New York Times,* May 23, 1993.

59 developments in other parts of the world: Bill Buford, "The Lads of the National Front," *New York Times Magazine,* April 26, 1992; John F. Burns, "New, Virulent Strains of Hatred in the Balkans and Beyond," *New York Times,* May 3, 1992; Alan Cowell, "Attacks on Immigrants Raising Concern in Italy," *New York Times,* February 9, 1992; "Racism's Back," *Economist,* November 16, 1991; Clyde H. Farnsworth, "To Battle Bigots, Help from South of the Border," *New York Times,* February 12, 1993; Clyde H. Farnsworth, "Canada Tightens Immigration Law," *New York Times,* December 22, 1992; Marlise Simons, "Anti-Racism Group Aids 'New French,' " *New York Times,* December 26, 1990; Jane Perlez, "Ethnic Violence Is Shaking Kenya," *New York Times,* March 29, 1992; and James Brooke, "As Centralized Rule Wanes, Ethnic Tension Rises in Soviet Georgia," *New York Times,* October 2, 1991.

59 and the Sierra Club: Deborah Sontag, "Calls to Restrict Immigration Come from Many Quarters," *New York Times,* December 13, 1992.

59 anti-Semitic incidents: Arthur Hertzberg, "Is Anti-Semitism Dying Out?," *New York Review of Books,* June 24, 1993.

59 more attacks on people than on property: "ADL 1992 Audit of Anti-Semitic Incidents: Overall Numbers Decrease but Campus Attacks

Are Up," *On the Frontline* (a monthly newsletter published by the Anti-Defamation League), February/March 1993.

60 rise in anti-Asian violence: "National Outcry as Anti-Asian Violence Continues to Rise," *Outlook* (publication of the Asian American Legal Defense and Education Fund), Winter 1993.

60 violence against homosexuals: "Anti-Gay Crimes Are Reported on Rise in 5 Cities," *New York Times*, March 20, 1992.

60 Allen R. Schindler: James Sterngold, "Killer Gets Life as Navy Says He Hunted Down Gay Sailor," *New York Times*, May 28, 1993.

61 "Clinton must pay": "3 Marines Are Acquitted of Assault at Gay Bar," *New York Times*, April 14, 1993.

61 ". . . homosexuality is wrong": "High School Council Passes a Gay Ban on Leaders," *New York Times*, May 16, 1993.

61 ". . . despised minority . . .": Jeffrey Schmalz, "Writing Against Time, Valiantly," *New York Times*, April 22, 1993.

61 "The album included . . .": Jon Pareles, "Rap After the Riot: Smoldering Rage and No Apologies," *New York Times*, December 13, 1992.

62 "Under the aegis . . ."; ". . . to affirmative action": Thomas Byrne Edsall and Mary D. Edsall, *Chain Reaction: The Impact of Race, Rights, and Taxes on American Politics* (New York: W. W. Norton, 1991), pp. 139–41.

63 "Bob stared . . .": Chandler Davidson, *Race and Class in Texas Politics* (Princeton, N.J.: Princeton University Press, 1990), pp. 222–23.

64 ". . . It's all slipping away": Reider, *Canarsie*, p. 98.

64 "explodes . . .": ibid., p. 102.

64 "Who's feeling sorry . . .": ibid.

65 A judicial commission: Jerry Gray, "Panel Says Courts Are 'Infested with Racism,' " *New York Times*, June 5, 1991.

65 three hundred car dealerships: William E. Schmidt, "White Men Get Better Deals on Cars, Study Finds," *New York Times*, December 13, 1990.

65 "Blacks are seen . . .": Lena Williams, "When Blacks Shop, Bias Often Accompanies Sale," *New York Times*, April 30, 1991.

65 heart-bypass surgery: "Fewer Heart Bypasses for Blacks on Medicare," *New York Times*, March 18, 1992.

65 minority students enrolled in medical school: Robert E. Tomasson, "Goals for Racial Inclusion Elude Latest Crop of Young Doctors," *New York Times*, April 1, 1992.

65 African-American Secret Service agents: "Black Agents Sue Denny's," *New York Times,* May 25, 1993.

65 In Boston: "Incident in Boston Taxi Fuels Debate on Racism," *San Francisco Chronicle,* December 26, 1992.

66 "There are problems . . .": David Margolick, "35 Law Firms in New York Pledge More Minority Hiring," *New York Times,* September 26, 1991.

66 And even in the military: Jason DeParle, "Bias Is Found at 6 U.S. Bases in Europe," *New York Times,* August 25, 1991.

67 "that segregation based on race . . .": Andrew Hacker, *Two Nations: Black and White, Separate, Hostile, Unequal* (New York: Scribner's Sons, 1992), p. 161.

67 National School Board Association: ibid., p. 163.

67 "I don't want . . ."; "I was called a nigger . . .": David J. Dent, "The New Black Suburbs," *New York Times Magazine,* June 14, 1992.

68 "When I heard . . ."; ". . . racial caste system": Isabel Wilkerson, "Middle-Class but Not Feeling Equal, Blacks Reflect on Los Angeles Strife," *New York Times,* May 4, 1993.

68 Data from the 1990 Census: Hacker, *Two Nations,* p. 97.

69 ". . . epidemic proportions"; ". . . violence against women": Lee Michael Katz, "Rapes Reach 'Epidemic' Rate in 1990," *USA Today,* March 22, 1991.

69 disbelieved for generations: Kimberle Crenshaw, "Whose Story Is It, Anyway? Feminist and Antiracist Appropriations of Anita Hill," in Toni Morrison, ed., *Race-ing Justice, En-gendering Power: Essays on Anita Hill, Clarence Thomas, and the Construction of Social Reality,* (New York: Pantheon, 1992), p. 412.

70 In a 1989 study: David Margolick, "Curbing Sexual Harassment in the Legal World," *New York Times,* November 9, 1990.

70 A survey of interns and residents: "Many Doctors Tell of Sex Harassment in Training," *New York Times,* February 4, 1993.

71 Another survey: Alison Bass, "Survey Finds Wide Sexual Harassment in Academic Science," *Boston Globe,* February 11, 1993.

71 A 1986 survey: ibid.

71 ". . . and female subservience": David W. Fisher, "A 'Remarkable' Woman," *Hospital Practice,* July 15, 1991.

72 In 1990 the Pentagon reported: Eric Schmitt, "2 Out of 3 Women in

Military Study Report Sexual Harassment Incidents," *New York Times,*
September 12, 1990.
72 ". . . stripping off their clothes": Eric Schmitt, "Wall of Silence
Impedes Inquiry into a Rowdy Navy Convention," *New York Times,*
June 14, 1992.
72 ". . . one officer shouted . . ."; ". . . of drunk aviators": ibid.
74 "breaks down . . ."; "Steeped in hatred . . .": Aljean Harmetz, " 'Falling Down' Takes Its Cues from the Headlines," *New York Times,* February 21, 1993.
74 "It's homicide . . .": *Homicide,* NBC, January 31, 1993.
74 "popular perceptions . . .": Andrew Ross, *No Respect: Intellectuals and
Popular Culture* (New York: Routledge, 1989), p. 4.
75 "While plain talk . . .": John Leland, "Rap and Race," *Newsweek,*
June 29, 1992, pp. 46–52.
75 "pure confrontation" . . . ; "Rap is an attempt . . .": ibid.
76 "black pride . . ."; ". . . what it has earned": Jon Pareles, "Hip-Hop's
Prophets of Rage Make Noise Again," *New York Times,* September 29,
1991.
76 ". . . no to racism and sexism": Peter Watrous, "When the Queen
Speaks, People Listen," *New York Times,* August 25, 1991.
76 The front-page article: Michael Marriott, "Rap's Embrace of 'Nigger'
Fires Bitter Debate," *New York Times,* January 24, 1993.
77 "That term . . .", "Does it signal . . .": ibid.
77 Phi Kappa Psi: "Rider College Is Closing Fraternity," *New York Times,*
January 30, 1993.

Chapter 3. Conflict Within the Ivory Tower

79 "Either/or dichotomous thinking . . .": Patricia Hill Collins, *Black
Feminist Thought: Knowledge, Consciousness, and the Politics of
Empowerment* (Boston: Unwin Hyman, 1990), pp. 68, 225.
80 "bastion of . . ."; "Racial epithets . . .": Isabel Wilkerson, "Racial
Tension Erupts Tearing a College Apart," *New York Times,* April 13,
1992.
81 "What is clear . . ."; "It was disgusting": ibid.
82 "Obviously . . ."; "Now she's gone": ibid.
82–84 "stiletto-style . . ."; ". . . to humiliate niggers": Diana Jean

Schemo, "Anger over List Divides Blacks and College Town," *New York Times*, September 27, 1992.

84 "an affront . . .": "College Official Who Released List of Black Students Is Demoted," *New York Times*, September 18, 1992.

84 "It was April 25, 1989 . . .": N'Tanya Lee, "Racism on College Campuses," *Focus* (monthly magazine of the Joint Center for Political Studies), Special Social Policy Issue, August/September 1989.

85 "Dese boys . . .": ibid.

85 "Support the K.K.K. College Fund . . .": Michele Collison, "For Many Freshmen, Orientation Now Includes Efforts to Promote Racial Understanding," *Chronicle of Higher Education*, September 7, 1988.

85 "Nigger, get out of here": Denise Goodman, "Racial Attack Jolts U. of Maine," *Boston Globe*, February 23, 1991.

85 A survey conducted in 1992: "Racism in Tigertown," *Princeton Alumni Weekly*, December 9, 1992, p. 11.

86 "I was stopped . . .": "Civil Rights Complaints Sought at Princeton," *New York Times*, February 13, 1993.

86 Simmons found that: *Princeton Alumni Weekly*, April 7, 1993, p. 5.

87 114, in 1992: "ADL 1992 Audit of Anti-Semitic Incidents: Overall Numbers Decrease but Campus Attacks Are Up," *On the Frontline* (monthly newsletter published by the Anti-Defamation League), March 1993.

87 "Israel Zionist": "Anti-Semitic Slurs Are Painted: Campus Reacts," *New York Times*, February 11, 1990.

87 "Hi' [sic] Hitler" and "Fuckin [sic] Jews": Sharon Kaplan, "Hillel Hut Vandalized with Anti-Semitic Grafitti," *Daily Sundial* (California State University, Northridge), September 26, 1991.

87 Dr. Leonard Jeffries, Jr.: James Barron, "Professor Steps off a Plane into a Furor over His Words," *New York Times*, August 15, 1991.

87 Syracuse University fraternity: "Anti-Gay Shirts Oust Syracuse Fraternity," *USA Today*, June 28, 1991.

87 *Peninsula:* "Magazine Issue on Homosexuality Leads to Rallies," *New York Times*, December 22, 1991.

88 University of Colorado: Dirk Johnson, "Coach's Anti-Gay Stand Ignites Rage," *New York Times*, March 15, 1992.

88 governor of Alabama: "Alabama Denies Aid to Gay Student Groups," *New York Times*, May 16, 1992.

88 photographs from *Penthouse:* "Nude Photographs Prompt Debate over Free Speech," *New York Times,* March 17, 1991.

88 George Mason University: "Constitution Protects An 'Ugly Woman' Skit," *New York Times,* May 13, 1993.

89 Carleton College: "Charge of Sexism Ends a Tradition by Football Team," *New York Times,* November 4, 1990.

89 U.S. Naval Academy: Carol Burke, "Dames at Sea," *New Republic,* August 17, 24, 1992, pp. 16–20.

90 "A group of fraternity brothers . . .": Katrina Foley, "Terror on Campus: Fraternities Training Grounds for Rape and Misogyny," *New Directions for Women,* September/October 1992, pp. 15, 29.

91 *Together:* ibid.

91 University of Rhode Island: William Celis, 3d, "After Rape Charge, 2 Lives Hurt and 1 Destroyed," *New York Times,* November 12, 1990.

92 the Rotunda: B. Drummond Ayres, Jr., "No Regrets, Says Organizer of Drug Raid at Virginia," *New York Times,* March 28, 1991.

92 "noisy, sloshy . . .": B. Drummond Ayres, Jr., "Drug Charges Embarrass U. of Virginia," *New York Times,* March 24, 1991.

92 "witnessed numerous instances . . .": ibid.

93 ". . . That's wrong": Michael deCourcy Hinds, "Myth of Fraternities as Sanctuaries Crumbles with Virginia Drug Raid," *New York Times,* March 29, 1991.

93 "Up there . . .": Ayres, "No Regrets."

93 University of Alabama: William Celis, 3d, "Hazing's Forbidden Rites Are Moving 'Underground,'" *New York Times,* January 27, 1993.

93 A 1991 survey: "Undergraduates Drink Heavily, Survey Discloses," *New York Times,* December 22, 1991.

94 According to a 1990 study: Hinds, "Myths of Fraternities."

94 A 1989–90 survey: "Study Finds Students at Small Colleges Drink More," *New York Times,* September 20, 1992.

95 "Two bull-necked boys . . ."; "This is a huge commuter school . . .": Anne Matthews, "The Campus Crime Wave," *New York Times Magazine,* March 7, 1993.

96 A national study of women: Peggy Reeves Sanday, *Fraternity Gang Rape: Sex, Brotherhood, and Privilege on Campus* (New York: New York University Press, 1990), pp. 23–24.

96 "There is no question . . .": Tamar Lewin, "Tougher Laws Mean More Cases Are Called Rape," *New York Times,* May 27, 1991.

96 ". . . the evening of March 1, 1990 . . .": E. R. Shipp, "St. John's Case Offers 2 Versions of Events," *New York Times,* July 6, 1991.

98 "pulling train" refers to: Sanday, *Fraternity Gang Rape,* p. 1.

98 Bernice Sandler: ibid.

98 "A vulnerable young woman . . .": ibid., pp. 1–2.

98 "four hits of LSD"; "barely conscious . . .": ibid., p. 6.

99 ". . . into masculine roles": ibid., pp. 8–9.

99 ". . . 'gays' or 'faggots' ": ibid., p. 11.

99 ". . . manipulated and controlled": Collins, *Black Feminist Thought,* p. 69.

Chapter 4. Coping with Bias

112 "Chinese Americans . . .": *The Diversity Project: Final Report* (Berkeley, Calif.: Institute for the Study of Social Change, University of California / Berkeley, 1991), p. 12.

113 ". . . never fully Americans": ibid., p. 24.

122 Eleven African-American males: Jung Yun, "Black Male Enrollment Drops," *Miscellany News* (newspaper of Vassar College), September 6, 1991.

124 "As a black male . . .": Jung Yun, "Diversity at Vassar: How Real Is It?," *Miscellany News,* September 6, 1991.

124 By April 1992: Alexandra Doumas, "Admissions Hopes for Better Year," *Miscellany News,* April 10, 1992.

Chapter 5. Speaking Out

133 ". . . women at MIT . . .": MIT Press Release, March 3, 1992.

144 "During Spring 1988 . . .": Task Force on Racism of the Associated Students of the University of Washington, *Report to the University: Racism and Discrimination in the College Environment* (Seattle: University of Washington, 1989), p. 1.

145 "All University schools . . .": ibid., p. 7.

146 "All students graduating . . .": Letter to the University of Washington

Faculty Senate, "Referendum Poll on American Pluralism Requirement," October 1, 1991.
146 ". . . to go down 80/20 . . .": personal communication.

Chapter 6. Leading Students

151 ". . . 'slam-dunkin' porch monkey": "There Is More Than One Way to
Say Nigger," *Badger Herald* (University of Wisconsin's "Independent
Student Newspaper"), August 31, 1992.
152 "mock slave auctions . . .": ibid.
152 "What's up, bro?"; "As I knocked . . .": ibid.
153 ". . . Uncle Remus?": Jake Lamar, *Bourgeois Blues: An American
Memoir* (New York: Plume, 1992), p. 94.
157 Some observers believe: Katie Roiphe, *The Morning After: Sex, Fear,
and Feminism on Campus* (Boston: Little, Brown, 1993).
163 "Wasn't it time . . .": Lorene Cary, *Black Ice* (New York: Alfred A.
Knopf, 1991), pp. 32–33.
164 ". . . not intend to fail": ibid., p. 53.
164 "*My* duty . . .": ibid., p. 58.
164 ". . . prayers of our ancestors": ibid., p. 59.
164 DuBois wrote about: W. E. B. DuBois, *The Souls of Black Folk* (New
York: New American Library, 1969), p. 45.
164 the "outsider within": Patricia Hill Collins, *Black Feminist Thought:
Knowledge, Consciousness, and the Politics of Empowerment* (Boston:
Unwin Hyman, 1990), p. 11.
164 ". . . be the *best* . . .": Cary, *Black Ice*, p. 202.
167 ". . . needs of black seniors": "Blacks Form Graduation Panel of
Their Own," *New York Times*, February 17, 1991.
168 "This college . . ."; "Commencement . . .": Lisa W. Foderaro, "At
Vassar, Expanded Role for Blacks at Commencement," *New York
Times*, May 10, 1991.
169 "I'd found Harvard . . .": Lamar, *Bourgeois Blues*, pp. 93–94.

Chapter 7. Walking in Two Worlds

199 "Would you rather . . .": Sara Rimer, "Campus Lesbians Step into
Unfamiliar Light," *New York Times*, June 5, 1993.

201 ". . . things do not mix?" Amy Tan, *The Joy Luck Club* (New York: Ivy, 1989), p. 289.

Chapter 9. A Matter of Survival

229 "As communities . . .": Charles Taylor et al., *Multiculturalism and "The Politics of Recognition"* (Princeton University Press, 1992), p. 23.

233 ". . . psychological depression . . .": Cornel West, *Race Matters* (Boston: Beacon, 1993), pp. 12–13.

234 ". . . reduced mode of being": Taylor et al., *Multiculturalism*, p. 25.

234 ". . . from its pall": Arthur Ashe and Arnold Rampersand, *Days of Grace: A Memoir* (New York: Alfred A. Knopf, 1993), pp. 127–28.

235 "hyphenated identification"; "In such a . . .": Troy Duster, "Understanding 'Self-Segregation' on Campus," *Cal Report*, Spring 1992, p. 24.

235–36 "Identity politics . . ."; ". . . amid shrinking resources": Todd Gitlin, "The Rise of 'Identity Politics': An Examination and a Critique," *Dissent*, Spring 1993, pp. 172–77.

238 Rauch . . . states forcefully: Jonathan Rauch, "Words Aren't Violence," *New York Times*, June 26, 1993.

239 "long romance with guns"; "Of course, guns . . .": Jeff Silverman, "Romancing the Gun," Arts & Leisure sec., *New York Times*, June 30, 1993.

240 According to Nannerl Keohane: "Message from the President," *Wellesley College Bulletin*, June 1993.

240 both Penn and Dartmouth: Michael deCourcy Hinds, "A Campus Case: Speech or Harassment?," *New York Times*, May 15, 1993; "Dartmouth Is Swept Up in Turmoil over Paper," *New York Times*, May 12, 1993.

242 "With the encouragement . . .": Dinesh D'Souza, *Illiberal Education: The Politics of Race and Sex on Campus* (New York: Free Press, 1991), pp. 242–43.

242 ". . . graduatin' Phi Beta Kappa": Louis Menand, "Illiberalisms," *New Yorker*, May 20, 1991, pp. 101–7.

243 "The cult of ethnicity . . .": Arthur M. Schlesinger, Jr., *The Disuniting*

of America: Reflections on a Multicultural Society (New York: W. W. Norton, 1992), p. 102.

243 Troy Duster points out: Duster, "Understanding 'Self-Segregation.' "

245 May 1993 . . . lawsuits: Sam Howe Verhovek, "Rich Schools, Poor Schools, Never-Ending Litigation," *New York Times*, May 30, 1993.

245 Alabama's schools: Peter Applebome, "Its Schools Ruled Inadequate, Alabama Looks for Answers," *New York Times*, June 9, 1993.

246 Philadelphia's schools: Michael deCourcy Hinds, "Belatedly, Philadelphia Faces Busing," *New York Times*, March 1, 1993.

246 "Equity . . .": George Judson, "In Hartford, Data Portray Schools in Crisis of Poverty," *New York Times*, January 2, 1993.

247 *Time* was a glorious place . . .": John Gregory Dunne, "Your Time Is My Time," *New York Review of Books*, April 23, 1992.

247 "During my first week . . .": Jake Lamar, *Bourgeois Blues: An American Memoir* (New York: Plume, 1992), p. 114.

248 the class of 1997: "University Admits Class of 1997," *Princeton Alumni Weekly*, May 12, 1993.

253 "We were all stunned . . ."; ". . . wondered, 'Now what?' ": Willa Panvini, "Exploring Transfer: Like an Outward Bound Program for the Mind," *Vassar Quarterly*, Summer 1992, pp. 10–15.

254 Willa Panvini reports: ibid.

255–56 "The peace and vitality . . ."; " 'Civility' . . .": Ralph B. Potter, "Civility, Citizenship, Custom, Community," *Religion & Values in Public Life: A Forum from Harvard Divinity School*, Spring 1993, p. 12.

257 ". . . among a downtrodden people": West, *Race Matters*, p. 19.

258 ". . . shared among groups": Gitlin, "The Rise of 'Identity Politics.' "

259 ". . . upperclass, racially homogeneous . . ."; ". . . bond between people": Eddie Olivera-Robles, "Seniors Reflect," *Princeton Alumni Weekly*, June 2, 1993, p. 17.

Selected Reading

Paul Berman, ed. *Debating P.C.: The Controversy over Political Correctness on College Campuses.* New York: Laurel, 1992.

Steven L. Carter. *Reflections of an Affirmative Action Baby.* New York: Basic, 1991.

Lorene Cary. *Black Ice.* New York: Alfred A. Knopf, 1991.

Patricia Hill Collins, *Black Feminist Thought: Knowledge, Consciousness, and the Politics of Empowerment.* Boston: Unwin Hyman, 1990.

Dinesh D'Souza. *Illiberal Education: The Politics of Race and Sex on Campus.* New York: Free Press, 1991.

Thomas Byrne Edsall and Mary D. Edsall. *Chain Reaction: The Impact of Race, Rights, and Taxes on American Politics.* New York: W. W. Norton, 1991.

Henry Louis Gates, Jr. *Loose Canons: Note on the Culture Wars.* New York: Oxford University Press, 1992.

Gerald Graff. *Beyond the Culture Wars: How Teaching the Conflicts Can Revitalize American Education.* New York: W. W. Norton, 1992.

Andrew Hacker. *Two Nations: Black and White, Separate, Hostile, Unequal.* New York: Scribner's Sons, 1992.

Roger Kimball. *Tenured Radicals: How Politics Has Corrupted Our Higher Education.* New York: Harper, 1991.

Jonathan Kozol. *Savage Inequalities: Children in America's Schools.* New York: HarperCollins, 1992.

Paul Krugman. *The Age of Diminished Expectations: U.S. Economic Policy in the 1990s.* Cambridge, Mass.: MIT Press, 1992.

Jake Lamar. *Bourgeois Blues: An American Memoir.* New York: Plume, 1992.

Michael Moffat. *Coming of Age in New Jersey: College and American Culture.* New Brunswick, N.J.: Rutgers University Press, 1989.

Paul Monette. *Becoming a Man: Half a Life Story.* New York: Harper, 1993.

Toni Morrison, ed. *Race-ing Justice, En-gendering Power: Essays on Anita*

Hill, Clarence Thomas, and the Construction of Social Reality. New York: Pantheon, 1992.

Michael Omi and Howard Winant. *Racial Formation in the United States: From the 1960s to the 1980s.* New York: Routledge, 1986.

Alejandro Portes and Ruben G. Rumbaut. *Immigrant America: A Portrait.* Berkeley, Calif.: University of California Press, 1990.

Robert B. Reich. *The Work of Nations.* New York: Vintage, 1992.

Jonathan Rieder. *Canarsie: The Jews and Italians of Brooklyn Against Liberalism.* Cambridge, Mass.: Harvard University Press, 1985.

Henry Rosovsky. *The University: An Owner's Manual.* New York: W. W. Norton, 1990.

Paula S. Rothenberg. *Race, Class, and Gender in the United States: An Integrated Study.* New York: St. Martin's Press, 1992.

Peggy Reeves Sanday. *Fraternity Gang Rape: Sex, Brotherhood, and Privilege on Campus.* New York: New York University Press, 1990.

Arthur M. Schlesinger, Jr. *The Disuniting of America: Reflections on a Multicultural Society.* New York: W. W. Norton, 1992.

Shelby Steele. *The Content of Our Character: A New Vision of Race in America.* New York: St. Martin's Press, 1990.

Charles Taylor et al. *Multiculturalism and "The Politics of Recognition."* Princeton, N.J.: Princeton University Press, 1992.

Barrie Thorne. *Gender Play: Girls and Boys in School.* New Brunswick, N.J.: Rutgers University Press, 1993.

Lois Weis and Michelle Fine, eds. *Beyond Silenced Voices: Class, Race, and Gender in United States Schools.* Albany, N.Y.: State University of New York Press, 1993.

Cornel West. *Race Matters.* Boston: Beacon, 1993.

Geoffrey Wolff. *The Final Club.* New York: Vintage, 1991.

Index